PRACTICE MAKES PERFECT®

T0003134

Complete Japanese Grammar

Premium Second Edition

Eriko Sato, PhD

Mc
Graw
Hill

New York Chicago San Francisco Athens London Madrid
Mexico City Milan New Delhi Singapore Sydney Toronto

3   4   5   6   7   8   9   LOV   26   25   24   23

ISBN   978-1-260-46321-7
MHID   1-260-46321-4

e-ISBN   978-1-260-46322-4
e-MHID   1-260-46322-2

McGraw Hill Language Lab App

Audio recordings and flashcards are available to support your study of this book. Go
to mhlanguagelab.com to access the online version of this application, or to locate
links to the mobile app for iOS and Android devices. More details about the features
of the app are available on the inside front and back covers.

McGraw Hill products are available at special quantity discounts to use as premiums and
sales promotions or for use in corporate training programs. To contact a representative,
please visit the Contact Us pages at www.mhprofessional.com.

Contents

Introduction

Practice Makes Perfect: Complete Japanese Grammar is designed as a study tool for elementary to intermediate students of Japanese or as a review for intermediate to advanced students of Japanese. It can serve as a helpful self-study tool or as a supplement for high school or college students. It starts with the basic sound and writing systems and covers complete major Japanese grammar, including conditionals and passive/causative constructions.

Chapters are organized in such a way that learners can understand the characteristics of each building block of Japanese sentences and then gradually gain insight into how these building blocks are combined to form complex sentences that are needed for authentic Japanese communication.

Each chapter includes a number of short units, each of which focuses on a single grammar concept, such as "Adverb + する **suru**/なる **naru** (change)." Each unit can be completed in 20 to 30 minutes and provides concise explanations and various authentic examples of sentences followed by exercises. All sentence examples are written in authentic Japanese script, accompanied by Romanization to clarify the ambiguity in the pronunciation of kanji (Chinese characters) and word boundaries, as well as to accommodate those who have not gained full command of using the Japanese scripts. They are also accompanied by English translations, so the user can learn new vocabulary in context.

Exercises are carefully presented so they can mostly be done using the vocabulary words included in sentence examples in the same unit or in the preceding units; short glossaries and sentence translations are occasionally provided wherever they might be helpful. Translations are also provided in the answer key whenever they might be helpful. Exercises vary from simple multiple-choice and fill-in-the-blank questions to open-ended questions that encourage readers to express themselves freely, which can be enjoyably done by applying the grammatical knowledge acquired in the unit and the help of a dictionary.

New to this edition is a final review chapter. Exercises are grouped by chapter and provide additional practice on key grammatical concepts covered throughout the book. Audio recordings of the answers of these, and many other exercises, are provided via the McGraw Hill Language Lab app to further aid your study.

Learning another language requires dedication, time, and frequent practice. By using *Practice Makes Perfect: Complete Japanese Grammar*, students at any level can gain or clarify grammatical concepts and strengthen their Japanese language skills through practice.

Only practice makes perfect.

Introducing Japanese sounds, word order, and writing systems

Japanese sounds are pretty easy to pronounce. In contrast, the Japanese writing system is quite complex. Sentences can be written horizontally or vertically. A Japanese sentence can be written by combining two sets of **kana** phonetic symbols, **hiragana** and **katakana**, as well as about 2,000 **kanji** characters, Chinese characters adapted to Japanese. In this chapter, you will learn the basic Japanese sound systems and writing systems. Japanese words are represented by **romaji** (Romanization) throughout this textbook, but authentic scripts will be gradually added in this chapter and then throughout in the rest of this book.

Basic sounds

Japanese has five basic vowels:

- **a**, which sounds like the vowel in *aha*
- **i**, which sounds like the vowel in *eat*
- **u**, which sounds like the vowel in *boot*, but without lip rounding
- **e**, which sounds like the vowel in *eight*
- **o**, which sounds like the vowel in *oat*

These vowels have long counterparts, which are specified by a macron above them, as in **ā, ī, ū, ē**, and **ō**.

Most consonants in English exist or are pronounced similarly in Japanese. However, note that **r** and **f** are quite different in Japanese than in English:

- Japanese **r** is made by tapping the tip of the tongue behind the upper teeth just once, like the brief flap sound *tt* in *letter* in American English.
- Japanese **f** is pronounced by bringing the upper and lower lips close to each other and blowing air between them gently.

Japanese has double consonants where a single consonant is preceded by a brief abrupt pause. They are represented by two letters in romaji—for example, **tt** and **ss**.

*Pronounce the following words written in romaji carefully and try to get used to Japanese sounds. The letter **n** with an apostrophe, **n'**, shows the separation from the following vowel or semi-vowel.*

1. **kokoro** (*heart*)

2. **e** (*painting*)

3. **take** (*bamboo*)

4. **tori** (*bird*)

5. **tōri** (*street*)

6. **ringo** (*apple*)

7. **fūfu** (*married couple*)

8. **oto** (*sound*)

9. **otto** (*husband*)

10. **kinen** (*anniversary*)

11. **kin'en** (*nonsmoking*)

12. **hon'yaku** (*translation*)

Pitch

Pitch can make a difference in word meanings in Japanese. For example, in Tokyo Japanese, the two-syllable word **ame** means *rain* if the first syllable is in high pitch and the second syllable is in low pitch, but it means *candy* if the first syllable is in low pitch and the second syllable is in high pitch.

Pronounce two words in each pair, paying attention to the pitch. H means high pitch and L means low pitch.

1. **shiro** (HL) (*white*)   **shiro** (LH) (*castle*)

2. **ame** (HL) (*rain*)   **ame** (LH) (*candy*)

3. **hashi** (HL) (*chopsticks*)   **hashi** (LH) (*bridge*)

4. **kami** (HL) (*god*)   **kami** (LH) (*paper*)

5. **kaki** (HL) (*oyster*)   **kaki** (LH) (*persimmon*)

Basic hiragana

Hiragana are used to represent grammatical items such as verb inflections and particles as well as content words that are not written in kanji or katakana. There are 46 basic hiragana characters, each of which represents a syllable sound. They are shown in the following table:

あ **a**	い **i**	う **u**	え **e**	お **o**
か **ka**	き **ki**	く **ku**	け **ke**	こ **ko**
さ **sa**	し **shi**	す **su**	せ **se**	そ **so**
た **ta**	ち **chi**	つ **tsu**	て **te**	と **to**
な **na**	に **ni**	ぬ **nu**	ね **ne**	の **no**
は **ha**	ひ **hi**	ふ **fu**	へ **he**	ほ **ho**
ま **ma**	み **mi**	む **mu**	め **me**	も **mo**
や **ya**	----	ゆ **yu**	----	よ **yo**
ら **ra**	り **ri**	る **ru**	れ **re**	ろ **ro**
わ **wa**	----	----	----	を **o (wo)**
ん **n**	----	----	----	----

The character を is pronounced as **o**, just like the character お, although some people pronounce it as **wo** when reading a hiragana table. を**o** is exclusively used as a grammatical particle. The character ん **n** forms an independent syllable for Japanese although it is a consonant. は is read as **wa** when used as a topic-marking particle, but it is read as **ha** in all other contexts. Similarly, へ is read as **e** when used as a direction-marking particle, but it is read as **he** in all other contexts.

EXERCISE 1·3

Read each of the 46 basic hiragana characters in the following hiragana table aloud, from left to right, from the top row to the bottom row. For example, あいうえおかきく.... Repeat as many times as you want.

あ	い	う	え	お
か	き	く	け	こ
さ	し	す	せ	そ
た	ち	つ	て	と
な	に	ぬ	ね	の
は	ひ	ふ	へ	ほ
ま	み	む	め	も
や	----	ゆ	----	よ
ら	り	る	れ	ろ
わ	----	----	----	を
ん	----	----	----	----

Diacritics for kana

By adding the diacritic ˝ or ° to the upper-right corner of some characters, you can make their beginning consonant voiced or change it to **p**, respectively. For example, ˝ changes **k** to **g**, **s** to **z**, and **t** to **d**. Note that ˝ changes **h** and **f** to **b**. On the other hand, ° changes **h** and **f** to **p**. All characters that can be marked by these diacritics are listed in the following table:

が **ga**	ぎ **gi**	ぐ **gu**	げ **ge**	ご **go**
ざ **za**	じ **ji**	ず **zu**	ぜ **ze**	ぞ **zo**
だ **da**	ぢ **ji**	づ **zu**	で **de**	ど **do**
ば **ba**	び **bi**	ぶ **bu**	べ **be**	ぼ **bo**
ぱ **pa**	ぴ **pi**	ぷ **pu**	ぺ **pe**	ぽ **po**

The syllables **ji** and **zu** are usually represented by じ and ず, respectively, but they are represented by ぢ and づ in some limited cases, as in the following examples:

- つづく **tsuzuku** (*to continue*)
- はなぢ **hanaji** (*nose bleeding*)
- ちぢむ **chijimu** (*to shrink*))

EXERCISE 1·4

Read each of the following words aloud, paying attention to the diacritics. For a greater challenge, cover the romaji as you work on this exercise.

1. じかん **jikan** (*time*)
2. げた **geta** (*a type of wooden clogs*)
3. ぎん **gin** (*silver*)
4. りんご **ringo** (*apple*)
5. ぶんがく **bungaku** (*literature*)
6. てんぷら **tenpura** (*tempura*)
7. おりがみ **origami** (*origami*)

Representing double consonants and long vowels

To express the brief abrupt pause found in double consonants, use the small つ **tsu**. For example, **kitte** (*postage stamp*) is written as きって. To represent a long vowel, just add a character that represents the same vowel. For example, **tōri** (*street*) is written as とおり. There are some discrepancies between kana and the actual pronunciation in some words for historical reasons. A kana character with a vowel **o** and the kana う **u** that directly follows it are read as one long syllable with the long vowel **ō**. For example, おとうさん (*father*) is pronounced as **otōsan**. Similarly, a kana character with a vowel **e** and the kana い **i** that directly follows it are read as one syllable with the long vowel **ē**. For example, せんせい (*teacher*) is pronounced as **sensē**. In this book, **ē** in such cases is still specified as **ei** in romaji, following the common practice in most romaji Japanese dictionaries.

*Read the following words out loud, paying attention to the pause represented by the small つ **tsu**. For a greater challenge, cover the romaji as you work on this exercise.*

1. きって   **kitte**   (*postage stamp*)

2. ざっし   **zasshi**   (*magazine*)

3. みっつ   **mittsu**   (*three pieces*)

4. きっぷ   **kippu**   (*train ticket*)

EXERCISE
1·6

Read the following words out loud, paying attention to long vowels. For a greater challenge, cover the romaji as you work on this exercise.

1. おかあさん   **okāsan**   (*mother*)

2. おとうさん   **otōsan**   (*father*)

3. おにいさん   **onīsan**   (*older brother*)

4. おねえさん   **onēsan**   (*older sister*)

5. せんせい   **sensei**   (*teacher*)

6. とおり   **tōri**   (*street*)

Representing palatalized sounds

Japanese syllables may begin with a palatalized consonant, a consonant pronounced with the body of the tongue raised toward the roof of the mouth. To express such syllables, use the hiragana that has the consonant you need and the vowel **i** and add small や **ya**, ゆ **yu**, or よ **yo**, depending on the vowel you need. For example, to represent **kya**, use the letter き **ki** because it has the consonant **k** and the vowel **i**, and add a small や**ya** because it has the vowel **a**. The following table lists all such palatalized syllables:

きゃ **kya**	きゅ **kyu**	きょ **kyo**
ぎゃ **gya**	ぎゅ **gyu**	ぎょ **gyo**
しゃ **sha**	しゅ **shu**	しょ **sho**
じゃ **ja**	じゅ **ju**	じょ **jo**
ちゃ **cha**	ちゅ **chu**	ちょ **cho**
ぢゃ **ja**	ぢゅ **ju**	ぢょ **jo**
にゃ **nya**	にゅ **nyu**	にょ **nyo**
ひゃ **hya**	ひゅ **hyu**	ひょ **hyo**
びゃ **bya**	びゅ **byu**	びょ **byo**
ぴゃ **pya**	ぴゅ **pyu**	ぴょ **pyo**
みゃ **mya**	みゅ **myu**	みょ **myo**
りゃ **rya**	りゅ **ryu**	りょ **ryo**

*Read each of the following Japanese words, paying attention to the small や **ya,** ゆ **yu,** or よ **yo.** For a greater challenge, cover the romaji as you work on this exercise.*

1. びょういん   **byōin**   (*hospital*)

2. しゃちょう   **shachō**   (*company president*)

3. とうきょう   **Tōkyō**   (*Tokyo*)

4. おちゃ   **ocha**   (*green tea*)

5. ちゅうごく   **Chūgoku**   (*China*)

6. きんぎょ   **kingyo**   (*goldfish*)

Katakana

Katakana are used to represent non-Chinese foreign names and words. They are also commonly used to represent onomatopoeic expressions. Katakana consists of 46 characters, just like hiragana, as shown in the following table:

ア **a**	イ **i**	ウ **u**	エ **e**	オ **o**
カ **ka**	キ **ki**	ク **ku**	ケ **ke**	コ **ko**
サ **sa**	シ **shi**	ス **su**	セ **se**	ソ **so**
タ **ta**	チ **chi**	ツ **tsu**	テ **te**	ト **to**
ナ **na**	ニ **ni**	ヌ **nu**	ネ **ne**	ノ **no**
ハ **ha**	ヒ **hi**	フ **fu**	ヘ **he**	ホ **ho**
マ **ma**	ミ **mi**	ム **mu**	メ **me**	モ **mo**
ヤ **ya**	----	ユ **yu**	----	ヨ **yo**
ラ **ra**	リ **ri**	ル **ru**	レ **re**	ロ **ro**
ワ **wa**	----	----	----	ヲ **o (wo)**
ン **n**	----	----	----	----

With katakana, you can use the same diacritics and conventions used with hiragana. However, unlike in hiragana, in katakana long vowels are represented by adding an elongation mark (ー). Note that the katakana system allows some combinations of characters that are not available in the hiragana system in order to approximate the pronunciation of foreign words. Such examples include ファ (**fa**), フィ (**fi**), フェ (**fe**), フォ (**fo**), ティ (**ti**),トゥ (**tu**), ディ (**di**), ドュ (**du**), ヴァ (**va**), ヴォ (**vo**),ヴェ (**ve**),ウォ (**wo**), ウェ (**we**), チェ (**che**), シェ (**she**), and ジェ (**je**).

Read each of the 46 basic katakana characters in the following table aloud, from left to right, from the top row to the bottom row. For example, アイウエオカキ.... Repeat as many times as you want.

ア	イ	ウ	エ	オ
カ	キ	ク	ケ	コ
サ	シ	ス	セ	ソ
タ	チ	ツ	テ	ト

ナ	ニ	ヌ	ネ	ノ
ハ	ヒ	フ	ヘ	ホ
マ	ミ	ム	メ	モ
ヤ	----	ユ	----	ヨ
ラ	リ	ル	レ	ロ
ワ	----	----	----	ヲ
ン	----	----	----	----

EXERCISE 1·9

Read the following words written in katakana aloud. For a greater challenge, cover the romaji as you work on this exercise.

1. アメリカ **Amerika** (*America*)
2. ボストン **Bosuton** (*Boston*)
3. チェロ **chero** (*cello*)
4. ソファー **sofā** (*sofa*)
5. ピザ **piza** (*pizza*)
6. キムチ **kimuchi** (*kimchee, Korean spicy pickled vegetables*)

EXERCISE 1·10

Read the following katakana words and guess what they mean. For a greater challenge, cover the romaji as you work on this exercise.

1. バス **basu** _____
2. ネクタイ **nekutai** _____
3. テレビ **terebi** _____
4. ラジオ **rajio** _____
5. カメラ **kamera** _____
6. アイロン **airon** _____

Kanji

Kanji characters are Chinese characters imported from China and adapted to Japanese. Japanese people learn about 2,000 kanji characters by the time they graduate from high school. Each kanji character represents a meaning rather than a sound. For example, the kanji character 人 represents *person*. Some kanji characters were created from pictures or signs. For example, 人 (*person*) was created from a picture of a standing person viewed side-on. Some were made from signs. For example, 三 (*three*) was created from three bars. Many kanji characters were created by combining two or more kanji. For example, 明 (*bright*) was created by combining 日 (*sun*) and 月 (*moon*). Remember that kanji characters that represent verbs and adjectives need to be followed by hiragana that show inflectional endings, as in 書く **kaku** (*to write*) and 書いた **kaita** (*wrote*). Most kanji characters have multiple pronunciations, some of which are the Japanese native way and others the Chinese way. For example, the Japanese way of pronouncing 人 is **hito**, and the Chinese way of pronouncing it is **nin** or **jin**. You need to learn how kanji are read in different contexts on a case-by-case basis. In this book, you will always know how kanji characters are read because romaji is provided after each phrase or sentence.

The following are some of the relatively simple and frequently used kanji characters. A hyphen is added in romaji to show the pronunciation of each kanji character separated from the surrounding kanji, hiragana, or katakana, if such a division is available.

人	*person*	人 **hito** (*person*); 日本人 **Ni-hon-jin** (*a Japanese person*); アメリカ人 **Amerika-jin** (*an American person*); 三人 **san-nin** (*three people*)
日	*sun*	日 **hi** (*the sun*); 日曜日 **Nichi-yō-bi** (*Sunday*); 明日 **asu** (*tomorrow*); 今日 **kyō** (*today*); 昨日 **kinō** (*yesterday*)
月	*moon*	月 **tsuki** (*the moon*); 月曜日 **Getsu-yō-bi** (*Monday*); 先月 **sen-getsu** (*last month*); 今月 **kon-getsu** (*this month*); 来月 **rai-getsu** (*next month*)
年	*year, age*	年 **toshi** (*year, age*); 去年 **kyo-nen** (*last year*); 今年 **kotoshi** (*this year*); 来年 **rai-nen** (*next year*)
学	*learn*	学ぶ **mana-bu** (*to learn*); 学生 **gaku-sei** (*student*); 学校 **gak-kō** (*school*); 大学 **dai-gaku** (*university*)
生	*live, birth*	生きる **i-kiru** (*to live*); 生まれる **u-mareru** (*to be born*); 先生 **sen-sei** (*teacher*); 学生 **gaku-sei** (*student*)
来	*to come*	来る **ku-ru** (*to come*); 来ない **ko-nai** (*not to come*); 来年 **rai-nen** (*next year*); 来週 **rai-shū** (*next week*)
高	*expensive, tall*	高い **taka-i** (*expensive*); 高校 **kō-kō** (*high school*); 高速道路 **kō-soku-dō-ro** (*highway*)
私	*I, me*	私 **watashi** (*I, me*); 私立大学 **shi-ritsu-dai-gaku** (*private university*)

EXERCISE

1·11

Read the following words aloud and identify their meanings by referring to the preceding table. For a greater challenge, cover the romaji as you work on this exercise.

1. 人   **hito**   _____

2. 日本人   **Nihonjin**   _____

3. 来る   **kuru**   _____

4. 来ない   **konai**   _____

5. 来年   **rainen**   _____

6. 高い   **takai**   _____

7. 学生   **gakusei**   _____

Try reading the following sentences written in Japanese script out loud by referring to the kanji table on page 8. For a greater challenge, cover the romaji as you work on this exercise.

1. 私は日本人です。

   Watashi wa Nihonjin desu.

   I'm Japanese.

2. あの人はアメリカ人です。

   Ano hito wa Amerika-jin desu.

   That person is an American.

3. 山田さんは来ないでしょう。

   Yamada-san wa konai deshō.

   Ms. Yamada won't come, I guess.

Basic word order and particles

The order between the subject and the object is flexible in Japanese. However, a verb needs to be placed at the end of a sentence. A sentence can be understood correctly regardless of the word order because the subject and the object are directly followed by the subject-marking particle が **ga** and the object-marking particle を **o**, respectively. For example, the following two sentences both mean *Ken invited Ann*:

> ケンがアンを誘った。
> **Ken ga An o sasotta.**

> アンをケンが誘った。
> **An o Ken ga sasotta.**

English prepositions such as *to, from, in, on, at*, and *with* correspond to postpositions, or particles placed after nouns, in Japanese. For example, the English preposition *to* corresponds to the Japanese particle に **ni** when expressing destinations. Instead of saying *to Toronto*, you need to say something like *Toronto to*—actually, トロントに **Toronto ni**, as in the following sentence:

> ケンがトロントに行った。
> **Ken ga Toronto ni itta.**
> *Ken went to Toronto.*

*Complete the sentences with が **ga,** を **o,** or に **ni**. For a greater challenge, cover the English translations as you work on this exercise.*

1. ジョン _____ ホットドッグ _____ 食べた。

   Jon _____ hottodoggu _____ tabeta.

   John ate hotdogs.

2. ジュース _____ メアリー_____ 飲んだ。

   Jūsu _____ Mearī _____ nonda.

   Mary drank juice.

3. トム _____ ボストン _____ 来た。

   Tomu _____ Bosuton _____ kita.

   Tom came to Boston.

Dropping pronouns

Some nouns in a sentence are usually dropped if understood in context, especially in conversation. So, you will hear many sentences without the subject noun. However, nouns are accompanied by a particle, so you will not have a problem understanding what they mean. For example, observe the following dialog between ビル **Biru** (*Bill*) and メアリー **Mearī** (*Mary*).

BILL 昨日、シカゴに行った。

Kinō, Shikago ni itta.

I went to Chicago yesterday.

MARY ああ、そう。だれと？

Ā, sō. Dare to?

Oh, okay. With whom?

BILL 友達と。

Tomodachi to.

With my friend.

MARY どうだった？

Dō datta?

How was it?

BILL よかった。

Yokatta.

It was good.

*Complete the following sentences with が **ga**, を **o**, or に **ni**. For a greater challenge, cover the English translations as you work on this exercise.*

1. シカゴ _____ 行った。

   Shikago _____ **itta.**

   (I) went to Chicago.

2. 友達 _____ 来た。

   Tomodachi _____**kita.** (来た **kita**: *came*)

   My friend came (here).

3. うち _____ 来た。

   Uchi _____ **kita.** (うち **uchi**: *home*)

   (He) came to my home.

4. たまご _____ 食べた。

   Tamago _____ **tabeta.** (たまご **tamago**: *egg*; 食べた **tabeta**: *ate*)

   (I) ate eggs.

The topic particle は **wa**

Japanese sentences often start with a noun marked by the particle は **wa**. It may be a subject noun, an object noun, a noun marked by a postposition such as に **ni**, or any noun if it serves as the topic of the sentence. There is no equivalent in English, but it can be thought to mean *as for* or *speaking of* . . . and represent a topic where the rest of the sentence is some statement about it. Consider these examples:

> メアリーはボストンに行った。
> **Mearī wa Bosuton ni itta.**
> *Mary went to Boston.* (Literally: *As for Mary, she went to Boston.*)

> すしは食べた。
> **Sushi wa tabeta.**
> *I ate sushi.* (Literally: *As for sushi, I ate it.*)

> シカゴには行かない。
> **Shikago ni wa ikanai.**
> *I will not go to Chicago.* (Literally: *As for to Chicago, I will not go there.*)

> 昨日は休んだ。
> **Kinō wa yasunda.**
> *I took a rest yesterday.* (Literally: *Speaking of yesterday, I rested.*)

Reorder the items in each set to form a grammatical sentence.

1. 東京 **Tōkyō**, 行った **itta**, に **ni**

   _____

2. すし **sushi**, 食べた **tabeta**, を **o**

   _____

3. 食べた **tabeta**, 友達 **tomodachi**, バナナ **banana**, が **ga**, を **o**

   _____

4. ボストン **Bosuton**, メアリー **Mearī**, 行った **itta**, は **wa**, に **ni**

   _____

The copular verb です **desu**

The Japanese copular verb です **desu** does not pattern like a verb at all because it was historically developed from a combination of the particle で **de** and the verb あります **arimasu**, which means *to exist*. です **desu** can directly follow a noun or an adjective to show equality. So, to say *A is B*, you can say AはBです **A wa B desu**. For example:

> メアリーはアメリカ人です。
> **Mearī wa Amerika-jin desu.**
> *Mary is an American. (Literally: As for Mary, (she) is an American.)*

Speech styles

There are three basic speech styles in Japanese: a plain/informal style, a polite/neutral style, and a formal style. For example, you can ask a question like *Did you buy it?* in three different ways:

- 買ったの。**Katta no.** (plain/informal)
- 買いましたか。**Kaimashita ka.** (polite/neutral)
- お買いになりましたか。**O-kai ni narimashita ka.** (formal)

Which style you use depends on the "social hierarchy," based on age, status, position, rank, and experiences and the "social grouping," such as family vs. non-family or colleagues vs. clients. To your siblings, parents, close friends, or assistants, you can use the plain/informal form, but to your teachers, clients, or superiors, you should use the formal style. If you are not sure, or if you're speaking to strangers or to your classmates or colleagues, it's safe to use the polite/neutral style, although you may also use the other two styles, depending on the context. For example, even when you are talking to a stranger, your speech style may depend on the location (for example, at a bar vs. at a conference). Be aware that formal styles show your respect to your addressees but also create some distance between you. Similarly, plain/informal styles sound very friendly but might also make you sound quite rude or childish. Which one to use depends on the context and your attitude.

For each of the following people, which speech style should be used: (a) plain/informal, (b) polite/neutral, or (c) formal?

1. Your younger sister _____

2. Your older sister _____

3. Your roommate _____

4. Your classmate _____

5. Your client _____

6. Your teacher _____

Nouns

Nouns are words that refer to people, things, and concepts. A noun can serve as the subject or the direct object in a sentence. Japanese nouns can be followed by particles or the copula です **desu** (*to be*). Unlike in English, Japanese nouns do not change forms depending on whether they are plural or singular.

Proper nouns

A proper noun names a specific item, such as a specific person, a specific institution, or a specific place. For example:

- Family names, such as 山田 **Yamada** (*Yamada*), 森 **Mori** (*Mori*), and スミス **Sumisu** (*Smith*)
- Male given names, such as 武 **Takeshi** (*Takeshi*) and ジョージ **Jōji** (*George*)
- Female given names, such as 陽子 **Yōko** (*Yoko*) and メアリー **Mearī** (*Mary*)
- Country names, such as 日本 **Nihon/Nippon** (*Japan*), アメリカ **Amerika** (*the United States*), and 中国 **Chūgoku** (*China*)
- City names, such as 東京 **Tōkyō** (*Tokyo*), トロント **Toronto** (*Toronto*), and ソウル **Sōru** (*Seoul*)
- Mountains, such as 富士山 **Fujisan** (*Mt. Fuji*)
- Corporations, such as ソニー **Sonī** (*Sony*)

EXERCISE

2·1

1. List Japanese city names that you know.

   _____

2. List Japanese family names that you know.

   _____

3. List Japanese company names that you know.

   _____

Respectful titles

When addressing or referring to someone, you add a respectful title after his or her name. The most neutral respectful title is さん **san**, which can be used after either a family name or a given name, regardless of the person's gender or marital status. For example:

- 田中さん **Tanaka-san** (*Mr./Ms./Mrs. Tanaka*)
- 陽子さん **Yōko-san** (*Yoko*)
- 田中陽子さん **Tanaka Yōko-san** (*Ms./Mrs. Yoko Tanaka*)
- マイクさん **Maiku-san** (*Mike*)
- スミスさん **Sumisu-san** (*Mr./Ms./Mrs. Smith*)

For young girls or boys, ちゃん **chan** can be used after the given name to show affection, but 君 **kun** is more commonly used for boys. 様 **sama** is used in extremely polite contexts but is typically used for addressing a business customer or client. If the person has a certain position or function, his or her professional title, such as 部長 **buchō** (*division manager*), 社長 **shachō** (*company president*), or 先生 **sensei** (*professor, teacher, medical doctor*, etc.), should be used after the family name instead of さん **san**. For example:

- 山田社長 **Yamada shachō** (*President Yamada*)
- スミス先生 **Sumisu sensei** (*Professor Smith*)

Do not use a respectful title or professional title when addressing yourself. When you tell your name, just say your name, without the respectful title. Adults usually say their family name, as in:

- 山田と申します。 **Yamada to mōshimasu.** (*I'm Yamada.*)
- 山田です。 **Yamada desu.** (*I'm Yamada.*)

EXERCISE
2·2

*Choose the most appropriate way to address **Yoko Yamada** in each of the following situations.*

1. She is your little sister's friend and is 5 years old.
   a. 陽子さん **Yōko-san**
   b. 陽子ちゃん **Yōko-chan**
   c. 山田ちゃん **Yamada-chan**

2. She is 25 years old and is your teacher in your high school.
   a. 山田さん **Yamada-san**
   b. 山田先生 **Yamada sensei**
   c. 山田ちゃん **Yamada-chan**

3. She is your customer at a department store.
   a. 山田様 **Yamada-sama**
   b. 山田さん **Yamada-san**
   c. 陽子様 **Yōko-sama**

4. She is your neighbor, a middle-aged woman.
   a. 山田さん **Yamada-san**
   b. 山田様 **Yamada-sama**
   c. 山田君 **Yamada-kun**

5. She is your student in high school.
   a. 山田先生 **Yamada sensei**
   b. 山田ちゃん **Yamada-chan**
   c. 山田さん **Yamada-san**

Common nouns

Unlike a proper noun that names a specific item, a common noun refers to a class of items, such as 学生 **gakusei** (*student/students*), 犬 **inu** (*dog/dogs*), 机 **tsukue** (*desk/desks*), 町 **machi** (*town/towns*), 川 **kawa** (*river/rivers*), and 大学 **daigaku** (*university/universities*). However, if you want to refer to a specific item without using a proper name, you can add a demonstrative adjective to a common noun. Different demonstrative adjectives are used, depending on where the item is in relation to the speaker and the listener's location. If the item is located near the speaker but not near the listener, use この **kono**. If it is near the listener but not near the speaker, use その **sono**. If it is far from either of them, use あの **ano**. If it is not clear which item, you can ask about it using どの **dono** (*which*). You can place one of these demonstrative adjectives before any common noun. For example:

   ◆ あの猫 **ano neko** (*that cat over there*)
   ◆ この犬 **kono inu** (*this dog*)
   ◆ そのカメラ **sono kamera** (*that camera near you*)
   ◆ どの本 **dono hon** (*which book*)

EXERCISE

2·3

Pretend that you are speaking with someone who is sitting across the coffee table from you in his living room. Choose the most appropriate answer from the options given.

1. You want to ask him about the book (本 **hon**) he is holding.
   a. この本 **kono hon**
   b. その本 **sono hon**
   c. あの本 **ano hon**
   d. どの本 **dono hon**

2. You want to talk about the painting (絵 **e**) hung in the next room.
   a. この絵 **kono e**
   b. その絵 **sono e**
   c. あの絵 **ano e**
   d. どの絵 **dono e**

3. You want to talk about the coffee cup (コーヒーカップ **kōhīkappu**) you are holding.
   a. このコーヒーカップ **kono kōhīkappu**
   b. そのコーヒーカップ **sono kōhīkappu**
   c. あのコーヒーカップ **ano kōhīkappu**
   d. どのコーヒーカップ **dono kōhīkappu**

4. Through the window, you see three cars in the driveway, and you want to ask him which one is his car.
   a. この車 **kono kuruma**
   b. その車 **sono kuruma**
   c. あの車 **ano kuruma**
   d. どの車 **dono kuruma**

Compound nouns

Some nouns were made by combining two or more nouns. They are called compound nouns. The following are some examples. Note that the consonant at the beginning of the second word of a compound is voiced in some cases:

* 貿易会社 **bōeki-gaisha** (*trading company*) ← 貿易 **bōeki** (*trading*) + 会社 **kaisha** (*company*)
* 女言葉 **onna-kotoba** (*female language*) ← 女 **onna** (*woman*) + 言葉 **kotoba** (*language*)
* ごみ箱 **gomi-bako** (*trash can*) ← ごみ **gomi** (*trash*) + 箱 **hako** (*box*)
* シャボン玉 **shabon-dama** (*soap bubble*) ← シャボン **shabon** (*soap*) + 玉 **tama** (*ball*)

The stems of some verbs can serve as nouns and are used to create many compound nouns. (See Chapter 4 for stem forms.) The following nouns contain a verb in the stem form and a noun:

* 食べ物 **tabe-mono** (*food*) ← 食べる **taberu** (*to eat*) + 物 **mono** (*thing*)
* 焼き肉 **yaki-niku** (*grilled meat*) ← 焼く **yaku** (*to grill*) + 肉 **niku** (*meat*)
* 飼い猫 **kai-neko** (*house cat*) ← 飼う **kau** (*feed and keep animals*) + 猫 **neko** (*cat*)

The following nouns are made of two verbs in the stem form:

* 読み書き **yomi-kaki** (*reading and writing*) ← 読む **yomu** (*to read*) + 書く **kaku** (*to write*)
* 立ち読み **tachi-yomi** (*reading books at a bookstore without buying them*) ← 立つ **tatsu** (*to stand*) + 読む **yomu** (*to read*)

The following nouns contain a **na** adjective in the stem form (see Chapter 8 for **na** adjectives):

* 酒好き **sake-zuki** (*alcohol lover*) ← 酒 **sake** (*alcohol*) + 好きな **suki na** (*like*)
* 人間嫌い **ningen-girai** (*those who hate people*) ← 人間 **ningen** (*human being*) + 嫌い **kirai** (*hate*)

EXERCISE
2·4

List the compound nouns that you know.

_____

_____

_____

_____

Demonstrative pronouns

To refer to items that the speaker and the listener can see, use a demonstrative pronoun. The following table lists demonstrative adjectives discussed earlier in this chapter and frequently used demonstrative pronouns:

		The Speaker's Domain (close to the speaker)	The Listener's Domain (close to the listener but far from the speaker)	Beyond the Speaker and the Listener's Domain (far from both the speaker and the listener)	Question Words
Demonstrative adjective		この **kono**...	その **sono**...	あの **ano**...	どの **dono**...
Demonstrative pronoun	Things and animals	これ **kore**	それ **sore**	あれ **are**	どれ **dore**
	Location	ここ **koko**	そこ **soko**	あそこ **asoko**	どこ **doko**
	Direction	こちら **kochira**	そちら **sochira**	あちら **achira**	どちら **dochira**

When referring to people you and your addressee can see, use a demonstrative adjective directly followed by a common noun like 人 **hito** (*person*) or 学生 **gakusei** (*student*). For example:

- あの人 **ano hito** (*that person*)
- この学生 **kono gakusei** (*this student*)

Alternatively, you can use the demonstrative pronouns こちら **kochira**, そちら **sochira**, or あちら **achira** in relatively formal contexts. If you use これ **kore**, それ **sore**, or あれ **are** to refer a person, you will sound very rude. These words and phrases can be placed before a topic particle は **wa** or the copula です **desu**. (See Chapter 1 for は **wa** and です **desu**.) For example:

あの人は学生です。
Ano hito wa gakusei desu.
That person is a student.

こちらは山田さんです。
Kochira wa Yamada-san desu.
This is Ms. Yamada.

この学生は日本人です。
Kono gakusei wa Nihonjin desu.
This student is Japanese.

Choose the appropriate answer from the items in parentheses.

1. (あの, あれ, nothing) 人は日本人です。

   (Ano, Are, nothing) hito wa Nihon-jin desu.

2. (あの, あれ, nothing) は犬です。(犬 **inu**: *dog*)

   (Ano, Are, nothing) wa inu desu.

3. (あの, あれ, nothing) 山田さんは学生です。

   (Ano, Are, nothing) Yamada-san wa gakusei desu.

4. (その, それ, nothing) は鉛筆です。(鉛筆 **enpitsu**: *pencil*)

   (Sono, Sore, nothing) wa enpitsu desu.

5. (この, これ, nothing) は机です。(机 **tsukue**: *desk*)

   (Kono, Kore, nothing) wa tsukue desu.

Personal pronouns

To refer to people in terms of first, second, and third person, use personal pronouns. Although English personal pronouns change form depending on the grammatical case (for example, *he* and *him*), Japanese personal pronouns do not because grammatical case is expressed by particles such as が **ga** and を **o**. (See Chapter 7 for particles.) The following table lists frequently used personal pronouns in Japanese:

	SINGULAR	PLURAL
First person, gender neutral	私 **watashi**	私達 **watashi-tachi**
First person, masculine	僕 **boku**	僕達 **boku-tachi**
Second person, gender neutral	あなた **anata**	あなた達 **anata-tachi**
Third person, masculine, or gender neutral	彼 **kare**	彼ら **karera**
Third person, feminine	彼女 **kanojo**	彼女ら **kanojora**

Note that personal pronouns are usually omitted when understood in the context in Japanese. In fact, you should avoid the use of あなた **anata** (*you*) either by dropping it or by replacing it with the name of the person.

Dropped pronouns and lack of articles and number specification

The Japanese prefer to drop words in a sentence if they are understood. So they rarely use pronouns such as *it*, *I*, *you*, and *he*. Articles like *a*, *an*, and *the* are absent, and the singular/plural distinction is not usually clarified. For example, the following sentence means *Did you brush your teeth?*, but there is no pronoun that corresponds to *you* or *your*, and there is no indication for whether it means *tooth* or *teeth*:

歯を磨きましたか。
Ha o migakimashita ka.

The particle の no

In Japanese, you can modify a noun by placing another noun before it. However, you need to add the particle の **no** at the end of the added noun to indicate that it is a modifier. For example, 学生 **gakusei** means *a student*, and 文学の学生 **bungaku no gakusei** means *a student of literature*. See how a noun can be modified in the following examples:

- 私の本 **watashi no hon** (*my book*)
- 日本語の本 **Nihongo no hon** (*a book written in Japanese, a book for Japanese language study*)
- 日本語の学生 **Nihongo no gakusei** (*a student who studies the Japanese language*)
- 日本人の学生 **Nihon-jin no gakusei** (*a Japanese student, a student who is Japanese*)
- 子供の本 **kodomo no hon** (*a children's book, a book for children*)
- アメリカの車 **Amerika no kuruma** (*a car made in the United States*)
- 田中さんの友達 **Tanaka-san no tomodachi** (*Mr. Tanaka's friend*)
- 東京の大学 **Tōkyō no daigaku** (*a university in Tokyo*)

You can add multiple such modifiers, as in this example:

> ボストンの大学の文学の学生
> **Bosuton no daigaku no bungaku no gakusei**
> *a student of literature in a university in Boston*

EXERCISE

2·6

Translate the following sentences into Japanese.

1. *Mr. Tanaka is my friend.*

   _____

2. *This is a children's book.*

   _____

3. *That one over there is Ms. Yamada's university.*

   _____

4. *That car over there is Ms. Yamada's friend's car.*

   _____

Omitting nouns after の no

You can omit the noun after the particle の **no** if it is the last noun in the noun phrase and it is understood in context. So, instead of saying 私の本です **Watashi no hon desu**, you can say 私のです **Watashi no desu**. Similarly, instead of saying 私の友達の本です **Watashi no tomodachi no hon desu**, you can say 私の友達のです **Watashi no tomodachi no desu**.

Create a grammatical sentence by reordering all the given items in each set but without adding any words.

1. は, あれ, 本, の, 私, です

   wa, are, hon, no, watashi, desu

   _____

2. は, その, の, 私, 車, です

   wa, sono, no, watashi, kuruma, desu

   _____

3. です, は, 父, 車, 日本, の, の

   desu, wa, chichi, kuruma, Nihon, no, no

   _____

4. の, 田中さん, この, 鉛筆, です, は

   no, Tanaka-san, kono, enpitsu, desu, wa

   _____

Kinship terms

There are two sets of kinship terms in Japanese: plain forms and polite forms. Plain forms are shorter and used when referring to one's own family members in front of a third person. Polite forms, which are longer, are used when referring to someone else's family members. For example, 母 **haha** is used to refer to one's own mother, and お母さん **okāsan** is used for referring to someone else's mother. The following table shows some of the essential Japanese kinship terms:

	PLAIN	POLITE
father	父 **chichi**	お父さん **otōsan**
mother	母 **haha**	お母さん **okāsan**
sibling(s)	兄弟 **kyōdai**	ご兄弟 **go-kyōdai**
older brother	兄 **ani**	お兄さん **onīsan**
older sister	姉 **ane**	お姉さん **onēsan**
younger brother	弟 **otōto**	弟さん **otōtosan**
younger sister	妹 **imōto**	妹さん **imōtosan**
grandfather	祖父 **sofu**	おじいさん **ojīsan**
grandmother	祖母 **sobo**	おばあさん **obāsan**
uncle	おじ **oji**	おじさん **ojisan**
aunt	おば **oba**	おばさん **obasan**
husband	主人 **shujin**; 夫 **otto**	ご主人 **go-shujin**
wife	家内 **kanai**; 妻 **tsuma**	奥さん **okusan**

Unless you need to emphasize or clarify, you don't need to say 私の **watashi no** (*my*) before a kinship term in the plain form because it is obvious.

Choose the correct answer from the items in parentheses.

1. 私の(お母さん, 母)は日本人です。

   Watashi no (okāsan, haha) wa Nihon-jin desu.

2. 陽子さんの(お母さん, 母)はアメリカ人です。

   Yōko-san no (okāsan, haha) wa Amerika-jin desu.

3. あの人は田中さんの(お父さん, 父)です。

   Ano hito wa Tanaka-san no (otōsan, chichi) desu.

4. 山田さんの友達の(兄, お兄さん)は空手の先生です。

   Yamada-san no tomodachi no (ani, onīsan) wa karate no sensei desu.

Complete the sentences with either は **wa** *or* の **no***. Make sure that you use* は **wa** *only once in each sentence.*

1. メアリーさん _____ 日本語 _____ 学生です。

   Mearī-san _____ Nihon-go _____ gakusei desu.

   Mary is a student of Japanese language.

2. スミスさん _____ 私 _____ 姉 _____ 友達です。

   Sumisu-san _____ watashi _____ ane _____ tomodachi desu.

   Mr. Smith is my older sister's friend.

3. 私 _____ 犬 _____ 日本 _____ 犬です。

   Watashi _____ inu _____ Nihon _____ inu desu.

   My dog is a Japanese dog.

4. 私 _____ 兄 _____ 友達 _____ 山田さん _____ 友達です。

   Watashi _____ ani _____ tomodachi _____ Yamada-san _____ tomodachi desu.

   My older brother's friend is Ms. Yamada's friend.

Numbers

■·3·

This chapter shows how numbers are pronounced independently and with counters such as *class counters*, *ordinal counters*, and *unit counters*. You will also learn how to express times and dates in Japanese.

Bare numbers based on the Chinese system

Numbers are usually expressed based on the Chinese system and written in Arabic numerals from left to right in modern Japanese, just like in English, although they can be written in kanji.

See how the numbers from 1 to 10 are written and pronounced in Japanese:

1	2	3	4	5	6	7	8	9	10
一	二	三	四	五	六	七	八	九	十
いち **ichi**	に **ni**	さん **san**	し **shi**, よん **yon**	ご **go**	ろく **roku**	しち **shichi**, なな **nana**	はち **hachi**	きゅう **kyū**, く **ku**	じゅう **jū**

The pronunciations **shi** (for *four*), **shichi** (for *seven*), and **ku** (for *nine*) are used only for reciting bare numbers, using them in physical exercises, or doing arithmetic. They are not usually used for counting things or specifying places in an ordered sequence. Note that **shi** also means *death* in Japanese and tends to be avoided.

From 10 to 19, numbers are compound words consisting of **jū** (*ten*) plus one of the other digits. For example, 11 is **jū-ichi**, 12 is **jū-ni**, and 19 is **jū-kyū**. The multiples of 10 (20, 30, 40, etc.) are compound words consisting of one of the digits plus **jū** (*ten*). For example, 20 is **ni-jū**, 30 is **san-jū**, and 90 is **kyū-jū**. Other numbers under 100 consist of the multiples of ten plus one of the other digits. For example, 21 is **ni-jū-ichi**, and 99 is **kyū-jū-kyū**.

25

Give the pronunciation of each of the following numbers.

1. 8 _____

2. 12 _____

3. 20 _____

4. 22 _____

5. 79 _____

The following table shows the multiples of 10, 100, 1,000, and 10,000. Notice many irregular sound changes with the multiples of 100 (百: ひゃく **hyaku**, びゃく **byaku**, or ぴゃく **pyaku**) and 1,000 (千: せん **sen** or ぜん **zen**):

10 十	じゅう **jū**	100 百	ひゃく **hyaku**	1,000 千	せん **sen**	10,000 一万	いちまん **ichi-man**
20 二十	にじゅう **ni-jū**	200 二百	にひゃく **ni-hyaku**	2,000 二千	にせん **ni-sen**	20,000 二万	にまん **ni-man**
30 三十	さんじゅう **san-jū**	300 三百	さんびゃく **san-byaku**	3,000 三千	さんぜん **san-zen**	30,000 三万	さんまん **san-man**
40 四十	よんじゅう **yon-jū**	400 四百	よんひゃく **yon-hyaku**	4,000 四千	よんせん **yon-sen**	40,000 四万	よんまん **yon-man**
50 五十	ごじゅう **go-jū**	500 五百	ごひゃく **go-hyaku**	5,000 五千	ごせん **go-sen**	50,000 五万	ごまん **go-man**
60 六十	ろくじゅう **roku-jū**	600 六百	ろっぴゃく **rop-pyaku**	6,000 六千	ろくせん **roku-sen**	60,000 六万	ろくまん **roku-man**
70 七十	ななじゅう **nana-jū**	700 七百	ななひゃく **nana-hyaku**	7,000 七千	ななせん **nana-sen**	70,000 七万	ななまん **nana-man**
80 八十	はちじゅう **hachi-jū**	800 八百	はっぴゃく **hap-pyaku**	8,000 八千	はっせん **has-sen**	80,000 八万	はちまん **hachi-man**
90 九十	きゅうじゅう **kyū-jū**	900 九百	きゅうひゃく **kyū-hyaku**	9,000 九千	きゅうせん **kyū-sen**	90,000 九万	きゅうまん **kyū-man**

Give the pronunciation of each of the following numbers.

1. 320 _____

2. 5,699 _____

3. 12,000 _____

4. 73,800 _____

5. 99,999 _____

The native Japanese number system

A native Japanese number system is often used for counting things in daily lives. It is actually a numeral and a counter つ **tsu** and goes only to 10 in modern Japanese. It is frequently used in informal contexts and rarely used in business and academics. See the following table for the numbers in the native Japanese system:

1つ	2つ	3つ	4つ	5つ	6つ	7つ	8つ	9つ	10
一つ	二つ	三つ	四つ	五つ	六つ	七つ	八つ	九つ	十
ひとつ	ふたつ	みっつ	よっつ	いつつ	むっつ	なな つ	やっつ	ここのつ	とお **tō**
hitotsu	**futatsu**	**mittsu**	**yottsu**	**itsutsu**	**muttsu**	**nanatsu**	**yattsu**	**kokonotsu**	

EXERCISE 3·3

Count aloud from 1 to 10 in the Japanese system until you memorize it.

Class counters

Class counters are used for general classes of things that aren't ordinarily divisible. In fact, the Japanese use a counter for counting almost everything. A counter is placed after a numeral. The choice of counter varies depending on the shape, size, and type of the item. For example:

- 人 **nin**: people
- 匹 **hiki**: small or medium-size animals
- 本 **hon**: cylindrically shaped long items such as pens and bananas
- 冊 **satsu**: bound items such as books, magazines, and notebooks
- 枚 **mai**: flat items such as sheets of paper, sheets, and postage stamps

Note that many counters cause minor sound changes or exceptional pronunciations, especially when they start with **s**, **h**, **t**, **ch**, **ts**, and **sh**. The following tables show how the counters 人 **nin**, 匹 **hiki**, 本 **hon**, 冊 **satsu**, and 枚 **mai** are combined with numbers:

COUNTING PEOPLE

1人 (一人)	2人 (二人)	3人 (三人)	4人 (四人)	5人 (五人)	6人 (六人)	7人 (七人)	8人 (八人)	9人 (九人)	10人 (十人)
ひとり **hito-ri**	ふたり **futa-ri**	さんにん **san-nin**	よにん **yo-nin**	ごにん **go-nin**	ろくにん **roku-nin**	ななにん / しちにん **nana-nin / shichi-nin**	はちにん **hachi-nin**	きゅうにん **kyū-nin**	じゅうにん **jū-nin**

COUNTING ANIMALS

1匹 (一匹)	2匹 (二匹)	3匹 (三匹)	4匹 (四匹)	5匹 (五匹)	6 匹 (六匹)	7匹 (七匹)	8匹 (八匹)	9 匹 (九匹)	10匹* (十匹)
いっぴ き ip-piki	にひき ni-hiki	さんび き san-biki	よんひ き yon-hiki	ごひ き go-hiki	ろっぴ き rop-piki	ななひき nana-hiki	はっぴ き hap-piki	きゅうひ き kyū-hiki	じゅっ ぴき jup-piki

COUNTING CYLINDRICAL ITEMS

1本 (一本)	2本 (二本)	3本 (三本)	4本 (四本)	5本 (五本)	6本 (六本)	7本 (七本)	8本 (八本)	9 本 (九本)	10本* (十本)
いっぽ ん ip-pon	にほん ni-hon	さんぼ ん san-bon	よんほ ん yon-hon	ごほん go-hon	ろっぽ ん rop-pon	ななほん nana-hon	はっぽ ん hap-pon	きゅうほ ん kyū-hon	じゅっ ぽん jup-pon

COUNTING BOUND ITEMS

1冊 (一冊)	2冊 (二冊)	3冊 (三冊)	4冊 (四冊)	5冊 (五冊)	6冊 (六冊)	7冊 (七冊)	8冊 (八冊)	9冊 (九冊)	10冊* (十冊)
いっさ つ is-satsu	にさつ ni-satsu	さんさ つ san-satsu	よんさ つ yon-satsu	ごさつ go-satsu	ろくさ つ roku-satsu	ななさ つ nana-satsu	はっさ つ has-satsu	きゅう さつ kyū-satsu	じゅっさ つ jus-satsu

COUNTING FLAT ITEMS

1枚 (一枚)	2枚 (二枚)	3枚 (三枚)	4枚 (四枚)	5枚 (五枚)	6枚 (六枚)	7枚 (七枚)	8枚 (八枚)	9枚 (九枚)	10枚 (十枚)
いちま い ichi-mai	にま い ni-mai	さんま い san-mai	よんま い yon-mai	ごまい go-mai	ろくまい roku-mai	ななまい nana-mai	はちまい hachi-mai	きゅう まい kyū-mai	じゅう まい jū-mai

*10匹 **jup-piki**, 10本 **jup-pon**, and 10冊 **jus-satsu** have a variation, **jip-piki**, **jip-pon**, and **jis-satsu**, respectively.

For counting medium-size objects such as apples and candies as well as some other inanimate items under 10, use the native numbers, which includes the counter つ **tsu**.

EXERCISE
3·4

Specify the number of each of the following items, using the example as a guide.

EXAMPLE   *two cats* 2匹 **ni-hiki**

1. *five pencils* _____

2. *three postage stamps* _____

3. *two dogs* _____

4. *five children* _____

5. *three apples* _____

6. *seven books* _____

Ordinal counters

Ordinal counters are used to specify the place in some order in time, location, or hierarchy. For example:

- 時 **ji**: . . . *o'clock* (e.g., 5時に行きます。 **Go-ji ni ikimasu.** *I'll go there at 5 o'clock.*)
- 分 **fun**: . . . *minutes* (e.g., 今、5時5分です。 **Ima, go-ji go-fun desu.** *It's 5:05 now.*)
- 年 **nen**: *year* (e.g., 2013年 **nisen-jū-san-nen** *2013*)
- ページ **pēji**: *page* . . . (e.g., 5ページを見てください。 **Go-pēji o mite kudasai.** *Please see page 5.*)
- 階 **kai**: . . . *th floor* (e.g., カフェテリアは5階です。 **Kafeteria wa go-kai desu.** *The cafeteria is on the fifth floor.*)
- 番 **ban**: *number* . . . (e.g., マイクさんはクラスで1番です。 **Maiku-san wa kurasu de ichi-ban desu.** *Mike is the top student in class.*)
- 位 **i**: . . . *th place* (e.g., 3位はビルさんでした。 **San-i wa Biru-san deshita.** *The third-place winner was Bill.*)

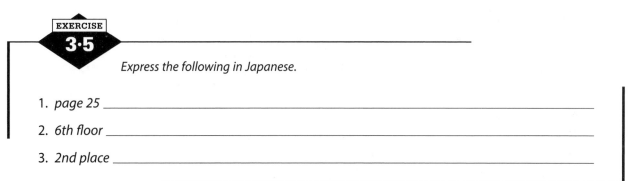

EXERCISE 3·5

Express the following in Japanese.

1. *page 25* _____

2. *6th floor* _____

3. *2nd place* _____

Expressing time

The following list shows how to express the time. Pay attention to irregular pronunciations.

1時 **ichi-ji** *1 o'clock*		1分 **ip-pun** *1 minute*	
2時 **ni-ji** *2 o'clock*		2分 **ni-fun** *2 minutes*	
3時 **san-ji** *3 o'clock*		3分 **san-pun** *3 minutes*	
4時 **yo-ji** *4 o'clock*		4分 **yon-pun** *4 minutes*	
5時 **go-ji** *5 o'clock*		5分 **go-fun** *5 minutes*	
6時 **roku-ji** *6 o'clock*		6分 **rop-pun** *6 minutes*	
7時 **shichi-ji** *7 o'clock*		7分 **nana-fun** *7 minutes*	
8時 **hachi-ji** *8 o'clock*		8分 **hap-pun** (**hachi-fun**) *8 minutes*	
9時 **ku-ji** *9 o'clock*		9分 **kyū-fun** *9 minutes*	
10時 **jū-ji** *10 o'clock*		10分 **jup-pun** (**jip-pun**) *10 minutes*	
11時 **jū-ichi-ji** *11 o'clock*		11分 **jū-ip-pun** *11 minutes*	
12時 **jū-ni-ji** *12 o'clock*		12分 **jū-ni-fun** *12 minutes*	

To indicate *AM*, add 午前 **gozen** before the time phrase. To indicate *PM*, add 午後 **gogo** after the time phrase. For example:

- 午前8時5分 **gozen hachi-ji go-fun** *8:05 AM*
- 午後3時 **gogo san-ji** *3 PM*

Give the pronunciations of the following phrases in hiragana or in romaji.

1. 3時 _____

2. 4時25分 _____

3. 7時10分 _____

4. 午前9時15分 _____

5. 午後12時12分 _____

Expressing months and days

The following list shows how to express the months and days in Japanese:

1月 **Ichi-gatsu** *January*	1日 **tsuitachi** *1st day*	16日 **jūroku-nichi** *16 days, 16th day*
2月 **Ni-gatsu** *February*	2日 **futsuka** *2 days, 2nd day*	17日 **jūshichi-nichi** *17 days, 17th day*
3月 **San-gatsu** *March*	3日 **mikka** *3 days, 3rd day*	18日 **jūhachi-nichi** *18 days, 18th day*
4月 **Shi-gatsu** *April*	4日 **yokka** *4 days, 4th day*	19日 **jūku-nichi** *19 days, 19th day*
5月 **Go-gatsu** *May*	5日 **itsuka** *5 days, 5th day*	20日 **hatsuka** *20 days, 20th day*
6月 **Roku-gatsu** *June*	6日 **muika** *6 days, 6th day*	21日 **nijū ichi-nichi** *21 days, 21st day*
7月 **Shichi-gatsu** *July*	7日 **nanoka** *7 days, 7th day*	22日 **nijū ni-nichi** *22 days, 22nd day*
8月 **Hachi-gatsu** *August*	8日 **yōka** *8 days, 8th day*	23日 **nijū san-nichi** *23 days, 23rd day*
9月 **Ku-gatsu** *September*	9日 **kokonoka** *9 days, 9th day*	24日 **nijū yokka** *24 days, 24th day*
10月 **Jū-gatsu** *October*	10日 **tōka** *10 days, 10th day*	25日 **nijū go-nichi** *25 days, 25th day*
11月 **Jūichi-gatsu** *November*	11日 **jūichi-nichi** *11 days, 11th day*	26日 **nijū roku-nichi** *26 days, 26th day*
12月 **Jūni-gatsu** *December*	12日 **jūni-nichi** *12 days, 12th day*	27日 **nijū shichi-nichi** *27 days, 27th day*
	13日 **jūsan-nichi** *13 days, 13th day*	28日 **nijū hachi-nichi** *28 days, 28th day*
	14日 **jūyokka** *14 days, 14th day*	29日 **nijū ku-nichi** *29 days, 29th day*
	15日 **jūgo-nichi** *15 days, 15th day*	30日 **sanjū-nichi** *30 days, 30th day*
		31日 **sanjūichi-nichi** *31 days, 31st day*

To ask questions using these ordinal numbers, use 何 **nan**, as in:

今、何時ですか。
Ima, nan-ji desu ka.
What time is it now?

今日は何日ですか。
Kyō wa nan-nichi desu ka.
What date is it today?

カフェテリアは何階ですか。
Kafeteria wa nan-kai desu ka.
Which floor is cafeteria located?

何ページから何ページまで読みましたか。
Nan-pēji kara nan-pēji made yomimashita ka.
From what page to what page did you read?

EXERCISE 3·7

Write the pronunciation of the following phrases using hiragana or romaji.

1. 3月 _____

2. 4月 _____

3. 5月5日 _____

4. 10月10日 _____

5. 9月24日 _____

EXERCISE 3·8

Answer the following questions about yourself in Japanese.

1. 今日は何日ですか。**Kyō wa nan-nichi desu ka.**

_____

2. 今、何時何分ですか。**Ima, nan-ji nan-pun desu ka.**

_____

3. 誕生日は何月何日ですか。**Tanjōbi wa nan-gatsu nan-nichi desu ka.**

_____

4. 何年に生まれましたか。**Nan-nen ni umaremashita ka.**

_____

Unit counters

Unit counters are used to refer to a quantity of something that is divisible, such as water, time, money, and distance. For example:

リットル **-rittoru** . . . *liters*
杯 **-hai** . . . *cups*
時間 **-jikan** . . . *hours*
分(間) **-fun(kan)** . . . *minutes*
週間 **-shūkan** . . . *weeks*
ヶ月 **-kagetsu** . . . *months*
グラム **-guramu** . . . *grams*
キロ(グラム) **-kiro(guramu)** . . . *kilograms*
メートル **-mētoru** . . . *meters*
キロ(メートル) **-kiro(mētoru)** . . . *kilometers*
センチ(メートル) **-senchi(mētoru)** . . . *centimeters*
ミリ(メートル) **-miri(mētoru)** . . . *millimeters*
マイル **-mairu** . . . *miles* (not used in Japan)
インチ **-inchi** . . . *inches* (not used in Japan)
ドル **-doru** . . . *dollars* (not used in Japan)
円 **-en** . . . *yen* (Japanese currency unit)

EXERCISE
3·9

Express the following in Japanese.

1. *3 o'clock* _____

2. *3 hours* _____

3. *100 yen* _____

4. *August* _____

5. *8 months* _____

6. *5 meters* _____

. . . 目 me

By adding the suffix 目 **-me** to a class or unit counter, you can create an ordinal counter. For example, 5人 **go-nin** means *five people*, and 5人目 **go-nin-me** means *the fifth person*. For example:

3人目の学生は日本人です。
San-nin-me no gakusei wa Nihonjin desu.
The third student is Japanese.

1冊目の本は面白かったです。
Is-satsu-me no hon wa omoshirokatta desu.
The first book was interesting.

2つ目の交差点を右に曲がってください。
Futat-tsu-me no kōsaten o migi ni magatte kudasai.
Please make a right turn at the second intersection.

このコーヒーは今日5杯目です。
Kono kōhī wa kyō go-hai-me desu.
This cup of coffee is the fifth one today.

2人目の子供は高校生です。
Futa-ri-me no kodomo wa kōkōsei desu.
My second child is a high school student.

EXERCISE
3·10

Express the following in Japanese.

1. *the third student* _____

2. *the second cup of coffee* _____

3. *the second intersection* _____

4. *the third child* _____

EXERCISE
3·11

Give the meaning of the following phrases in English.

1. 4時 **yo-ji** _____

2. 4時間 **yo-jikan** _____

3. 4時間目 **yo-jikan-me** _____

4. 4月 **shi-gatsu** _____

5. 4ケ月目 **yon-kagetsu-me** _____

Basic verb forms

Unlike English verbs, Japanese verbs do not change their forms based on person, gender, or number, but they change their forms based on the formality of speech (plain or polite), polarity (affirmative or negative), and tense (non-past or past).

Plain forms are used in a plain/informal speech context. Polite forms are used in a neutral/polite speech context. Polite forms are longer than plain forms, and they end in ます **masu**, です **desu**, and their variations. Japanese has two major tenses: past and non-past. The past tense is also called *perfect*. It refers to actions that took place in the past or that have completed. The non-past tense is also called *present tense* or *imperfect*. The non-past tense refers to future actions, habitual actions, and actions that have not started yet. These terms will be explained case by case later in this chapter.

Dictionary form

The dictionary form is the shortest verb form that can end a sentence. It is actually the plain non-past affirmative form but is called the "dictionary" form because it is the verb form used for listing verbs in dictionaries. A dictionary form ends in the vowel **u**. For example, the dictionary form of the Japanese verb for *to write* is 書く**kaku**, which means *will write*, *write*, or *writes*, depending on the context.

Masu form

The **masu** form is the polite version of the dictionary form. It is actually the polite non-past affirmative form. For example, the **masu** form of the Japanese verb for *to write* is 書きます **kakimasu**, which means *will write*, *write*, or *writes*, depending on the context.

Nai form

The **nai** form is the negative counterpart of the dictionary form or, more precisely, the plain non-past negative form. The **nai** forms all end in ない **nai**. For example, the **nai** form of the Japanese verb for *to write* is 書かない **kakanai**, which means *will not write*, *do not write*, or *does not write*, depending on the context.

Stem form

The stem form is the shortest pronounceable verb form, but it cannot end a sentence. Its major function is to serve as the stem of a complex word, being combined with a variety of suffixes, including the polite suffix ます **masu**, discussed earlier. The stem form always ends in the vowel **i** or **e**. For example, the stem forms of 書く **kaku** (*to write*) and 食べる **taberu** (*to eat*) are 書き **kaki** and 食べ **tabe**, respectively. See how they are combined with the polite suffix ます **masu**:

書きます **kaki-masu** (*will write, write,* or *writes*)
食べます **tabe-masu** (*will eat, eat,* or *eats*)

The stem form is often called the "pre-**masu**" form because it is the form used before **masu**. Stem forms and pre-**masu** forms diverge only for some verbs, such as くださる **kudasaru** (*to give*) and いらっしゃる **irassharu** (*to exist*). See Chapter 15 for their exceptional forms.

Ru verbs and u verbs

There are two classes of regular verbs: **ru** verbs and **u** verbs. (Here **u** in **u** verbs is pronounced as "oo.") They are also called **ru**-dropping verbs and **u**-dropping verbs because the first step of verb conjugation involves dropping of **ru** and **u** from their dictionary forms. In fact, by removing **ru** or **u**, you are revealing the barest form of a verb, which is called the "root." The root of a **ru** verb always ends in the vowel **e** or **i**. The root of an **u** verb always ends in one of the nine consonants **s**, **k**, **g**, **m**, **n**, **b**, **r**, **t**, or **w**. That is why all **ru** verbs end in **eru** or **iru** and all **u** verbs end in **su**, **ku**, **gu**, **mu**, **nu**, **bu**, **(w)u** (where **w** is not audible), **ru**, or **tsu**.

The dictionary form of a **ru** verb ends in **eru** or **iru**, and the rest of the forms can be made by removing the final **ru** and adding something (if needed). For example, 食べる **taberu** (*to eat*) is a **ru** verb. Its **masu** form can be created just by dropping the final **ru** and adding **masu** (食べます **tabe-masu**). Its **nai** form is created by dropping the final **ru** and adding **nai** (食べない **tabe-nai**). Its stem form can be created just by dropping the final **ru**.

By contrast, **u** verbs are the verbs whose dictionary form ends in **su**, **ku**, **gu**, **mu**, **nu**, **bu**, **(w)u** (where **w** is not audible), **ru**, or **tsu**, and the rest of the forms can be made by dropping the final **u** and adding something. For example, 書く **kaku** (*to write*) is a **u** verb. Its **masu** form can be created by dropping the final **u** and adding **imasu** (書きます **kak-imasu**). Its **nai** form can be created by dropping the final **u** and adding **anai** (書かない **kak-anai**). Its stem form can be created by dropping the final **u** and adding **i** (書き **kak-i**).

In most cases, you can tell a verb's class very easily just by looking at the ending of its dictionary forms. Here's the rule you should remember:

If a verb's dictionary form does *not* end in **eru** or **iru**, it is definitely an **u** verb. If it ends in **eru** or **iru**, it can be either a **ru** verb or an **u** verb.

So, you can safely conclude that the following verbs are all **u** verbs:

書く **kaku** (*write*)　　u verb
読む **yomu** (*read*)　　u verb
売る **uru** (*sell*)　　u verb
とる **toru** (*take*)　　u verb
なる **naru** (*become*)　　u verb

On the other hand, if a verb ends in **eru** or **iru**, it can be either a **ru** verb or an **u** verb because there are some **u** verbs that end in **eru** or **iru**. For example, the following verbs all end in either **eru** or **iru**, but some of them are **ru** verbs and others are **u** verbs, and they conjugate differently:

たべる **taberu** (*eat*) **ru** verb　　たべない **tabenai**　　たべます **tabemasu**
かえる **kaeru** (*change*) **ru** verb　　かえない **kaenai**　　かえます **kaemasu**

かえる **kaeru** (*return*) **u** verb	かえらない **kaeranai**	かえります **kaerimasu**
みる **miru** (*watch*) **ru** verb	みない **minai**	みます **mimasu**
はしる **hashiru** (*run*) **u** verb	はしらない **hashiranai**	はしります **hashirimasu**
いる **iru** (*exist*) **ru** verb	いない **inai**	います **imasu**
いる **iru** (*need*) **u** verb	いらない **iranai**	います **irimasu**
はいる **hairu** (enter) **u** verb	はいらない **hairanai**	はいります **hairimasu**

EXERCISE

4·1

*State whether each of the following verbs is a **ru** verb or an **u** verb, based on the ending. If it is ambiguous, say so. You do not need to know their meanings for now.*

1. かす **kasu** _____

2. いる **iru** _____

3. はこぶ **hakobu** _____

4. おる **oru** _____

5. かえる **kaeru** _____

6. かる **karu** _____

7. つくる **tsukuru** _____

It is helpful to know that *most* **eru/iru**-ending verbs are **ru** verbs. So, you can just memorize a handful of frequently used **eru/iru**-ending **u** verbs, such as the following:

- **U** verbs that end with **eru**:
  帰る **kaeru** (*return*)
  しゃべる **shaberu** (*chat*)
  減る **heru** (decrease)
  蹴る **keru** (*kick*)
  滑る **suberu** (*slide*)
  練る **neru** (*knead*)
  照る **teru** (*shine*)

- **U** verbs that end with **iru**:
  いる **iru** (*need*)
  入る **hairu** (*enter*)
  知る **shiru** (*get to know*)
  切る **kiru** (*cut*)
  走る **hashiru** (*run*)
  参る **mairu** (*go*, honorific)
  煎る **iru** (*roast*)
  散る **chiru** (*scatter*)
  混じる **majiru** (*mix*)
  限る **kagiru** (*limit*)
  ねじる **nejiru** (*twist*)

It is also helpful to know that you can deduce the verb class if you compare the most frequently used two forms—the dictionary form and the **masu** form. Just remove る **ru** and

ます **masu**. If what remains is exactly the same, you can conclude that it is a **ru** verb. Otherwise, it is an **u** verb. See the following example:

	DICTIONARY FORM	MASU FORM
Ru verb	きる (*wear*)	きます
U verb	きる (*cut*)	きります

EXERCISE 4·2

Compare the two forms of each verb and determine its verb class.

1. ねる **neru** (*sleep*), ねます **nemasu** _____

2. ねる **neru** (*knead*), ねります **nerimasu** _____

3. しる **shiru** (*get to know*), しります **shirimasu** _____

4. すぎる **sugiru** (*pass*), すぎます **sugimasu** _____

5. はしる **hashiru** (*run*), はしります **hashirimasu** _____

Irregular verbs

There are two major irregular verbs: くる **kuru** (*to come*) and する **suru** (*to do*). Their **masu** form, **nai** form, and stem form are as follows:

くる **kuru** (*come*)	きます **kimasu**	こない **konai**	き **ki**
する **suru** (*do*)	します **shimasu**	しない **shinai**	し **shi**

Several **u** verbs have a slight irregularity with one of their forms. For example, the verb ある **aru** patterns like an **u** verb, except that its negative form is ない **nai**:

ある **aru** (*exist*)	あります **arimasu**	ない **nai**	あり **ari**

EXERCISE 4·3

Choose the correct conjugated form of the irregular verb.

1. くる **kuru**
   a. くます **kumasu**　　b. きます **kimasu**　　c. こます **komasu**

2. くる **kuru**
   a. くない **kunai**　　b. きない **kinai**　　c. こない **konai**

3. する **suru**
   a. すます **sumasu**　　b. します **shimasu**

4. する **suru**
   a. すない **sunai**　　b. しない **shinai**

Conjugation patterns

The following table lists representative **ru** verbs, **u** verbs, and the two major irregular verbs in dictionary form, **masu** form, **nai** form, and stem form:

	Ending of the Dictionary Form	Dictionary Form	**Masu** Form	**Nai** Form	Stem Form
Ru verbs	-eる **-eru**	かえる **kaeru** (*change*)	かえます **kaemasu**	かえない **kaenai**	かえ **kae**
	-iる **-iru**	きる **kiru** (*wear*)	きます **kimasu**	きない **kinai**	き **ki**
U verbs	-す **-su**	はなす **hanasu** (*speak*)	はなします **hanashimasu**	はなさない **hanasanai**	はなし **hanashi**
	-く **-ku**	かく **kaku** (*write*)	かきます **kakimasu**	かかない **kakanai**	かき **kaki**
	-ぐ **-gu**	およぐ **oyogu** (*swim*)	およぎます **oyogimasu**	およがない **oyoganai**	およぎ **oyogi**
	-む **-mu**	よむ **yomu** (*read*)	よみます **yomimasu**	よまない **yomanai**	よみ **yomi**
	-ぬ **-nu**	しぬ **shinu** (*die*)	しにます **shinimasu**	しなない **shinanai**	しに **shini**
	-ぶ **-bu**	とぶ **tobu** (*jump*)	とびます **tobimasu**	とばない **tobanai**	とび **tobi**
	-う **-w(u)**	かう **kau** (*buy*)	かいます **kaimasu**	かわない **kawanai**	かい **kai**
	-る **-ru**	きる **kiru** (*cut*)	きります **kirimasu**	きらない **kiranai**	きり **kiri**
	-つ **-tsu**	まつ **matsu** (*wait*)	まちます **machimasu**	またない **matanai**	まち **machi**
Irregular verbs		くる **kuru** (*come*)	きます **kimasu**	こない **konai**	き **ki**
		する **suru** (*do*)	します **shimasu**	しない **shinai**	し **shi**

To conjugate a verb, check the ending syllable and the class of the verb and follow the pattern of one of the verbs in the previous table. Pay attention to the **w** sound that surprisingly appears in the **nai** form of an **u** verb whose dictionary form ends in an independent syllable う **u**. The root of such a verb ends in **w**, which is audible only when followed by the vowel **a**.

Conjugate the following **ru** verbs into the **masu** form and the **nai** form.

	MASU FORM	NAI FORM
1. たべる **taberu** (*eat*)	_____	_____
2. ねる **neru** (*sleep*)	_____	_____
3. みる **miru** (*look*)	_____	_____
4. あげる **ageru** (*give*)	_____	_____
5. かりる **kariru** (*borrow*)	_____	_____
6. おしえる **oshieru** (*teach*)	_____	_____

Conjugate the following **u** verbs into the **masu** form and the **nai** form.

	MASU FORM	NAI FORM
1. のむ **nomu** (*drink*)	_____	_____
2. あう **au** (*meet*)	_____	_____
3. かつ **katsu** (*win*)	_____	_____
4. いく **iku** (*go*)	_____	_____
5. およぐ **oyogu** (*swim*)	_____	_____
6. うる **uru** (*sell*)	_____	_____
7. しぬ **shinu** (*die*)	_____	_____
8. はなす **hanasu** (*speak*)	_____	_____
9. あそぶ **asobu** (*play*)	_____	_____

Complete the following verb conjugations. When a verb ends in **eru** or **iru**, you need to figure out whether it is a **ru** verb or an **u** verb by comparing two forms.

EXAMPLE	*write*	かく **kaku**	かきます kakimasu	かかない kakanai
1.	*eat*	たべる **taberu**	たべます **tabemasu**	_____
2.	*look*	みる **miru**	みます **mimasu**	_____
3.	*cut*	きる **kiru**	きります **kirimasu**	_____
4.	*wear*	きる **kiru**	_____	きない **kinai**
5.	*sell*	うる **uru**	_____	_____
6.	*jump*	とぶ **tobu**	_____	_____
7.	*wait*	まつ **matsu**	_____	_____
8.	*buy*	かう **kau**	_____	_____
9.	*do*	する **suru**	_____	_____
10.	*come*	くる **kuru**	_____	_____

Te form

The **te** form ends in て **te** or で **de**. For example, the **te** form of かく **kaku** (*write*) is かいて **kaite**, and the **te** form of よむ **yomu** (*read*) is よんで **yonde**. When listing actions in the same sentence, you need to use the **te** form for all verbs except the last verb. That is, the **te** form means *do/did . . . and*. For this reason, the **te** form is also called "continuing form." So, かいて **kaite** means *write and*. Accordingly, the **te** form cannot end a sentence; it must be followed by another verb or by an auxiliary adjective in order for the sentence to be complete. (See Chapter 6 for auxiliary verbs and auxiliary adjectives.) For example:

書いて読みます。**Kaite yomimasu.** (*I will write and read.*)
書いて読みました。**Kaite yomimashita.** (*I wrote and read.*)
書いてください。**Kaite kudasai.** (*Please write it.*)
書いてほしいです。**Kaite hoshii desu.** (*I want you to write it.*)
書いてしまいました。**Kaite shimaimashita.** (*I wrote it up!*)

To create the **te** form from a dictionary form, follow these rules:

- For **ru** verbs, drop the final る**ru** and add て **te**.
- For **u** verbs that end in す**su**, change the final syllable to して **shite**.
- For **u** verbs that end in く**ku**, change the final syllable to いて **ite**; for **u** verbs that end in ぐ **gu**, change the final syllable to いで **ide**.
- For **u** verbs that end in う**(w)u**, る **ru**, or つ **tsu**, change these final syllables to って **tte**.
- For **u** verbs that end in む **mu**, ぬ **nu**, or ぶ **bu**, change these final syllables to んで **nde**.
- Keep in mind that the verb いく **iku** is slightly irregular, and its **te** form is いって **itte**.
- The **te** forms of the irregular verbs する **suru** and くる **kuru** are して **shite** and きて **kite**.

The following table shows examples of these rules:

	Ending	Dictionary Form	Te Form
Ru verbs	-eる -eru	かえる kaeru (*change*)	かえて kaete
	-iる -iru	きるkiru (*wear*)	きて kite
U verbs	-す -su	はなす hanasu (*speak*)	はなして hanashite
	-く -ku	かく kaku (*write*)	かいて kaite
	-く -ku (exception)	いく iku (*go*)	いって itte
	-ぐ -gu	およぐ oyogu (*swim*)	およいで oyoide
	-む -mu	よむ yomu (*read*)	よんで yonde
	-ぬ -nu	しぬ shinu (*die*)	しんで shinde
	-ぶ -bu	とぶ tobu (*jump*)	とんで tonde
	-う -(w)u	かう kau (*buy*)	かって katte
	-る -ru	きる kiru (*cut*)	きって kitte
	-つ -tsu	まつ matsu (*wait*)	まって matte
Irregular verbs		くる kuru (*come*)	きて kite
		する suru (*do*)	して shite

EXERCISE

4·7

*Indicate the **te** form of each of the following verbs.*

1. かく **kaku** (*write*) _____

2. いく **iku** (*go*) _____

3. かう **kau** (*buy*) _____

4. かつ **katsu** (*win*) _____

5. とぶ **tobu** (*jump*) _____

6. する **suru** (*do*) _____

7. くる **kuru** (*come*) _____

You can create the negative **te** form of a verb by replacing **nai** in its **nai** form with **nakute** (e.g., **tabenakute**) or by adding **de** to its **nai** form (e.g., **tabenai de**). Which negative **te** form to use depends on the context. See Chapter 12 for the difference between the two types of negative **te** forms for verbs.

Ta form

The **ta** form is the short name of the plain past affirmative form. It ends in either **ta** or **da**. For example, the **ta** form of たべる **taberu** (*to eat*) is たべた **tabeta** (*ate*). You can make a **ta** form very easily if you know how to make a **te** form. Simply change the final vowel **e** in the **te** form to an **a**. For example, the **te** form of かく **kaku** (*to write*) is かいて **kaite** (*write and*), and its **ta** form is かいた **kaita** (*wrote*). Similarly, the **te** form of よむ **yomu** (*to read*) is よんで **yonde** (*read and*), and its **ta** form is よんだ **yonda** (*read*).

EXERCISE
4·8

*Indicate the **ta** form of each of the following verbs.*

1. かく **kaku** (*write*) _____

2. いく **iku** (*go*) _____

3. かう **kau** (*buy*) _____

4. かつ **katsu** (*win*) _____

5. とぶ **tobu** (*jump*) _____

6. する **suru** (*do*) _____

7. くる **kuru** (*come*) _____

Nakatta form

To create the negative counterpart of a **ta** form, which is the plain past negative form, replace ない **nai** in the **nai** form with なかった **nakatta**. For example, the **nai** form of the verb かく **kaku** is かかない **kakanai**, and the plain past negative form is かかなかった **kakanakatta**.

EXERCISE
4·9

*Indicate the **nakatta** form of each of the following verbs.*

1. かく **kaku** (*write*) _____

2. いく **iku** (*go*) _____

3. かう **kau** (*buy*) _____

4. かつ **katsu** (*win*) _____

5. とぶ **tobu** (*jump*) _____

6. する **suru** (*do*) _____

7. くる **kuru** (*come*) _____

Conjugating verbs in the plain form

The four forms—dictionary form, **nai** form, **ta** form, and **nakatta** form—are all the "plain" forms. Plain forms are the shortest verb forms that can end a sentence. They can be used in an informal context to complete sentences. The following table shows the four plain forms of the verb かく **kaku** (*to write*):

	AFFIRMATIVE	NEGATIVE
NON-PAST	かく **kaku**	かかない **kakanai**
PAST	かいた **kaita**	かかなかった **kakanakatta**

EXERCISE
4·10

*In informal contexts, you can drop the question particle か **ka** and ask questions by raising the intonation at the end of a statement sentence. Verbs are in the plain forms, はい **hai** is replaced by うん **un**, and いいえ **īe** is replaced by うんんん **Unnn**. Complete the responses to the following questions.*

1. A: 行く？ **Iku?**

   B: うんんん、＿＿＿＿＿＿＿＿＿。 **Unnn,** ＿＿＿＿＿＿＿＿＿**.**

2. A: 借りる？ **Kariru?**

   B: うんんん、＿＿＿＿＿＿＿＿＿。 **Unnn,** ＿＿＿＿＿＿＿＿＿**.**

3. A: 買う？ **Kau?**

   B: うん、＿＿＿＿＿＿＿＿＿。 **Un,** ＿＿＿＿＿＿＿＿＿**.**

4. A: 書いた？ **Kaita?**

   B: うん、＿＿＿＿＿＿＿＿＿。 **Un,** ＿＿＿＿＿＿＿＿＿**.**

5. A: 読んだ？ **Yonda?**

   B: うんんん、＿＿＿＿＿＿＿＿＿。 **Unnn,** ＿＿＿＿＿＿＿＿＿**.**

Plain forms are also used in some grammatical structures even in polite contexts.

Conjugating verbs in the polite form

The polite suffix can be used in both non-past and past forms as well as in both affirmative and negative forms, while maintaining the same stem form of the verb. The following table summarizes the polite forms of the verb かく **kaku** (*to write*):

	AFFIRMATIVE	NEGATIVE
NON-PAST	かきます **kakimasu**	かきません **kakimasen** (or 書かないです **kakanaidesu**)
PAST	かきました **kakimashita**	かきませんでした **kakimasendeshita** (or 書かなかったです **kakanakatta desu**)

EXERCISE
4·11

Complete the responses to the following questions asked in a polite context. Note that はい *hai means* Yes *and* いいえ *Īe means* No. *The particle* か *ka at the end of the sentence indicates a question.*

1. A: 行きますか。 **Ikimasu ka.**

   B: いいえ、＿＿＿＿＿＿＿＿＿。 **Īe, ＿＿＿＿＿＿＿＿＿＿.**

2. A: 食べますか。 **Tabemasu ka.**

   B: はい、＿＿＿＿＿＿＿＿＿。 **Hai, ＿＿＿＿＿＿＿＿＿＿.**

3. A: 書きましたか。 **Kakimashita ka.**

   B: --いいえ、＿＿＿＿＿＿＿＿＿。 **Īe, ＿＿＿＿＿＿＿＿＿＿.**

4. A: 読みましたか。 **Yomimashita ka.**

   B: はい、＿＿＿＿＿＿＿＿＿。 **Hai, ＿＿＿＿＿＿＿＿＿＿.**

5. A: 休みましたか。 **Yasumimashita ka.**

   B: いいえ、＿＿＿＿＿＿＿＿＿。 **Īe, ＿＿＿＿＿＿＿＿＿＿.**

Progressive form

To express ongoing actions, use the **te** form followed by the auxiliary verb いる **iru** (*exist*). For example, 飲んでいる **nonde iru** or 飲んでいます **nonde imasu** means *I am drinking*. On the other hand, 飲んでいた **nonde ita** or 飲んでいました **nonde imashita** means *I was drinking*. This construction can also express one's habitual or regular activities.

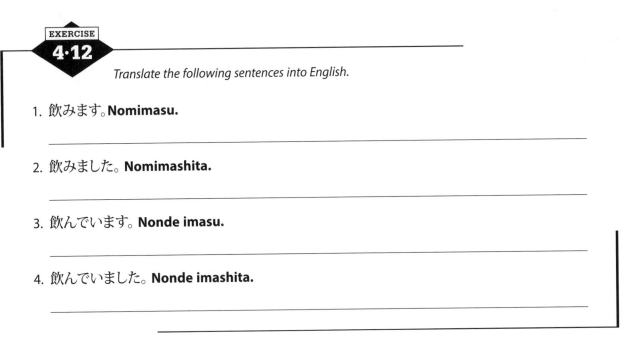

EXERCISE
4·12

Translate the following sentences into English.

1. 飲みます。 **Nomimasu.**

   ＿＿＿＿＿＿＿＿＿＿＿＿＿＿＿＿＿＿＿＿＿＿＿＿＿＿＿＿＿＿＿

2. 飲みました。 **Nomimashita.**

   ＿＿＿＿＿＿＿＿＿＿＿＿＿＿＿＿＿＿＿＿＿＿＿＿＿＿＿＿＿＿＿

3. 飲んでいます。 **Nonde imasu.**

   ＿＿＿＿＿＿＿＿＿＿＿＿＿＿＿＿＿＿＿＿＿＿＿＿＿＿＿＿＿＿＿

4. 飲んでいました。 **Nonde imashita.**

   ＿＿＿＿＿＿＿＿＿＿＿＿＿＿＿＿＿＿＿＿＿＿＿＿＿＿＿＿＿＿＿

Potential form

To express one's ability and potential, conjugate a verb into the potential form. For **ru** verbs, drop the final **ru** from the dictionary form and add **rareru**. For example, the potential form of the verb たべる **taberu** (to eat) is たべられる **taberareru** (to be able to eat). (Note that more and more Japanese add just **reru** instead of **rareru** today, saying たべれる **tabereru** instead of たべられる **taberareru**.) For **u** verbs, drop the final **u** and add **eru**. For example, the potential form of the verb のむ **nomu** (drink) is のめる **nomeru** (to be able to drink). The potential form of the verb くる **kuru** (come) is こられる **korareru** (to be able to come). To express the potential form of the verb する **suru** (do), use the verb できる **dekiru** (to be able to do). See Chapter 5 for the verb できる **dekiru**. To conjugate a verb in the potential form, look at the following table and follow the pattern of the verb in the same class and with the same ending:

	Ending	Dictionary Form	Potential Form
Ru verbs	-eる -eru	かえる**kaeru** (change)	かえられる **kaerareru** (be able to change)
	-iる -iru	きる**kiru** (wear)	きられる **kirareru** (be able to wear)
U verbs	-す -su	はなす **hanasu** (speak)	はなせる **hanaseru** (be able to speak)
	-く -ku	かく **kaku** (write)	かける **kakeru** (be able to write)
	-ぐ -gu	およぐ **oyogu** (swim)	およげる **oyogeru** (be able to swim)
	-む -mu	よむ **yomu** (read)	よめる **yomeru** (be able to read)
	-ぬ -nu	しぬ **shinu** (die)	しねる **shineru** (be able to die)
	-ぶ -bu	とぶ **tobu** (jump)	とべる **toberu** (be able to jump)
	-う-(w)u	かう **kau** (buy)	かえる **kaeru** (be able to buy)
	-る -ru	きる **kiru** (cut)	きれる **kireru** (be able to cut)
	-つ -tsu	まつ **matsu** (wait)	まてる **materu** (be able to wait)
Irregular verbs		くる **kuru** (come)	こられる **korareru** (be able to come)
		する **suru** (do)	できる **dekiru** (be able to do)

The potential verbs can be conjugated like **ru** verbs. The direct object particle を **o** is usually replaced with the particle が **ga** when the verb is in the potential form. For example:

私はカタカナで名前が書けます。
Watashi wa katakana de namae ga kakemasu.
I can write my name in katakana.

今日は映画がただで見られます。
Kyō wa eiga ga tada de miraremasu.
Today, we can see movies for free.

If the verb is できる **dekiru** (to be able to do), you must replace を **o** with が **ga**. For example:

スミスさんは空手ができます。
Sumisu-san wa karate ga dekimasu.
Mr. Smith can do karate.

An alternative way of expressing one's potential is to use ことができる **koto ga dekiru** (*to be able to do*), for example. See Chapter 10 for ことができる **koto ga dekiru**.

See Chapter 10 for ことができる **koto ga dekiru**.

EXERCISE

4·13

Indicate the potential form of each of the following verbs.

1. かく **kaku** (*write*) _____

2. いう **iu** (*say*) _____

3. よむ **yomu** (*read*) _____

4. かう **kau** (*buy*) _____

5. くる **kuru** (*come*) _____

6. たべる **taberu** (*eat*, **ru** verb) _____

Conjugating the copular verb です **desu**

Use です **desu** to express *to be* or *to be equal to* to show the identity or the state of things and people. (See Chapter 1 for more about です **desu**.) The following table shows how it is used after a noun, such as 犬 **inu** (*dog*), in both plain and polite speech styles:

	Polite		Plain	
	Affirmative	**Negative***	**Affirmative**	**Negative***
Non-past	犬です **inu desu** (*is a dog / are dogs*)	犬じゃありません **inu ja arimasen** (or 犬じゃないです **inu ja nai desu**) (*isn't a dog / aren't dogs*)	犬だ **inu da** (*is a dog / are dogs*)	犬じゃない **inu ja nai** (*isn't a dog / aren't dogs*)
Past	犬でした **inu deshita** (*was a dog / were dogs*)	犬じゃありませんでした **inu ja arimasendeshita** (or 犬じゃなかったです **inu ja nakatta desu**) (*wasn't a dog / weren't dogs*)	犬だった **inu datta** (*was a dog / were dogs*)	犬じゃなかった **inu ja nakatta** (*wasn't a dog / weren't dogs*)

_____

* In the negative forms in this table, じゃ **ja** is the contracted form of では **de wa**. You use it in a formal situation or in writing like the following:

犬ではありません **Inu de wa arimasen.**

犬ではない **Inu de wa nai.** (*isn't a dog / aren't dogs*)

犬ではありませんでした **Inu de wa arimasendeshita.** (*wasn't a dog / weren't dogs*)

犬ではなかった **Inu de wa nakatta.** (*wasn't a dog / weren't dogs*)

Convert the following Japanese sentences into polite counterparts.

1. 昨日は金曜日だった。

   Kinō wa Kinyōbi datta.

   Yesterday was Friday.

   _____

2. あれは猫じゃない。

   Are wa neko ja nai.

   That one over there is not a cat.

   _____

3. あの人はスミスさんだ。

   Ano hito wa Sumisu-san da.

   That person is Mr. Smith.

   _____

4. 昨日の晩ご飯はてんぷらじゃなかった。

   Kinō no ban-gohan wa tenpura ja nakatta.

   Yesterday's dinner was not tempura.

   _____

Verb types

When you learn verbs, in order to use them correctly, it is important to know what kinds of words and particles they require and what sort of restrictions they have. This chapter explains some types of Japanese verbs that you should be aware of.

する **suru verbs**

する **suru** is a verb that means *to do*, but it can be used with a variety of words. For example:

弟は毎日コンピューターゲームをしています。
Otōto wa mainichi konpyūtā gēmu o shite imasu.
My younger brother plays computer games every day.

よくテニスと水泳をします。
Yoku tenisu to suiei o shimasu.
I often play tennis and swim.

私はてんぷらにします。
Watashi wa tenpura ni shimasu.
I'll have tempura.

父は弁護士をしています。
Chichi wa bengoshi o shite imasu.
My father is a lawyer.

いい匂いがしますね。
Ii nioi ga shimasu ne.
It smells good, doesn't it?

この椅子はグラグラしています。
Kono isu wa guragura shite imasu.
This chair wiggles.

部屋をきれいにしてください。
Heya o kirei ni shite kudasai.
Please make your room clean (and neat).

この靴は3万円しました。
Kono kutsu wa 30,000 en shimashita.
This pair of shoes cost 30,000 yen.

However, する **suru** also directly follows a noun that has a verb-like meaning. For example, it can follow Chinese compounds or words borrowed from English. In many cases, the particle を **o** can optionally intervene between these words and する **suru**:

掃除 (を) する **sōji (o) suru** (*to clean*)
勉強 (を) する **benkyō (o) suru** (*to study*)
コピー (を) する **kopī (o) suru** (*to make a copy*)
メモする **memo suru** (*to take a note*)
チェックインする **chekkuin suru** (*to check in*)

The intervening を **o** is not allowed if there is another instance of を **o** that marks a direct object. So, in the following examples, sentences (a) to (c) are grammatical, but (d) is not:

(a) よく勉強します。 **Yoku benkyō shimasu.** *I study very hard.*
(b) よく勉強をします。 **Yoku benkyō o shimasu.** *I study very hard.*
(c) よく数学を勉強します。 **Yoku sūgaku o benkyō shimasu.** *I study mathematics very hard.*
(d) ✗よく日本語を勉強をします。 **Yoku nihongo o benkyō o shimasu.** (Ungrammatical)

EXERCISE 5·1

*The following verbs are made of words borrowed from English and the verb する **suru**. Guess what they mean.*

1. ログインする **roguin suru** _____

2. メールする **mēru suru** _____

3. スタートする **sutāto suru** _____

4. オーダーする **ōdā suru** _____

5. デートする **dēto suru** _____

Existential verbs ある **aru** and いる **iru**

The verbs ある **aru** and いる **iru** literally mean *to exist*. To express the existence of inanimate items, use ある **aru**. To express the existence of animate items such as people and animals, use いる **iru**. Items that exist are marked by the particle が **ga**, and the location is marked by the particle に **ni**. However, one of them should be conveyed as the old shared information, being marked by the topic particle は **wa**, so the other can be conveyed as the new information. This makes the sentence clear and natural. If you want to convey the location of an item as the new information, place the noun for the item at the beginning of the sentence and mark it with the topic particle は **wa**, and then place the location noun and mark it with the particle に **ni**. If you want to convey the existence of an item as the new information, place the location noun at the beginning of the sentence and mark it with the topic particle は **wa**, and then place the noun for the item and mark it with the particle が **ga**. (See Chapter 7 for the topic particle は **wa**.) For example: テレビはリビングルームにあります。

Terebi wa ribingurūmu ni arimasu.
The TV is in the living room.
(The location *living room* is the new information.)

リビングルームにはテレビがあります。
Ribingurūmu ni wa terebi ga arimasu.
There is a TV in the living room.
(The existence of the TV is the new information.)

この建物には警察官がいます。
Kono tatemono ni wa keisatsukan ga imasu.
There is a police officer in this building.
(The existence of the police officer is the new information.)

警察官はあそこにいます。
Keisatsukan wa asoko ni imasu.
The police officer is over there.
(The location *over there* is the new information.)

Precise locations of things are expressed using relative location terms. For example, 上 **ue** is a relative location term that is actually a noun that means *upper/top (area)*. Importantly, the reference item precedes the relative location term to clarify the location, as in 机の上 **tsukue no ue** (*the upper/top area of the desk*). It is used in a sentence as shown in this example:

辞書は机の上にあります。
Jisho wa tsukue no ue ni arimasu.
The dictionary is on the desk.

The following table lists some of the essential relative location terms:

Relative Location Term	Meaning	Usage Example
上 **ue**	*upper/top*	辞書は机の上にあります。 **Jisho wa tsukue no ue ni arimasu.** *The dictionary is on the desk.*
下 **shita**	*lower area*	猫はテーブルの下にいます。 **Neko wa tēburu no shita ni imasu.** *The cat is under the table.*
中 **naka**	*inside*	携帯はかばんの中にあります。 **Keitai wa kaban no naka ni arimasu.** *The cell phone is in the bag.*
右 **migi**	*right*	かばんは机の右にあります。 **Kaban wa tsukue no migi ni arimasu.** *The bag is on the right of the desk.*
左 **hidari**	*left*	銀行は病院の左にあります。 **Ginkō wa byōin no hidari ni arimasu.** *The bank is to the left of the hospital.*
前 **mae**	*front*	田中さんは山田さんの前にいます。 **Tanaka-san wa Yamada-san no mae ni imasu.** *Mr. Tanaka is in front of Ms. Yamada.*
後ろ **ushiro**	*rear, back*	高橋さんは山田さんの後ろにいます。 **Takahashi-san wa Yamada-san no ushiro ni imasu.** *Mr. Takahashi is behind Ms. Yamada.*

Relative Location Term	Meaning	Usage Example
間 **aida**	*between*	郵便局は病院と銀行の間にあります。 **Yūbinkyoku wa byōin to ginkō no aida ni arimasu.** *The post office is between the hospital and the bank.*
近く **chikaku**, そば **soba**	*vicinity, near*	本屋は大学の近くにあります。 **Hon'ya wa daigaku no chikaku ni arimasu.** 本屋は大学のそばにあります。 **Hon'ya wa daigaku no soba ni arimasu.** *The bookstore is near the university.*
横 **yoko**	*side*	本箱は机の横にあります。 **Honbako wa tsukue no yoko ni arimasu.** *The bookcase is on the side of the desk.*
隣 **tonari**	*next to*	マイクさんは私の隣にいます。 **Maiku-san wa watashi no tonari ni imasu.** *Mike is next to me.* 銀行はスーパーの隣にあります。 **Ginkō wa sūpā no tonari ni arimasu.** *The bank is next to the supermarket.*

EXERCISE

5·2

Translate the following sentences into Japanese.

1. *My book is in the bag.*

   _____

2. *My bag is behind the chair.*

   _____

3. *The dog is under the desk.*

   _____

4. *The cat is next to the dog.*

   _____

You can also use the verb ある **aru** to express your plans, duties, events, incidents, and experiences. For example:

今日はクラスがあります。したは面接があります。
Kyō wa kurasu ga arimasu. Ashita wa mensetsu ga arimasu.
I have a class today. I have an interview tomorrow.

来週は名古屋で会議があります。
Raishū wa Nagoya de kaigi ga arimasu.
We will have a conference in Nagoya next week.

今日大阪で地震がありました。
Kyō Osaka de jishin ga arimashita.
There was an earthquake in Osaka today.

富士山を見たことがあります。
Fujisan o mita koto ga arimasu.
I have seen Mt. Fuji.

The locations of events and incidents are marked by the particle で **de**. See Chapter 7 for particles. You express your experience by using a verb in the **ta** form and ことがあります **koto ga arimasu**. See Chapter 10 for this construction.

The verb いる **iru** can also express human relationships. For example:

私は兄が3人います。
Watashi wa ani ga san-nin imasu.
I have three older brothers.

兄はフランス人の友達がいます。
Ani wa Furansujin no tomodachi ga imasu.
My older brother has a French friend.

The verbs ある **aru** and いる **iru** can also function as auxiliary verbs that follow another verb in the **te** form. See Chapter 6 for auxiliary verbs.

EXERCISE 5·3

For each of the following, choose the appropriate answer from the options in the parentheses.

1. 桜通りで家事が（ありました, いました）。

   Sakura-dōri de kaji ga (arimashita, imashita).

   There was a fire in Sakura Street.

2. 伊藤さんは兄弟が3人（あります, います）。

   Itō-san wa kyōdai ga san-nin (arimasu, imasu).

   Ms. Ito has three siblings.

3. あしたは数学の試験が（あります, います）。

   Ashita wa sūgaku no shiken ga (arimasu, imasu).

   I have a math exam tomorrow.

4. うなぎを食べたことが（ありますか, いますか）。

   Unagi o tabeta koto ga (arimasu ka, imasu ka).

   Have you ever had eel?

5. 猫はどこに（ありますか, いますか）。

   Neko wa doko ni (arimasu ka, imasu ka).

   Where is the cat?

Transitive and intransitive verbs

A *transitive verb* is a verb that can take a direct object. In English, a direct object immediately follows a verb, without an intervening preposition. For example, the verb *to make* is a transitive verb in English. First, this verb makes sense only when *someone makes something*. Second, you cannot say only *I made*, even if what you made is contextually understood. You have to say, for example, *I made this cake* or *I made it*. A direct object does not have to be an inanimate object but can be a person or an animal. For example, in the sentence *Mary invited John*, the direct object is *John*, because this name immediately follows the verb.

By contrast, the verb *to go* is not a transitive verb because it cannot be immediately followed by a noun. For example, you can say *He will go to Tokyo*, but you cannot say *He will go Tokyo*. A verb that cannot take a direct object is called an *intransitive verb*.

In Japanese, if a verb can have a noun marked by the particle を **o**, it is a transitive verb. The particle を **o** is the direct object marker. The following sentences use transitive verbs. See the direct object marked by を **o** in each of them.

母がすしを作ります。
Haha ga sushi o tsukurimasu.
My mother will make sushi.

新聞を読みました。
Shinbun o yomimashita.
(I) read the newspaper.

メアリーさんを招待します。
Mearī-san o shōtai shimasu.
(I) will invite Mary.

By contrast, the following sentences contain intransitive verbs:

兄は毎日図書館に行きます。
Ani wa mainichi toshokan ni ikimasu.
My older brother goes to the library every day.

子供がよくこの公園で遊びます。
Kodomo ga yoku kono kōen de asobimasu.
Children often play in this park.

EXERCISE
5·4

Identify the direct object in each of the following sentences, if any.

1. 昨日はうちに田中さんが来ました。

   Kinō wa uchi ni Tanaka-san ga kimashita.

   Mr. Tanaka came to my house yesterday.

2. 姉はてんぷらを作りました。

   Ane wa tenpura o tsukurimashita.

   My sister made tempura.

3. メアリーさんはマイクさんを招待しました。

   Mearī san wa Maiku-san o shōtai shimashita.

   Mary invited Mike.

4. あしたはボストンに行きます。

   Ashita wa Bosuton ni ikimasu.

   I'll go to Boston tomorrow.

Transitive and intransitive pairs

In English, some pairs of verbs (e.g., *to raise* and *to rise*) have similar meanings and sound similar, but they differ in whether the relevant item serves as the direct object or as the subject. For example, consider *I will raise the flag* vs. *The flag will rise*. The flag is the direct object of the verb *to raise*, but it is the subject of the verb *to rise*. Therefore, *to raise* is a transitive verb, and *to rise* is an intransitive verb. Another example of a transitive and intransitive pair of verbs in English is *to lay* and *to lie*. There are not many pairs like this in English, but there are many in Japanese. For example, こわす **kowasu** is a transitive verb (*to break*), and こわれる **kowareru** is an intransitive verb (*to break*). The item broken is marked by the direct object particle を **o** when the verb is こわす **kowasu**, but it is marked by the subject particle が **ga** when the verb is こわれる **kowareru**.

> 弟が父のカメラをこわしました。
> **Otōto ga chichi no kamera o kowashimashita.**
> *My younger brother broke my father's camera.*

> 父のカメラがこわれました。
> **Chichi no kamera ga kowaremashita.**
> *My father's camera broke down.*

The following are only a few of the many transitive and intransitive pairs in Japanese:

Transitive Verb	Intransitive Verb
(. . . を) 上げる (. . . **o**) **ageru** *raises (something)*	(. . . が) 上がる (. . . **ga**) **agaru** *(Something) rises*
(. . . を) 開ける (. . . **o**) **akeru** *opens (something)*	(. . . が) 開く (. . . **ga**) **aku** *(Something) opens*
(. . . を) 出す (. . . **o**) **dasu** *lets (something) out*	(. . . が) 出る (. . . **ga**) **deru** *(Something) goes out*
(. . . を) 始める (. . . **o**) **hajimeru** *begins (something)*	(. . . が) 始まる (. . . **ga**) **hajimaru** *(Something) begins*
(. . . を) 入れる (. . . **o**) **ireru** *puts (something) in, lets (someone) in*	(. . . が) 入る (. . . **ga**) **hairu** *(Something) is placed in, (someone) enters*

Transitive Verb	Intransitive Verb
(...を) 消す **(... o) kesu** *turns (something) off*	(...が) 消える **(... ga) kieru** *(Something) turns off*
(...を) 壊す **(... o) kowasu** *breaks (something)*	(...が) 壊れる **(... ga) kowareru** *(Something) breaks down*
(...を) 回す **(... o) mawasu** *turns (something)*	(...が) 回る **(... ga) mawaru** *(Something) turns*
(...を) 閉める **(... o) shimeru** *closes (something)*	(...が) 閉まる **(... ga) shimaru** *(Something) closes*
(...を) つける **(... o) tsukeru** *turns (something) on*	(...が) つく **(... ga) tsuku** *(Something) turns on*

EXERCISE 5·5

For each of the following, choose the appropriate answer from the options in the parentheses.

1. ドア(が, を)開きました。

   Doa (ga, o) akimashita.

2. 本(が, を)かばんに入れました。

   Hon (ga, o) kaban ni iremashita.

3. クラス(が, を)始まりました。

   Kurasu (ga, o) hajimarimashita.

4. パソコン(が, を)壊れました。

   Pasokon (ga, o) kowaremashita.

5. テレビ(が, を)消してください。

   Terebi (ga, o) keshite kudasai.

Inherently potential verbs

Some verbs, such as 見える **mieru** (*to see*), 聞こえる **kikoeru** (*to hear*), 分かる **wakaru** (*to understand*), and できる **dekiru** (*can do*), inherently include "potential" meaning and express the state that is available (possible) for the speaker. The understood direct objects of these verbs are marked by the particle が**ga** rather than the particle を **o**. For example:

> あ、富士山が見えますよ。
> **A, Fujisan ga miemasu yo.**
> *Oh, we can see Mt. Fuji!*

あれ？足音が聞こえますよ。
Are? Ashioto ga kikoemasu yo.
Oh, I hear footsteps.

日本語が分かりますか。
Nihongo ga wakarimasu ka.
Do you understand Japanese?

まだ運転ができません。
Mada unten ga dekimasen.
I still cannot drive.

These verbs cannot be used with the potential suffix (**rareru** or **eru**) because they already include the potential meaning. (See Chapter 4 for potential forms.) 見える **mieru** and 聞こえる **kikoeru** have a slightly different nuance from 見られる **mirareru** and 聞こえる **kikoeru**, which are the potential forms of 見る **miru** (*watch*) and 聞く**kiku** (*listen*). Whereas 見える **mieru** and 聞こえる **kikoeru** express what is spontaneously available for the speaker, 見られる **mirareru** and 聞ける **kikeru** express what the speaker can consciously do, if he wants to do it. For example:

2,000円のチケットを買えばショーが見られます。
ni-sen-en no chiketto o kaeba shō ga miraremasu.
If you buy a 2,000-yen ticket, you can see a show.

ヘッドホンを使えば音楽が聞けます。
Heddohon o tsukaeba ongaku ga kikemasu.
If you use headphones, you can listen to music.

EXERCISE 5·6

For each of the following, choose the appropriate answer from the options in the parentheses.

1. 富士山（を, が）見ました。

   Fujisan (o, ga) mimashita.

2. 富士山（を, が）見えました。

   Fujisan (o, ga) miemashita.

3. 富士山が（見られました, 見ました）。

   Fujisan ga (miraremashita, mimashita).

4. からて（を, が）できます。

   Karate (o, ga) dekimasu.

Verbs with hidden *become/get*

Many states that you can express with a simple adjective or verb in English have to be expressed using verbs and the auxiliary verb いる **iru** in Japanese. This is the case because some Japanese verbs have a hidden meaning *become* or *get*. (See Chapter 6 for the auxiliary verb いる **iru**.) For example, to say you *know* someone, you cannot say 知ります **shirimasu**, but you have to say 知っています **shitte imasu**. It is a good idea to know the following verbs:

Verb	Example of Usage
晴れる **hareru** *to become cleared (sky)*	今日は晴れていますね。 **Kyō wa harete imasu ne.** *It's nice [sky condition] today.*
結婚する **kekkon suru** *to get married*	姉は結婚しています。 **Ane wa kekkon shite imasu.** *My sister is married.*
混む **komu** *to become crowded*	このバスは混んでいます。 **Kono basu wa konde imasu.** *This bus is crowded.*
おこる **okoru** *to get angry*	母はいつも怒っています。 **Haha wa itsumo okotte imasu.** *My mother is always angry.*
知る **shiru** *to get to know*	田中さんを知っていますか。 **Tanaka-san o shitte imasu ka.** *Do you know Mr. Tanaka?*
疲れる **tsukareru** *to get tired*	ちょっと疲れています。 **Chotto tsukarete imasu.** *I'm a bit tired.*
喜ぶ **yorokobu** *to get delighted*	父はとても喜んでいます。 **Chichi wa totemo yorokonde imasu.** *My father is very pleased.*

Verbs of giving and receiving

You express giving and receiving by using three verbs in Japanese: あげる **ageru** (*to give*), くれる **kureru** (*to give*), and もらう **morau** (*to receive*). They have honorific counterparts: 差し上げる **sashiageru**, 下さる **kudasaru**, and 頂く **itadaku**, respectively. Which one of these verbs you use depends on who the giver and the receiver are and what their relationship is. Here, the notion of in-group and out-group plays an important role. Your family are always your in-group members, whereas the others are usually your out-group members. However, if you feel very close to your friend, he or she can be your in-group member. Similarly, if you are in a business context, the members in your company can be your in-group members whereas your clients are your out-group members. In fact, the giver and the receiver are often omitted in conversations because the choice of verbs can clarify who is the giver and who is the receiver.

The verb くれる **kureru** means *to give*, but the receiver of the item must be the speaker, or it must be the speaker's in-group member when the giver is his out-group member. If the giver is the speaker's in-group member, the receiver must be the speaker himself or his in-group member, who is closer to the speaker than the giver. That is, the verb くれる **kureru** shows the giving takes place in the inward direction. However, in a question sentence, the second person can be the receiver. For example:

> 山田さんは私に花をくれました。
> **Yamada-san wa watashi ni hana o kuremashita.**
> *Ms. Yamada gave me flowers.*

> 山田さんは私の妹に花をくれました。
> **Yamada-san wa watashi no imōto ni hana o kuremashita.**
> *Ms. Yamada gave my little sister flowers.*

叔父は母に花瓶をくれました。
Oji wa haha ni kabin o kuremashita.
My uncle gave my mother a vase.

田中さんはあなたに何をくれましたか。
Tanaka-san wa anata ni nani o kuremashita ka.
What did Mr. Tanaka give to you?

In all other contexts, あげる **ageru** is used. For example:

私は由美子さんに辞書をあげます。あなたには本をあげます。
Watashi wa Yumiko-san ni jisho o agemasu. Anata ni wa hon o agemasu.
I'll give Yumiko a dictionary. I'll give you a book.

トムさんは美香さんに本をあげました。あなたは美香さんに何をあげましたか。
Tomu-san wa Mika-san ni hon o agemashita. Anata wa Mika-san ni nani o agemashita ka.
Tom gave Mika a book. What did you give to Mika?

In a formal context, use honorific counterparts of these verbs. Use 下さる **kudasaru** instead of くれる **kureru** when the giver is higher in social status than the receiver. Use 差し上げる **sashiageru** instead of あげる **ageru** when the receiver is higher in status than the giver. The relative social status can be decided by a variety of factors including age and occupational position. Remember the slight irregularity in the conjugated form of 下さる **kudasaru**: its stem form is 下さり**kudasari**, but its final syllable り **ri** changes to い **i** when followed by polite suffixes such as ます **masu** and ました **mashita**. For example:

先生が私に辞書を下さいました。私は先生に花を差し上げました。
Sensi ga watashi ni jisho o kudasaimashita. Watashi wa sensei ni hana o sashiagemashita.
The teacher gave me a dictionary. I gave my teacher flowers.

When you are talking about giving to animals or plants, you can use やる **yaru** instead of あげる **ageru**. You can also use やる **yaru** when you speak of giving something to your child or younger sibling. For example:

花に水をやりました。
Hana ni mizu wo yarimashita.
I watered my flowers.

弟に古い服をやりました。
Otōto ni furui fuku o yarimashita.
I gave my old clothes to my younger brother.

**EXERCISE
5·7**

For each of the following, choose the appropriate answer from the options in the parentheses.

1. 私は山田さんに本を（あげました, くれました）。

   Watashi wa Yamada-san ni hon o (agemashita, kuremashita).

2. 山田さんは私に本を（あげました, くれました）。

   Yamada-san wa watashi ni hon o (agemashita, kuremashita).

3. 山田さんは母に本を（あげました, くれました）。

   Yamada-san wa haha ni hon o (agemashita, kuremashita).

4. 山田さんは田中さんに本を(あげました, くれました)。

Yamada-san wa Tanaka-san ni hon o (agemashita, kuremashita).

5. 先生は私に本を(くれました, 下さいました)。

Sensei wa watashi ni hon o (kuremashita, kudasaimashita).

The verb もらう **morau** means *to receive*. The receiver appears as the subject of the sentence and is marked by the particle が **ga**, if not by the topic marker は **wa**. The giver is marked by the particle からkara or に**ni** when the verb is もらう**morau**. For example:

私は山田さんに本をもらいました。
Watashi wa Yamada-san ni hon o moraimashita.
I received a book from Ms. Yamada.

妹は田中さんからクッキーをもらいました。
Imōto wa Tanaka-san kara kukkī o moraimashita.
My younger sister received cookies from Mr. Tanaka.

Remember that the receiver must be closer to the speaker than to the giver. So, for example, if you want to say *Ms. Yamada received cookies from my mother*, you should not say:

山田さんは母にクッキーをもらいました。
Yamada-san wa haha ni kukkī o moraimashita.

Instead, say:

母は山田さんにクッキーをあげました。
Haha wa Yamada-san ni kukkī o agemashita.
My mother gave Ms. Yamada cookies.

You replace もらう **morau** with 頂く**itadaku** when the giver is someone to whom you wish to show respect. For example:

私は先生に辞書を頂きました。
Watashi wa sensei ni jisho o itadakimashita.
I received a dictionary from my teacher.

EXERCISE
5·8

For each of the following, choose the appropriate answer from the options in the parentheses.

1. これは母から(もらいました, 頂きました)。

Kore wa haha kara (moraimashita, itadakimashita).

2. これは先生から(もらいました, 頂きました)。

Kore wa sensei kara (moraimashita, itadakimashita).

3. 私は父(で, に)お金を もらいました。

Watashi wa chichi (de, ni) okane o moraimashita.

4. (山田さん, 兄)は母から本をもらいました。

(Yamada-san, ani) wa haha kara hon o moraimahsita.

The verbs of giving and receiving—あげる **ageru** (*to give*), くれる **kureru** (*to give*) and もらう **morau** (*to receive*)—their honorific counterparts—差し上げる **sashiageru,** 下さる **kudasaru,** and 頂く **itadaku**—and the verb やる **yaru** (*to give*) can also function as auxiliary verbs, following another verb in the **te** form to implicitly show who was helping whom. For example, if your mother made cookies and it was for you, say:

母がクッキーを作ってくれました。
Haha ga kukkī o tsukutte kuremashita.

See Chapter 6 for auxiliary verbs.

EXERCISE
5·9

Look at the following illustrations. In Japanese, describe what happened in each one. There may be more than one way of stating the same facts. If so, state them all.

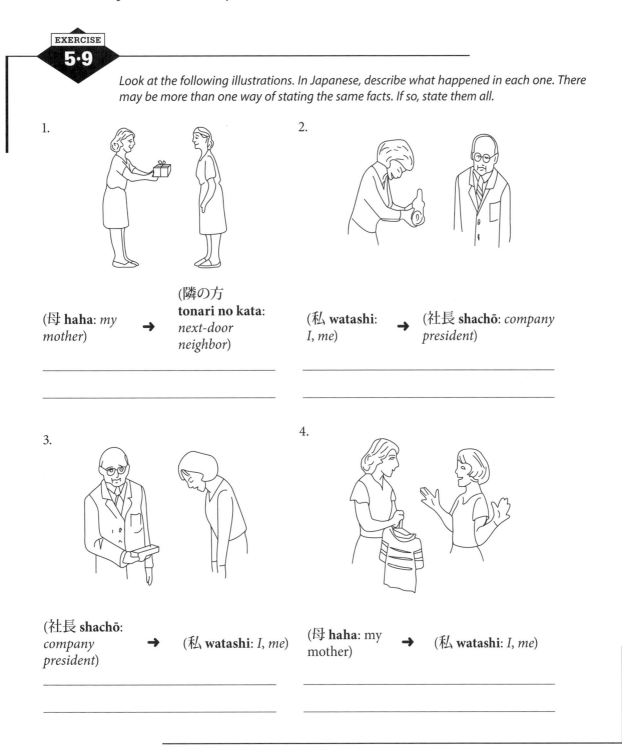

1.

(母 **haha:** *my mother*) → (隣の方 **tonari no kata:** *next-door neighbor*)

_____

_____

2.

(私 **watashi:** *I, me*) → (社長 **shachō:** *company president*)

_____

_____

3.

(社長 **shachō:** *company president*) → (私 **watashi:** *I, me*)

_____

_____

4.

(母 **haha:** *my mother*) → (私 **watashi:** *I, me*)

_____

_____

Auxiliaries that follow verbs in the **te** form

Some verbs and adjectives also function as auxiliary verbs or auxiliary adjectives following a verb in the **te** form. The basic meaning they add is *do . . . and . . .*, and they provide additional meanings, refinements, or implications.

. . . て **te** + あげる **ageru**, etc. (helpfulness)

All verbs of giving and receiving introduced in Chapter 5 can be used as auxiliaries. These verbs—あげる **ageru** (*to give*), くれる **kureru** (*to give*), やる **yaru** (*to give*), and もらう **morau** (*to receive*), and their honorific counterparts 差し上げる **sashiageru**, 下さる **kudasaru**, and 頂く **itadaku**—not only imply the closeness of the relevant people but also imply who is being helpful to whom. Which one of these verbs you use depends on who the giver and the receiver are and what their relationship is. Just remember that the source of help is marked by に **ni** but not by から **kara** if 頂く **itadaku** and もらう **morau** are used as auxiliary verbs. For example:

あなたの部屋を掃除してあげましたよ。
Anata no heya o sōji shite agemashita yo.
I cleaned your room (as a help)!

山田さんが本当のことを私に話してくれました。
Yamada-san ga hontō no koto o watashi ni hanashite kuremashita.
She told me the truth (and I appreciate it).

先生が推薦状を書いてくださいました。
Sensei ga suisenjō o kaite kudasaimashita.
My teacher wrote a recommendation letter (as a kindness/help).

先生に推薦状を書いていただきました。
Sensei ni suisenjō o kaite itadakimashita.
I (received a kindness of) my teacher's writing a recommendation letter for me.

弟の宿題を手伝ってやりました。
Otōto no shukudai o tetsudatte yarimashita.
I helped my younger brother do his homework.

Complete these sentences appropriately.

1. 先生が推薦状を書いて _____ ました。

   Sensei ga suisenjō o kaite _____ mashita.

2. 先生に推薦状を書いて _____ ました。

   Sensei ni suisenjō o kaite _____ mashita.

3. 母がクッキーを作って _____ ました。

   Haha ga kukkī o tsukutte _____ mashita.

4. 父の車を洗って _____ ました。(洗う **arau**: *to wash*)

   Chichi no kuruma o aratte _____ mashita.

5. 妹の部屋を掃除して _____ ました。

   Imōto no heya o sōji shite _____ mashita.

...て te + いる iru (progressive, resulting, and habitual states)

The verb いる **iru** means *to exist*. Although it is a verb, it represents a state rather than an action.

Likewise, the auxiliary verb いる **iru** represents a state, which is a progressive state, a habitual state, or a resulting state. For example, マイクさんは飲んでいます **Maiku-san wa nonde imasu** has the following three possible meanings, all of which are about the current state:

◆ *Mike is drinking (now).*
   (Progressive state: An activity progressively continues over a period of time.)
◆ *Mike drinks (regularly).*
   (Habitual state: An activity takes place regularly, such as every day or every week.)
◆ *Mike had some drinks (and he is drunk now).*
   (Resulting state: An activity took place in the past and still influences the current state.)

The context can help you figure out the meaning of a sentence. It's a good idea to pay close attention to other phrases in the same sentence, particularly adverbs such as 今 **ima** (*now*), 毎日 **mainichi** (*every day*), ずっと **zutto** (*continuously*), and まだ **mada** (*yet*). It is also useful to know that some verbs can express actions that can be repeated and prolonged, such as *drinking* and *walking*, but others can only express one-time action or change-of-state actions, such as *getting married*, *going*, or *opening*. The latter kind of verbs cannot express progressive state. The following are examples of these three states:

私は今ピザを食べています。
Watashi wa ima piza o tabete imasu.
I am eating pizza now. (progressive state)

昨日の3時は友達とコーヒーを飲んでいました。
Kinō no san-ji wa tomodachi to kōhī o nonde imashita.
I was having coffee with my friend at 3 o'clock yesterday. (progressive state in the past)

兄は毎朝 1 時間走っています。

Ani wa maiasa ichi-jikan hashitte imasu.

My older brother jogs for one hour every morning. (habitual state)

妹はコンピューターゲームばかりしています。

Imōto wa konpyūtāgēmu bakari shite imasu. (ばかり **bakari**: *does nothing but*)

My younger sister does nothing but plays computer games. (habitual state)
(See Chapter 7 for ばかり **bakari**.)

母は大学で英語を教えています。父は銀行で働いています。弟は高校に行っています。

Haha wa daigaku de eigo o oshiete imasu. Chichi wa ginkō de hataraite imasu. Otōto wa kōkō ni itte imasu.

My mother teaches English at a college. My father works at a bank. My younger brother goes to high school. (habitual state)

田中さんは言葉をよく知っていますね。本をたくさん読んでいるんでしょう。

Tanaka-san wa kotoba o yoku shitte imasu ne. Hon o takusan yonde iru n deshō. (んでしょう **n deshō**: *I guess*)

Mr. Tanaka knows a lot of words. (resulting state) *He reads a lot of books.* (habitual state) / *He has read a lot of books.* (resulting state)

田中さんはまだ来ていません。変ですね。

Tanaka-san wa mada kite imasen. Hen desu ne.

Mr. Tanaka hasn't come yet. It's strange. (resulting state)

すみません。父は今大阪に行っています。あしたはうちに帰ります。

Sumimasen. Chichi wa ima Ōsaka ni itte imasu. Ashita wa uchi ni kaerimasu.

I'm sorry. My father has gone to Osaka. He'll come home tomorrow. (resulting state)

姉は結婚しています。

Ane wa kekkon shite imasu.

My older sister is married. (resulting state)

EXERCISE
6·2

Which state do the underlined phrases represent: progressive state, habitual state, or resulting state?

1. A: お姉さんは学生さんですか。 **Onēsan wa gakusei-san desu ka.**

   B: はい、姉は<u>大学に行っています</u>。 **Hai, ane wa <u>daigaku ni itte imasu</u>.**

   _____

2. A: お兄さんは今うちにいらっしゃいますか。 **Onī san wa ima uchi ni irasshaimasu ka.**

   B: いいえ、<u>今大阪に行っています</u>。 **Īe, ima <u>Osaka ni itte imasu</u>.**

   _____

3. A: 弟さんは今うちにいらっしゃいますか。 **Otōto-san wa ima uchi ni irasshaimasu ka.**

   B: いいえ、<u>今高校でテニスをしています</u>。 **Īe, ima kōkō de <u>tenisu o shite imasu</u>.**

   _____

4. A: テニスは 好きですか。 **Tenisu wa suki desu ka.**

   B: はい、毎朝弟とテニスをしています。 **Hai, maiasa otōto to <u>tenisu o shite imasu</u>.**

   _____

5. A: 山田さんはクラスに来ていますか。 **Yamada-san wa kurasu ni kite imasu ka.**

   B: いいえ、まだ来ていません。 **Īe, mada <u>kite imasen</u>.**

   _____

...て te + しまう shimau (completion)

The auxiliary verb しまう **shimau** emphasizes the completion of action and expresses satisfaction or regret, depending on the context. For example:

> ダイエットをしているのに、昨日の晩ケーキを3つ食べてしまいました。
> **Daietto o shite iru noni, kinō no ban kēki o mit-tsu tabete shimaimashita.**
> *Although I'm on diet, I ate three pieces of cake last night.* (regret)

> 宿題を全部やってしまいました。
> **Shukudai o zenbu yatte shimaimashita.**
> *I did all homework!* (satisfaction)

> 違う電車に乗ってしまいました。
> **Chigau densha ni notte shimaimashita.**
> *I got on a wrong train.* (regret)

> 漢字を忘れてしまいました。
> **Kanji o wasurete shimaimashita.**
> *I forgot kanji.* (regret)

> **EXERCISE**
> **6·3**

In Japanese, share two things you think you should not have done in the past week.

1. _____

2. _____

...て te + おく oku (preparation)

The auxiliary verb おく **oku** implies that the action is for the preparation for some future event, for future convenience, or for avoiding potential future problems. For example:

> ホテルを予約しておいてください。
> **Hoteru o yoyaku shite oite kudasai.**
> *Please go ahead and reserve a hotel room (so we don't have to worry about it later).*

> 掃除をして、ワインを買っておきます。
> **Sōji o shite, wain o katte okimasu.**
> *I'll clean the room and buy some bottles of wine (for today's party).*

メールアドレスをメモしておきます。
Mēru adoresu o memo shite okimasu.
I'll take a note of his email address (so I won't forget it).

このことは秘密にしておいてくださいね。
Kono koto wa himitsu ni shite oite kudasai ne.
Please keep this matter a secret (because otherwise, it would cause a problem).

EXERCISE 6·4

Complete the following passage appropriately.

あしたはうちに山田さんと田中さんが来ます。いっしょにすき焼きを食べます。今日は部屋を
_____ おきます。それから、飲み物を _____ おきます。肉と
野菜はあした買います。

Ashita wa uchi ni Yamada-san to Tanaka-san ga kimasu. Isshoni sukiyaki o tabemasu.

Kyō wa heya o _____ okimasu. Sorekara, nomimono o _____

okimasu. Niku to yasai wa ashita kaimasu.

Ms. Yamada and Mr. Tanaka will come to my home tomorrow. We will have sukiyaki together. I will clean my room today. Then, I will buy drinks. I will buy meat and vegetables tomorrow.

...て te + みる miru (trial)

The auxiliary verb みる **miru** means *to do . . . and see* or *to try . . . ing*. For example:

おいしいですから食べてみてください。
Oishii desu kara tabete mite kudasai.
It's delicious, so please try eating it.

このドレスを着てみてもいいですか。
Kono doresu o kite mite mo ii desu ka.
Is it okay to wear this dress?

EXERCISE 6·5

Choose from the following list of verbs to complete the sentences. Make sure to conjugate each verb appropriately.

使う **tsukau** (*to use*)　　会う **au** (*to meet*)　　考える **kangaeru** (*to consider*)　　着る **kiru** (*to put on*)

1. いい人ですから _____ みてください。

   Ii hito desu kara _____ mite kudasai.

   (He) is a nice person, so please try meeting (him).

2. _____ みましたが、ちょっと不便でした。

   _____ **mimashita ga, chotto fuben deshita.**

   I tried using it, but it was a bit inconvenient.

Auxiliaries that follow verbs in the te form　**67**

3. _____ みましたが、ちょっと短かったです。

_____ **mimashita ga, chotto mijikakatta desu.**

(I) tried putting it on, but it was a bit short.

4. この仕事はよくありませんよ。もう一度 _____ みてください。

Kono shigoto wa yoku arimasen yo. Mōichido _____ mite kudasai.

This job is not very good. Please try thinking about it one more time.

Complete the following sentences appropriately.

1. あしたはテストがあるので _____ おきます。

Ashita wa tesuto ga aru node _____ okimasu.

I have a test tomorrow, so I'll study.

2. また漢字を _____ しまいました。

Mata kanji o _____ shimaimashita.

I forgot the kanji again.

3. あしたはマリーさんの誕生日ですから _____ おきます。

Ashita wa Marī-san no tanjōbi desu kara _____ okimasu. (誕生日 **tanjōbi:** *birthday*)

Tomorrow is Marie's birthday, so I will buy a present.

4. 宿題を _____ しまいましょう!

Shukudai o _____ shimaimashō!

Let's finish doing our homework.

5. 便利ですよ。 _____ みてください。

Benri desu yo. _____ mite kudasai.

It's convenient. Please try using it.

...て te + いく iku and くる kuru (progress)

Some auxiliary verbs express the progress of an action or a change. The auxiliary verb いく **iku** shows the initiation of the action or change at the time of the speech and its continuation thereafter. It is often used with the verb なる **naru** or する **suru**, which expresses a change. For example:

> もう3月です。これからだんだん暖かくなっていきますよ。
> **Mō San-gatsu desu. Korekara dandan atatakaku natte ikimasu yo.**
> *It's already March. It will gradually become warmer and warmer.*

これからは頑張っていきます。
Korekara wa ganbatte ikimasu.
From now on, I will start trying my best (and will continue to do so).

毎年試験の問題を難しくしていきます。
Maitoshi shiken no mondai o muzukashiku shite ikimasu.
Every year, I shall make the questions in the exam gradually more difficult.

The auxiliary verb くる **kuru** shows the initiation of the action or change prior to the time of the speech and its continuation until the time of the speech. Again, it is often used with the verb なる **naru** or する **suru** to express a change. For example:

寒くなってきましたね。
Samuku natte kimashita ne.
It is getting colder, isn't it?

日本語の文法が分かってきました。
Nihongo no bunpō ga wakatte kimashita.
I have come to understand Japanese grammar.

最近だんだん慣れてきました。
Saikin dandan narete kimashita.
Recently, I started to get accustomed to it little by little.

EXERCISE
6·7

For each of the following, choose the appropriate answer from the options in the parentheses.

1. やっと文法が分かって（いきます、いきました、きました）。先生、ありがとうございました。

   Yatto bunpō ga wakatte (ikimasu, ikimashita, kimashita). Sensei, arigatō gozaimashita.

   I started to understand grammar. Thank you, teacher.

2. これからも頑張って勉強して（いきます、いきました、きました）。これからも宜しくお願いします。

   Korekara mo ganbatte benkyō shite (ikimasu, ikimashita, kimashita). Korekara mo yoroshiku onegai shimasu.

   I will continue to try my best and study from now on also. Thank you in advance for your (support).

3. これからは暑くなって（いきますよ、きましたよ）。

   Korekara wa atsuku natte (ikimasu yo, kimashita yo).

   It will gradually become hot from now on.

4. 最近暑くなって（いきますね、きましたね）。

   Saikin atsuku natte (ikimasu ne, kimashita ne).

   It started to become hot recently.

5. 値段を毎年高くして（いく、くる）つもりです。

   Nedan o maitoshi takaku shite (iku, kuru) tsumori desu. (値段 **nedan**: *price*)

   I plan to increase the price every year.

...て te + ある aru (resulting state)

The auxiliary verb ある **aru** follows a transitive verb in the **te** form, to express the state of something (or someone) that has resulted from a past action. The item can be marked by が **ga** or を **o**. However, if marked by を **o**, it implies that the action was performed by the speaker. If the verb is an intransitive verb, いる **iru** is used instead of ある **aru**. In this case, there is no implication about who performed the action. (See Chapter 5 for transitive and intransitive verbs.) For example:

> ドアが閉めてあります。
> **Doa ga shimete arimasu.**
> *The door is closed. (Somebody closed it.)*
>
> ドアを閉めてあります。
> **Doa o shimete arimasu.**
> *The door is closed. (I closed it.)*
>
> ドアが閉まっています。
> **Doa ga shimatte imasu.**
> *The door is closed. (It was closed.)*

EXERCISE 6·8

Following the example, convert the sentences to include あります *arimasu.*

EXAMPLE　だれかがテーブルの上に花瓶を置きました。→ テーブルの上に花瓶が置いてあります。

Dareka ga tēburu no ue ni kabin o okimashita. → Tēburu no ue ni kabin ga oite arimasu.

Someone placed a vase on the table. → A vase is placed on the table.

1. だれかが壁にポスターを貼りました。　→　_____

   Dareka ga kabe ni posutā o harimashita.　→　_____

   Someone glued a poster on the wall.　→　*A poster is glued on the wall.*

2. だれかがシャツを壁に掛けました。　→　_____

   Dareka ga shatsu o kabe ni kakemashita.　→　_____

   Someone hung a shirt on the wall.　→　*A shirt is hung on the wall.*

3. だれかが窓を開けました。　→　_____

   Dareka ga mado o akemashita.　→　_____

   Someone opened the window.　→　*The window is open.*

4. だれかが電気をつけました。　→　_____

   Dareka ga denki o tsukemashita.　→　_____

   Someone turned on the light.　→　*The light is on.*

5. だれかが味噌汁を作りました。　→　_____

   Dareka ga misoshiru o tsukurimashita.　→　_____

   Someone made miso soup.　→　*Miso soup has been made.*

... て te + ほしい hoshii (desire)

Whereas you use the adjective ほしい **hoshii** to express your desire for something, you use the auxiliary adjective ほしい **hoshii** to express what you want someone else to do. The person who performs the action is marked by the particle に **ni**. To express what you do not want the person to do, use the verb in the **nai** form followed by the particle で **de**. For example:

> あの人にはどこかに行ってほしいです。もううちには来ないでほしいです。
> **Ano hito ni wa dokoka ni itte hoshii desu. Mō uchi ni wa konai de hoshii desu.**
> *I want that person to go somewhere. I want him not to come to my house anymore.*

However, you can also express such a request by using the auxiliary verb もらう **morau**, whose verb version means *to receive*, along with the adjective formative たい **tai** (*to want*). For example, the following sentence means the same as the above sentence:

> あの人にはどこかに行ってもらいたいです。もううちには来ないでもらいたいです。
> **Ano hito ni wa dokoka ni itte morai-tai desu. Mō uchi ni wa konai de moraitai desu.**
> (See Chapter 5 for the verb もらう **morau**. See Chapter 10 for the suffix たい **tai**.)

EXERCISE

6·9

Complete the Japanese passage so it has the following meaning.

My younger brother's room is dirty. I want him to make it cleaner. I don't want him to put his clothes on the floor. I want him to put trash in a trash can. I want him to wash the used coffee cups and plates. And I want him to open the window sometimes.

弟の部屋はきたないです。もう少しきれいに ＿＿＿＿＿＿＿＿＿ ほしいです。洋服は床の

上に ＿＿＿＿＿＿＿＿＿ ほしいです。ゴミはゴミ箱に ＿＿＿＿＿＿＿＿＿ ほしいです。

使ったコーヒーカップや皿は ＿＿＿＿＿＿＿＿＿ ほしいです。それから、ときどき窓を

＿＿＿＿＿＿＿＿＿ ほしいです。

Otōto no heya wa kitanai desu. Mō sukoshi kireini ＿＿＿＿＿＿＿＿＿ hoshii desu.

Yōfuku wa yuka no ue ni ＿＿＿＿＿＿＿＿＿ hoshii desu. Gomi wa gomi-bako ni

＿＿＿＿＿＿＿＿＿ hoshii desu. Tsukatta kōhīkappu ya sara wa ＿＿＿＿＿＿＿＿＿

hoshii desu. Sorekara, tokidoki mado o ＿＿＿＿＿＿＿＿＿ hoshii desu.

Particles

In this chapter, you will learn the essential functions of many useful particles. Some particles, such as が **ga** and を **o**, are placed after a noun and show the relationship between the noun and the verb in a sentence. Such particles are called *structural particles*. Their function is essential for understanding the meaning of a sentence because word order is flexible in Japanese. (See Chapter 1 for the flexible word order in Japanese.)

Some particles, such as は **wa** and も **mo**, are placed after a noun and its structural particle in order to add some pragmatic or contextual information, based on the speaker and the listener's understanding. These are called *pragmatic particles*.

Some structural and pragmatic particles can also appear after a verb or an adjective. They are discussed individually in other chapters.

を o (direct object)

The particle を **o** specifies the direct object of a verb. There is no counterpart for を **o** in English. However, in English, the direct object is the noun that immediately follows a verb, without an intervening preposition. In most cases the direct object is the thing or the person to which the action applies directly. In either language, only some verbs can take a direct object, and such verbs are called *transitive verbs*. (See Chapter 5 for transitive verbs.) For example:

> 父が弟を叱った。
> **Chichi ga otōto o shikatta.**
> *My father scolded my brother.*

> 名前を言った。
> **Namae o itta.**
> *(He) said (his) name.*

> すしを食べた。
> **Sushi o tabeta.**
> *(I) ate sushi.*

You can easily figure out what type of item can be the direct object of a verb based on the meaning of the verb. From the following list, choose the appropriate direct object for each phrase.

1. _____ を飲む **o nomu** (*drink*)
2. _____ を勉強する **o benkyō-suru** (*study*)
3. _____ を読む **o yomu** (*read*)
4. _____ を招待する **o shōtai-suru** (*invite*)
5. _____ を作る **o tsukuru** (*make*)

a. ケーキ **kēki** (*cake*)
b. 水 **mizu** (*water*)
c. デイビッドさん **Deibiddo-san** (*David*)
d. 化学 **kagaku** (*chemistry*)
e. 新聞 **shinbun** (*newspaper*)

The particle を **o** also marks items that cannot easily be thought of as direct objects, such as the location covered by some movements, the location that one leaves, and occupations when expressed by the verb する **suru** (*do*). For example:

この道をまっすぐ行ってください。
Kono michi o massugu itte kudasai.
Go straight on this street, please.

交差点を右に曲がってください。
Kōsaten o migi ni magatte kudasai.
Please make a right turn at the intersection.

うちを出ました。
Uchi o demashita.
(I) left home.

車を降りました。
Kuruma o orimashita.
I got off the car.

姉は教師をしています。
Ane wa kyōshi o shite imasu.
My older sister is a teacher.

Translate each of the following sentences into English.

1. 銀行を過ぎました。

Ginkō o sugimashita.

2. 山を登りました。

   Yama o noborimashita.

   _____

3. 空を飛びました。

   Sora o tobimashita.

   _____

4. 公園を歩きました。

   Kōen o arukimashita.

   _____

5. 銀座をブラブラしました。

   Ginza o burabura shimashita.

   _____

が **ga** (subject)

The particle が **ga** specifies the subject of a sentence. There is no counterpart for が **ga** in English, but the subject is a noun that precedes a verb in English, and every sentence has a subject in English. In many cases, the subject is the person or the animal that performs an action if the sentence expresses some action, but an inanimate item can also be the subject of a sentence. In Japanese, when the item has already been introduced in the context, が **ga** tends to be covered by the topic particle は **wa**. (The topic particle は **wa** is discussed later in this chapter.) However, depending on the context, you might see the particle が **ga**. For example:

> 田中さんが来た。
> **Tanaka-san ga kita.**
> *Mr. Tanaka came.*
>
> クラスがある。
> **Kurasu ga aru.**
> *There is a class. (Literally: A class exists.)*
>
> 雨が降った。
> **Ame ga futta.**
> *It rained. (Literally: Rain fell.)*
>
> 何が難しいですか。
> **Nani ga muzukashii desu ka.**
> *What is difficult?*

Choose the correct translation of each Japanese sentence.

1. トムがマイクをたたいた。

   Tomu ga Maiku o tataita.

   a. *Mike hit Tom.*

   b. *Tom hit Mike.*

2. 犬を猫がからかった。

   Inu o neko ga karakatta.

   a. *The dog teased the cat.*

   b. *The cat teased the dog.*

3. 安子をリチャードが批判した。

   Yasuko o Richādo ga hihan-shita.

   a. *Yasuko criticized Richard.*

   b. *Richard criticized Yasuko.*

Complete each of the following sentences with the particle が **ga** or を **o.**

1. ハンバーガー _____ 食べました。(ハンバーガー **hanbāgā**: *hamburger*)

   Hanbāgā _____ tabemashita.

2. ハンバーガー _____ あります。

   Hanbāgā _____ arimasu.

3. _____ 買いました。(傘 **kasa**: *umbrella*)

   Kasa _____ kaimashita.

4. 犬 _____ います。

   Inu _____ imasu.

5. 林さん _____ 来ました。

   Hayashi-san _____ kimashita.

The particle が **ga** marks an item that might appear to be a direct object when the predicate is an adjective or a verb that expresses potentials. For example:

私は犬が好きです。
Watashi wa inu ga suki desu.
I like dogs.

私は車がほしいです。
Watashi wa kuruma ga hoshii desu.
I want a car.

マイクさんは漢字が書けます。
Maiku-san wa kanji ga kakemasu.
Mike can write kanji.

EXERCISE
7·5

*Complete each of the following sentences with が **ga** or を **o**.*

1. 映画 _____ 見ます。(映画 **eiga**: *movie*)

   Eiga _____ mimasu.

   I'll watch a movie.

2. 漢字 _____ 書きます。

   Kanji _____ kakimasu.

   I will write kanji.

3. 漢字 _____ 書けます。

   Kanji _____ kakemasu.

   I can write kanji.

4. 交差点 _____ 曲がってください。

   Kōsaten _____ magatte kudasai.

   Please make a turn at the intersection.

5. 車 _____ ほしいです。

   Kuruma _____ hoshii desu.

   I want a car.

6. 車 _____ 買います。

   Kuruma _____ kaimasu.

   I will buy a car.

7. すし _____ 好きです。

   Sushi _____ suki desu.

   I like sushi.

に ni (*at, in, to*)

The particle に **ni** specifies the target of an action such as coming, going, giving, or placing. For example:

東京に行く。
Tōkyō ni iku.
I will go to Tokyo.

空港に着いた。
Kūkō ni tsuita.
I arrived at the airport.

妹にスカーフをあげた。
Imōto ni skāfu o ageta.
(I) gave a scarf to my sister.

花はあそこに置く。
Hana wa asoko ni oku.
(I) will place the flowers over there.

The particle に **ni** also specifies the location where people and things exist. For example:

慶応大学は東京にある。
Keiō daigaku wa Tōkyō ni aru.
Keiō University is in Tokyo.

姉は大阪に住んでいる。
Ane wa Ōsaka ni sunde iru.
My older sister lives in Osaka.

It also specifies the absolute time of an event, as in these examples:

月曜日に試験がある。
Getsuyōbi ni shiken ga aru.
There is an exam on Monday.

2月に中国に行った。
Ni-gatsu ni Chūgoku ni itta.
(I) went to China in February.

EXERCISE
7·6

Complete each of the following sentences with the particles に **ni** *and* を **o.**

1. 7時 _____ サンフランシスコ _____ 出ました。

Shichi-ji _____ Sanfuranshisuko _____ demashita. (サンフランシスコ **Sanfuranshisuko**:
San Francisco)

(I) left San Francisco at 7 o'clock.

2. ロサンゼルス _____ 行きました。

Rosanzerusu _____ ikimashita. (ロサンゼルス **Rosanzerusu**: *Los Angeles*)

(I) went to Los Angeles.

3. 山田さん _____ 花 _____ あげました。

   Yamada-san _____ hana _____ agemashita. (花 **hana**: *flower*)

   (I) gave flowers to Ms. Yamada.

4. 交差点 _____ 右 _____ 曲がってください。

   Kōsaten _____ migi _____ magatte kudasai.

   Please make a right turn at the intersection.

で **de** *(at, by, in, with)*

The particle で **de** specifies the location, the tool, the method, or the condition used for an action.
For example:

> 東京で勉強する。
> **Tōkyō de benkyō-suru.**
> *(I) study in Tokyo.*

> フォークで食べる。
> **Fōku de taberu.**
> *(I) eat with fork.*

> 日本語で話す。
> **Nihongo de hanasu.**
> *(I) speak in Japanese.*

> セールで買った。
> **Sēru de katta.**
> *(I) bought (it) on sale.*

> 着物でパーティーに行った。
> **Kimono de pātī ni itta.**
> *(I) went to the party in a kimono.*

EXERCISE 7·7

Complete each of the following sentences with the particles に **ni** and で **de**.

1. 図書館 _____ 行きます。(図書館 **toshokan**: *library*)

   Toshokan _____ ikimasu.

   (I) will go to the library.

2. 図書館 _____ 本を読みます。

   Toshokan _____ hon o yomimasu.

   (I) will read a book at the library.

3. マイクさんは図書館 _____ います。

   Maiku-san wa toshokan _____ imasu.

   Mike is at the library.

4. 箸 ＿＿＿＿ 食べます。(箸 **hashi**: *chopsticks*)

   Hashi ＿＿＿＿ tabemasu.

   (I) eat with chopsticks.

5. 車 ＿＿＿＿ ボストン ＿＿＿＿ 行きます。

   Kuruma ＿＿＿＿ Bosuton ＿＿＿＿ ikimasu.

   (I) will go to Boston by car.

Complete each of the following sentences with the particle を **o**, に **ni**, *or* で **de**.

1. すし ＿＿＿＿ 食べます。

   Sushi ＿＿＿＿ tabemasu.

   (I) eat sushi.

2. シカゴ ＿＿＿＿ 帰ります。

   Shikago ＿＿＿＿ kaerimasu. (シカゴ **Shikago**: *Chicago*)

   (I) will return to Chicago.

3. 手 ＿＿＿＿ 食べます。

   Te ＿＿＿＿ tabemasu. (手 **te**: *hand*)

   (I) eat with hand.

4. ドレス ＿＿＿＿ 買います。

   Doresu ＿＿＿＿ kaimasu. (ドレス**doresu**: *dress*)

   (I) will buy a dress.

5. 大学 ＿＿＿＿ バス ＿＿＿＿ 来ました。

   Daigaku ＿＿＿＿ basu ＿＿＿＿ kimashita.

   (I) came to the university by bus.

6. パソコン ＿＿＿＿ 使います。

   Pasokon ＿＿＿＿ tsukaimasu. (パソコン **pasokon**: *computer, PC*)

   (I) use a computer.

へ e (*toward, to*)

The particle へ, which is read as **e**, specifies the direction of coming and going. The particle へ **e** can be replaced by the particle に **ni**, but に **ni** cannot always be replaced by へ **e** because the particle に **ni** has many more functions than へ **e**. For example:

> こちらへ来てください。
> **Kochira e kite kudasai.**
> *Please come here.*

> ボストンへ行った。
> **Bosuton e itta.**
> *I went to Boston.*

EXERCISE

7·9

For each of the following, choose the appropriate answer from the options in the parentheses. There might be more than one correct answer for some sentences.

1. 大阪(に, へ)行きましょう。

   Ōsaka (ni, e) ikimashō.

   Let's go to Osaka.

2. 9時(に, へ)うち(に, へ)着きました。

   Ku-ji (ni, e) uchi (ni, e) tsukimashita.

   We got home at 9 PM.

3. 母の日(に, へ)母(に, へ)プレゼントをあげました。

   Haha no hi (ni, e) haha (ni, e) purezento o agemashita.

   I gave a present to my mother on Mother's Day.

4. 車の鍵はうち(に, へ)あります。

   Kuruma no kagi wa uchi (ni, e) arimasu.

   The car key is at home.

から kara (*from*)

The particle から **kara** specifies the source, origin, or starting point. For example:

> タイから来ました。
> **Tai kara kimashita.**
> *(I) came from Thailand.*

> 田中さんから聞いた。
> **Tanaka-san kara kiita.**
> *(I) heard (about it) from Mr. Tanaka.*

> 初級から始めた。
> **Shokyū kara hajimeta.**
> *(I) started from the beginner's level.*

まで **made** (*until*)

The particle まで **made** specifies the ending point of a continuous action. For example:

> 2ページから5ページまで読んだ。
> **Ni-pēji kara go-pēji made yonda.**
> *I read from page 2 to page 5.*

> 11時までおきていた。
> **Jūichi-ji made okite ita.**
> *I stayed up until 11 PM.*

> 郵便局まで走った。
> **Yūbinkyoku made hashitta.**
> *I ran to the post office.*

EXERCISE 7·10

For each of the following, choose the appropriate answer from the options in the parentheses.

1. 東京(で, へ)行きます。

   Tōkyō (de, e) ikimasu.

   (I) will go to Tokyo.

2. 東京(で, から)来ました。

   Tōkyō (de, kara) kimashita.

   (I) came from Tokyo.

3. スーパー(まで, に)歩きます。(スーパー **sūpā**: *supermarket*)

   Sūpā (made, ni) arukimasu.

   (I) will walk to the supermarket.

4. スーパー(で, に)行きます。

   Sūpā (de, ni) ikimasu.

   (I) will go to the supermarket.

5. 地下鉄(を, で)行きます。

   Chikatetsu (o, de) ikimasu. (地下鉄 **chikatetsu**: *subway*)

   (I) will go there by subway.

の **no** (*of, 's*)

The particle の **no** creates a phrase along with the preceding noun, which qualifies the following noun. For example, 日本人の学生 means a Japanese student. It is possible for a noun to be modified by multiple phrases created by の **no**. (See Chapter 2 for more about the particle の **no**.)

と to, や ya, and か ka (listing nouns)

The particles と **to**, や **ya**, and か **ka** can be used to list nouns. と **to** is used to exhaustively list nouns, as in *A, B, and C*; や **ya** is used to list nouns as examples, as in *A, B, C, etc.*; and か **ka** is used to list alternatives, as in *A, B, or C*. For example:

> クッキーと、ケーキと、チョコレートを食べます。
> **Kukkī to, kēki to, chokorēto o tabemasu.**
> *(I) eat cookies, cakes, and chocolate.*

> クッキーや、ケーキや、チョコレートを食べます。
> **Kukkī ya, kēki ya, chokorēto o tabemasu.**
> *(I) eat cookies, cakes, chocolate, etc.*

> クッキーか、ケーキか、チョコレートを食べます。
> **Kukkī ka, kēki ka, chokorēto o tabemasu.**
> *(I) eat cookies, cakes, or chocolate.*

See Chapter 12 for additional examples of how to list nouns.

The particle と **to** can also specify the person or animal that performs an action with the person or animal specified by the subject noun. It can also indicate a reciprocal relationship. For example:

> 私は友達とテニスをしました。
> **Watashi wa tomodachi to tenisu o shimashita.**
> *I played tennis with my friend.*

> 車がトラックとぶつかった。
> **Kuruma ga torakku to butsukatta.**
> *A car collided with a truck.*

> 兄は弟と似ている。
> **Ani wa otōto to nite iru.**
> *My older brother resembles my younger brother.*

EXERCISE

7·11

Indicate the Japanese you would use in the following situations.

1. You want to say that you bought a math book and an economics book. (*mathematics:* 数学 **sūgaku**; *economics:* 経済学 **keizaigaku**)

   _____

2. You want to say that you will go to Tokyo, Osaka, etc.

   _____

3. You want to say that you made tempura with your mother.

   _____

は wa (topic)

The particle は is pronounced as **wa**. As discussed in Chapter 1, は **wa** shows that an item is what the speaker wants to talk about, and so the item must already be known to the speaker and the listener. It doesn't matter whether the item is the subject, direct object, or destination. Usually, such a noun is placed at the beginning of a sentence. は **wa** can follow structural particles, but が **ga** and を **o** need to be dropped when followed by は **wa**. Other structural particles, such as に **ni** and から **kara**, may or may not be present before は **wa**. For example:

> 東京には去年行きました。
> **Tōkyō ni wa kyonen ikimashita.**
> *As for (to) Tokyo, I went there last year.*

> このクラスは宿題がありません。
> **Kono kurasu wa shukudai ga arimasen.**
> *In this class, homework is not assigned.*

> メアリーは日本語の学生です。
> **Mearī wa Nihon-go no gakusei desu.**
> *Mary is a student of Japanese.*

> すしは食べません。
> **Sushi wa tabemasen.**
> *I don't eat sushi.*

は **wa** is also used to highlight some nouns that are in contrast to one another. It is also used to mark the item to which the action does not apply when the verb is in the negative form. For example:

> 私は猫は好きです。でも、犬は嫌いです。
> **Watashi wa neko wa suki desu. Demo, inu wa kirai desu.**
> *I like cats. However, (I) hate dogs.*

> 私はコーヒーは飲みません。
> **Watashi wa kōhī wa nomimasen.**
> *I do not drink coffee.*

も mo (addition)

The particle も **mo** marks an item that is in addition to another item introduced in the context. It means *also* or *too*. It is a pragmatic particle just like は **wa** and may follow structural particles except for が **ga** and を **o**. For example:

> うちには猫がいます。犬もいます。鳥もいます。
> **Uchi ni wa neko ga imasu. Inu mo imasu. Tori mo imasu.**
> *We have a cat in our home. We also have a dog. We also have a bird.*

> 兄は私のクッキーを食べました。妹のクッキーも食べました。
> **Ani wa watashi no kukkī o tabemashita. Imōto no kukkī mo tabemashita.**
> *My older brother ate my cookies. He also ate my little sister's cookies.*

> 京都に行きました。奈良にも行きました。
> **Kyōto ni ikimashita. Nara ni mo ikimashita.**
> *I went to Kyoto. I also went to Nara.*

For each of the following, choose the appropriate answer from the options in the parentheses.

1. 韓国に行きました。中国（には, にも, はに, もに）行きました。

    Kankoku ni ikimashita. Chūgoku (ni wa, ni mo, wa ni, mo ni) ikimashita. (韓国 **Kankoku**: *South Korea*; 中国 **Chūgoku**: *China*)

    (I) went to South Korea. I also went to China.

2. 韓国に行きました。でも、中国（には, にも, はに, もに）行きませんでした。

    Kankoku ni ikimashita. Demo, Chūgoku (ni wa, ni mo, wa ni, mo ni) ikimasendeshita.

    (I) went to South Korea. However, (I) did not go to China.

3. メアリーさんが来ました。レベッカさん（がも, もが, も, は）来ました。

    Mearī-san ga kimashita. Rebekka-san (ga mo, mo ga, mo, wa) kimashita.

    Mary came. Rebecca also came.

4. 兄はてんぷらを食べました。すし（を, は, も）食べました。

    Ani wa tempura o tabemashita. Sushi (o, wa, mo) tabemashita.

    My older brother ate tempura. He also ate sushi.

5. 兄はてんぷらを食べました。姉もてんぷら（を, は, も）食べました。

    Ani wa tempura o tabemashita. Ane mo tempura (o, wa, mo) tabemashita.

    My older brother ate tempura. My older sister also ate tempura.

ばかり **bakari** (*nothing but . . .*)

The particle ばかり **bakari** is used to show that an action applies to an item exclusively and excessively. It gives a negative connotation. Like other pragmatic particles, ばかり **bakari** can follow structural particles other than が **ga** and を **o**. For example:

> 兄はビールばかり飲んでいます。
> **Ani wa bīru bakari nonde imasu.**
> *My older brother drinks nothing but beer.*

> 学はパチンコにばかり行っています。
> **Manabu wa pachinko ni bakari itte imasu.**
> *Manabu goes nowhere but to a pachinko parlor.*

It can also follow verbs in the **te** form. For example:

> 兄は寝てばかりいます。
> **Ani wa nete bakari imasu.**
> *My older brother does nothing but sleep.*

Theoretically, ばかり **bakari** can be added at the end of a noun or at the end of the verb in the **te** form. For example, the following examples are both grammatical:

> コーヒを飲んでばかりいます。
> **Kōhī o nonde bakari imasu.**

> コーヒばかり飲んでいます。
> **Kōhī bakari nonde imasu.**

The difference is whether the choice of beverage or the choice of action is extreme. However, native Japanese speakers do not usually notice such a difference and tend to add ばかり **bakari** after the noun.

EXERCISE
7·13

Translate the following sentences into Japanese.

1. *My little brother does nothing but play. (to play:* 遊ぶ **asobu)**

   _____

2. *My little sister reads nothing but comic books. (comic books:* マンガ **manga)**

   _____

3. *My older sister does nothing but shop. (to go shopping:* 買い物をする **kaimono o suru)**

   _____

しか shika (*only*)

しか **shika** means *only* and expresses that the quantity, amount, or range of items is too few, little, or limited for the given context. Just like other pragmatic particles, such as は **wa**, も **mo**, and ばかり **bakari**, しか **shika** can be placed after structural particles except が **ga** and を **o**. The predicate must be negative if **shika** is used in a sentence. For example:

> ケビンさんにしか言いませんでした。
> **Kebin-san ni shika iimasendeshita.**
> *(I) only told Kevin about it.*

EXERCISE
7·14

Recast the following sentences using しか **shika** *for the underlined item.*

1. 明子さんは<u>みち子さん</u>と話します。

   Akiko-san wa <u>Michiko-san</u> to hanashimasu.

   Akiko talks with Michiko.

   _____

   _____

2. チケットが<u>一枚</u>あります。

Chiketto ga <u>ichi-mai</u> arimasu.

There is one ticket.

_____

_____

3. <u>自転車</u>があります。

<u>Jitensha</u> ga arimasu.

I have a bicycle.

_____

_____

4. <u>ラーメン</u>を食べました。

<u>Rāmen</u> o tabemashita.

I ate ramen noodles.

_____

_____

だけ **dake** (*just/only*)

だけ **dake** means *just* or *only*. When だけ **dake** occurs with a noun, the particle that is used for the noun can be placed before or after だけ **dake**, except for the particles が **ga** and を **o**, which can optionally occur only after だけ **dake**. Unlike with しか **shika**, the predicate can be either affirmative or negative. For example:

> ケビンさんにだけ言いました。
> **Kebin-san ni dake iimashita.**
> *(I) told about it just to Kevin.*

> ケビンさんにだけ言いませんでした。
> **Kebin-san ni dake iimasendeshita.**
> *(I told everyone about it), but not Kevin.*

> ケビンさんだけに言いました。
> **Kebin-san dake ni iimashita.**
> *(I) told about it just to Kevin.*

When the emphasis is on the lack of additional quantity, amount, or number of items, しか **shika** should be used rather than だけ **dake**. For example:

> 10ドルしかありません。ですから、無理です。
> **Jū-doru shika arimasen. Desukara, muri desu.**
> *(I) have only 10 dollars. So, it's impossible.*

> 10ドルだけあります。ですから、だいじょうぶです。
> **Jū-doru dake arimasu. Desukara, daijōbu desu.**
> *(I) have just 10 dollars. So, we can manage it.*

Complete each of the following sentences with しか **shika** *or* だけ **dake.**

1. 母に _____ 言いました。

   Haha ni _____ iimashita.

   (I) only told my mother (about it).

2. 祖母は私に _____ お金をくれました。

   Sobo wa watashi ni _____ o-kane o kuremashita.

   My grandmother gave money just to me.

3. 父はステーキ _____ 食べません。

   Chichi wa sutēki _____ tabemasen.

   My father only eats steak.

4. チケットが2枚 _____ ありません。ですから、2人しか行けません。

   Chiketto ga ni-mai _____ arimasu. Desukara, futa-ri shika ikemasen.

   There are only two tickets. So, only two people can go.

5. チケットが2枚 _____ あります。ですから、いっしょに行きましょう。

   Chiketto ga ni-mai _____ arimasu. Desukara, isshoni ikimashō.

   There are just two tickets. So, let's go (there) together.

でも **demo** (*even*)

でも **demo** means *even* and implies that the speaker considers the item to be one of the least expected items in the given situation. For example:

> これは簡単です。子どもでもできます。
> **Kore wa kantan desu. Kodomo demo dekimasu.**
> *This is easy. Even a child can do it.*

> これは難しいです。大人でもできません。
> **Kore wa muzukashii desu. Otona demo dekimasen.**
> *This is difficult. Even an adult cannot do it.*

From the following list, choose the appropriate option for each sentence.

1. 姉は _____ でも食べません。

   Ane wa _____ demo tabemasen.

2. 兄は _____ でも食べます。

   Ani wa _____ demo tabemasu.

3. 父は _____ でも買いません。

   Chichi wa _____ demo kaimasen.

4. 兄は _____ でも買います。

   Ani wa _____ demo kaimasu.

5. 弟は _____ でも読みません。

   Otōto wa _____ demo yomimasen.

a. おもしろい本 **omoshiroi hon** (*interesting books*)

b. おいしい物 **oishii mono** (*delicious things*)

c. まずい物 **mazui mono** (*things that are not delicious*)

d. 安い物 **yasui mono** (*cheap things*)

e. 高い物 **takai mono** (*expensive things*)

Adjectives and adverbs · 8 ·

Adjectives describe the property and the state of things and people. Adverbs, on the other hand, describe the manner of actions. This chapter shows how adjectives and adverbs are used, what forms they take, and how they can form a variety of comparative sentences.

Adjective types

Adjectives modify nouns. In fact, verbs and nouns can also modify nouns: Verbs in the plain form can be placed before a noun; nouns can be followed by the particle の **no** and placed before a noun. For example:

> これは日本で売っている本です。
> **Kore wa Nihon de utte iru hon desu.**
> *This is a book sold in Japan.*

> これは日本の本です。
> **Kore wa Nihon no hon desu.**
> *This is a Japanese book.*

However, adjectives have distinct endings when placed before nouns as modifiers. They all end in either い **i** or な **na**. For example:

> これは高い本です。
> **Kore wa takai hon desu.**
> *This is an expensive book.*

> これは高価な本です。
> **Kore wa kōka na hon desu.**
> *This is an expensive book.*

Adjectives that end in い **i** when placed before a noun are called **i** adjectives. Adjectives that end in な **na** when placed before a noun are called **na** adjectives. For example, 高い **takai** and 高価な **kōka na** in the examples above both mean *expensive*, but the former is an **i** adjective and the latter is a **na** adjective. Some adjectives were created from words borrowed from other languages. Such adjectives all belong to **na** adjectives. For example:

シンプルなドレス	**sinpuru na doresu**	*a simple dress*
エレガントなドレス	**ereganto na doresu**	*an elegant dress*
デリケートな肌	**derikēto na hada**	*delicate skin*

There is a third category of adjectives that some linguists call *no-type adjectives*. In this book, however, such an adjective is treated as a noun followed by の **no**, as in 病気の人 **byōki no hito** (*sick person*).

Basic adjective forms

The part of an adjective without the ending い **i** or な **na** (e.g., 高 **taka** and 高価 **kōka**) is called the *stem*. The stem of a **na** adjective patterns just like a noun: It can be followed by all forms of the copular verb, including です **desu**, じゃありません **ja arimasen**, だ **da**, and だった **datta**, when used as part of a sentence predicate, just like a noun. Because of this, **na** adjectives are also called *adjectival nouns*. The stem of an **i** adjective is followed by unique inflectional endings, including い **i**, く **ku**, and かった **katta**, when used as a sentence predicate. They can end sentences without being followed by the copular verb. For this reason, **i** adjectives are sometimes called *adjectival verbs*. In this case, the copular verb is not needed except to make the phrase polite.

The following table summarizes how adjectives pattern as sentence predicates:

			I Adjectives (高-い **taka-i**)	Na Adjectives (高価な **kōka na**)
Plain	**Non-past**	Affirmative	Stem + い **i** 高い **takai**	Stem + だ **da** 高価だ **kōka da**
		Negative (**nai** form)	Stem + くない **ku nai** 高くない **takaku nai**	Stem + じゃない **ja nai*** 高価じゃない **kōka ja nai***
	Past	Affirmative (**ta** form)	Stem + かった **katta** 高かった **takakatta**	Stem + だった **datta** 高価だった **kōka datta**
		Negative (**nakatta** form)	Stem + くなかった **ku nakatta** 高くなかった **takaku nakatta**	Stem + じゃなかった **ja nakatta*** 高価じゃなかった **kōka ja nakatta***
Polite	**Non-past**	Affirmative	Stem + いです **i desu** 高いです **takai desu**	Stem + です **desu** 高価です **kōka desu**
		Negative	Stem + くありません **ku arimasen** (*or* くないです **ku nai desu**) 高くありません **takaku arimasen** (高くないです **takaku nai desu**)	Stem + じゃありません **ja arimasen** (*or* じゃないです **ja nai desu**)* 高価じゃありません **kōka ja arimasen*** (高価じゃないです **kōka ja nai desu**)*
	Past	Affirmative	Stem + かったです **katta desu** 高かったです **takakatta desu**	Stem + でした **deshita** 高価でした **kōka deshita**
		Negative	Stem + くありませんでした **ku arimasendeshita** (*or* くなかったです **ku nakatta desu**) 高くありませんでした **takaku arimasendeshita** (高くなかったです **takaku nakatta desu**)	Stem + じゃありませんでした **ja arimasendeshita** (*or* じゃなかったです **ja nakatta desu**)* 高価じゃありませんでした **kōka ja arimasendeshita*** (高価じゃなかったです **kōka ja nakatta desu**)*

*じゃ **ja** in the negative forms in this table can be では **de wa**.

The negative form of いい **ii** is よくありません **yoku arimasen**, or よくないです **yoku nai desu**. 大きい **ōkii** and 小さい **chīsai** are **i** adjectives, but when used as prenominal modifiers, they have the additional forms 大きな **ōki na** and 小さな **chīsa na**.

EXERCISE

8·1

Change the following sentences, using the example as a guide.

EXAMPLE これは高い本です。 **Kore wa takai hon desu.** *This is an expensive book.*

→ これは高いです。 **Kore wa takai desu.** *This is expensive.*

1. ジョージさんはまじめな人です。

   Jōji-san wa majime na hito desu.

   George is a serious person.

   _____

   _____

   _____

2. 幸子さんの家は大きい家です。

   Sachiko-san no ie wa ōkii ie desu.

   Sachiko's house is a big house.

   _____

   _____

   _____

3. 私の部屋は広い部屋です。

   Watashi no heya wa hiroi heya desu.

   My room is a spacious room.

   _____

   _____

   _____

4. 兄の車は新しい車です。

   Ani no kuruma wa atarashii kuruma desu.

   My older brother's car is a new car.

   _____

   _____

   _____

5. これは便利な辞書です。

   Kore wa benri na jisho desu.

   This is a convenient dictionary.

   _____

   _____

   _____

6. 恵子さんはきれいな人です。

   Keiko-san wa kirei na hito desu.

   Keiko is a pretty person.

   _____

   _____

   _____

**EXERCISE
8·2**

Convert the following sentences into negatives.

1. 親切です。

   Shinsetsu desu.

   (He) is kind.

   _____

   _____

   _____

2. 優しいです。

   Yasashii desu.

   (He) is kind.

   _____

   _____

   _____

3. 意地悪です。

   Iijiwaru desu.

   (He) is mean.

   _____

   _____

   _____

4. こわいです。

   Kowai desu.

   (He) is scary.

   _____

   _____

   _____

5. かっこいいです。

   Kakkoii desu.

   (He) is good looking.

   _____

   _____

   _____

6. きれいです。

   Kirei desu.

   (She) is pretty.

   _____

   _____

   _____

EXERCISE

8·3

Convert the following phrases into the past tense.

1. 難しいです。

   Muzukashii desu.

   (It) is difficult.

   _____

   _____

   _____

2. 簡単です。

   Kantan desu.

   (It) is easy.

   _____

   _____

   _____

3. 面白いです。

Omoshiroi desu.

(It) is fun/interesting.

_____

_____

_____

4. 大変です。

Taihen desu.

(It) is hard.

_____

_____

_____

5. つまらないです。

Tsumaranai desu.

(It) is boring.

_____

_____

_____

Multiple subjects

Japanese adjectives often require two subjects, the first of which is marked by the topic particle は **wa**, creating a construction like . . . は **wa** . . . が **ga** . . . . In some cases, the second subject narrows the focus for the modifier. For example, compare the following two sentences:

陽子さんは きれいです。
Yōko-san wa kirei desu.
Yoko is pretty.

陽子さんは目がきれいです。
Yōko-san wa me ga kirei desu.
Yoko is pretty as far as her eyes are concerned. (Yoko has beautiful eyes.)

The second subject can also show the item to which an emotional property such as desire and preferences directly applies. For example:

私はアイスクリームが好きです。
Watashi wa aisukurīmu ga suki desu.
I like ice cream.

私はアイスクリームがほしいです。
Watashi wa aisukurīmu ga hoshii desu.
I want ice cream.

You might want to use the particle を **o** to mark *ice cream* in the above sentences because *ice cream* is the direct object in English translations, but を **o** can be used only if there is a transitive verb. Because the predicate of this sentence is not a verb, but is an adjective, there is no way to have the particle を **o** in these sentences.

EXERCISE
8·4

Translate the following sentences into Japanese.

1. *I like dogs.*

2. *I do not like cats.*

3. *I hate bugs. (bugs:* 虫 **mushi**)

4. *I want a new printer.*

Te forms of adjectives

To list two or more adjectives in the same sentence, you convert all adjectives in the sentence except the last one to the **te** form. (Remember that the particle と **to** can list only nouns; it cannot list verbs and adjectives.) To form a **te** form of an **i** adjective, add くて **kute** to its stem (e.g., 高い **takai** → 高くて **takakute**). To form a **te** form of a **na** adjective, add で **de** to its stem (きれいな **kirei na** → きれいで **kirei de**). The **te** form of the adjective いい **ii** is よくて **yokute**. The last adjective in a sentence can be in the usual form. For example:

> マイクさんは 頭がよくて、 やさしくて、 かっこいいです。
> **Maiku-san wa atama ga yokute, yasashikute, kakko ii desu.**
> *Mike is smart, kind, and cool.*

> トーマスさんは意地悪で、 ひどい人です。
> **Tōmasu-san wa ijiwaru de, hidoi hito desu.**
> *Thomas is a mean and terrible person.*

To form a negative **te** form of an **i** adjective, add くなくて **ku nakute** to its stem (e.g., 高い **takai** → 高くなくて **takaku nakute**). To form a negative **te** form of a **na** adjective, add じゃなくて **ja nakute** to its stem (e.g., きれいな **kirei na** → きれいじゃなくて **kirei ja nakute**). For example:

> あまり高くなくて、おいしいです。
> **Amari takaku nakute, oishii desu.**
> *It's not so expensive, and is delicious.*

> あまりきれいじゃなくて、よくありません。
> **Amari kirei ja nakute, yoku arimasen.**
> *It's not so pretty and not good.*

If the listed adjectives express contrasting properties, they should be listed in different clauses related by the conjunction particle が **ga**, as in the following example:

交通が便利じゃなくて、家賃が高いですが、とてもきれいなアパートです。
Kōtsū ga benri ja nakute, yachin ga takai desu ga, totemo kirei na apāto desu.
The commute is not convenient, and the rent is expensive, but it's a very beautiful apartment.

The **te** forms of adjectives, both affirmative and negative, are summarized in the following table:

	I Adjectives (高い **takai**)	**Na Adjectives** (高価な **kōka na**)
Affirmative	Stem + くて 高くて **takakute**	Stem + で 高価で **kōka de**
Negative	Stem + くなくて 高くなくて **takaku nakute**	Stem + じゃなくて 高価じゃなくて **kōka janakute**

You can mix adjectives and verbs in the same sentence by using the **te** form. Depending on the context, they may express a cause-and-effect relationship. For example:

仕事が大変でやめました。
Shigoto ga taihen de yamemashita.
Because the job was hard, I quit it.

おいしくなくて食べられませんでした。
Oishiku nakute taberaremasendeshita.
Because it was not delicious, I could not eat it.

頭が痛くて薬をのみました。
Atama ga itakute, kusuri o nomimashita.
I had a headache, and I took medicine.

EXERCISE
8·5

Complete the following sentences creatively.

1. 田中さんは _____,いい人です。

   Tanaka-san wa _____, ii hito desu.

2. 加藤さんは意地悪で、_____ 人です。

   Kato-san wa ijiwaru de, _____ hito desu.

3. 頭が _____, クラスに行けませんでした。

   Atama ga _____, kurasu ni ikemasendeshita.

4. _____, 買えませんでした。

   _____, **kaemasendeshita.**

5. あのレストランはとても _____, きれいですよ。

   Ano resutoran wa totemo _____, kirei desu yo.

Degree adverbs

To indicate the degree of some property expressed by adjectives, use the following degree adverbs:

- とても **totemo** (*very much*)
- まあまあ **māmā** (*more or less*)
- 少し **sukoshi** (*slightly*)
- ちょっと **chotto** (*a little*)
- あまり **amari** ((*not*) *very much*)
- ぜんぜん **zenzen** ((*not*) *at all*)

ぜんぜん **zenzen** and あまり **amari** must be used with a negative adjective, whereas other adverbs (とても **totemo**, まあまあ **māmā**, ちょっと **chotto**, and 少し **sukoshi**) are used with an affirmative adjective. For example:

> ぜんぜんきれいじゃありません。
> **Zenzen kirei ja arimasen.**
> *It's not pretty at all.*

> とてもきれいです。
> **Totemo kirei desu.**
> *It's very pretty.*

まあまあ **māmā** is used only when the speaker's feeling toward the state is favorable, whereas ちょっと **chotto** and 少し **sukoshi** are used when the speaker's feeling is unfavorable. For example:

> まあまあきれいです。
> **Māmā kirei desu.**
> *It is more or less pretty (and I am happy with it).*

> ちょっときたないです。
> **Chotto kitanai desu.**
> *It is slightly dirty.*

Frequency adverbs

To indicate the frequency of the action, use some of the following adverbs:

- よく **yoku** (*often*)
- ときどき **tokidoki** (*sometimes*)
- あまり **amari** ((*not*) *very often*)
- ぜんぜん **zenzen** ((*not*) *at all*)
- いつも **itsumo** (*always*)
- たいてい **taitei** (*usually*)

Note that ぜんぜん **zenzen** and あまり **amari** must be used with a negative verb. For example:

> 本屋にはよく行きます。
> **Hon'ya ni wa yoku ikimasu.**
> *I often go to bookstores.*

> 本屋にはあまり行きません。
> **Hon'ya ni wa amari ikimasen.**
> *I don't go to a bookstore very often.*

Complete the following sentences by conjugating the given verbs correctly.

1. 昨日はあまり _____。(食べる **taberu**: *eat*)

   Kinō wa amari _____.

2. よく大学まで _____。(歩く **aruku**: *walk*)

   Yoku daigaku made _____.

3. ビールはぜんぜん _____。(飲む **nomu**: *drink*)

   Bīru wa zenzen _____.

4. ときどき _____。(泣く **naku**: cry)

   Tokidoki _____.

Adverbs derived from adjectives

You can create adverbs from adjectives by adding に **ni** to the stem of a **na** adjective and adding く**ku** to the stem of an **i** adjective. The adverb version of いい **ii** is よく **yoku**. For example:

大きく書いてください。
Ōkiku kaite kudasai.
Please write a bit bigger.

きれいに書いてください。
Kirei ni kaite kudasai.
Please write neatly.

よく考えましたか？
Yoku kangaemashita ka?
Did you think about it carefully?

Convert the following adjectives into adverbs.

1. はやい **hayai** (*early* or *fast*) _____

2. 静かな **shizuka na** (*quiet*) _____

3. まじめな **majima na** (*serious*) _____

4. 小さい **chīsai** (*small*) _____

Adverb + する suru/なる naru (change)

When the verb する **suru** (*to do*) is used with an adverb, it means to change the state of something in a specified way. When the verb なる **naru** (*to become*) is used instead of する **suru**, it shows what change is made without drawing attention to the causer of the change. For example:

> 部屋をきれいにしました。
> **Heya o kirei ni shimashita.**
> *I made my room neat.*

> 部屋がきれいになりました。
> **Heya ga kirei ni narimashita.**
> *My room became neater.*

The item that changes is often unspoken if it is understood in context. It could be something obvious in the context, and it could also be the speaker or the listener. For example:

> 安くしてください。
> **Yasuku shite kudasai.**
> *Make (the price) cheaper.*

> 静かにしてください。
> **Shizuka ni shite kudasai.**
> *(Please) make (yourself) quiet.* or *Please be quiet.*

EXERCISE

8·8

Translate the following sentences into Japanese.

1. *Please study quietly.*

   _____

2. *Please eat quickly.*

   _____

3. *Please make your room clean.*

   _____

4. *Please be quiet.*

   _____

Adverbs made from onomatopoeia and mimetic words

Japanese has a large inventory of words whose sounds are intended to describe actions and states. They are categorized into onomatopoeia and mimetic words. Onomatopoeia describes auditory properties. Mimetic words describe non-auditory properties such as manners, actions, states, and the appearance of people and things. Most of them consist of a repetition of one or two syllables and can be used as adverbs in a sentence, occasionally followed by the particle と **to** or に **ni**. They are often written in katakana, especially in comic books. Note that it is very difficult to translate these words into English. For example:

> 子どもがゲラゲラ笑っていました。
> **Kodomo ga geragera waratte imashita.**
> *The children were laughing loudly.*

> 蛇がにょろにょろ（と）近づいてきた。
> **Hebi ga nyoronyhoro (to) chikadzuite kita.**
> *The snake slithered toward me.*

> 靴をぴかぴかに磨きました。
> **Kutsu o pikapika ni migakimashita.**
> *I polished my shoes (until they were) shiny.*

EXERCISE 8·9

For each of the following, choose the meaning of the underlined words from the options in the parentheses based on how you feel about the sounds of these words.

1. 弟はいつも<u>だらだら</u>しています。

   Otōto wa itsumo <u>daradara</u> shite imasu.

   (*energetic, quiet, lazy*)

2. 母はいつも<u>ぷんぷん</u>しています。

   Haha wa itsumo <u>punpun</u> shite imasu.

   (*loving, kind, upset*)

3. 父はいつも<u>にこにこ</u>しています。

   Chichi wa itsumo <u>nikoniko</u> shite imasu.

   (*serious, smiling, nervous*)

Comparing two items

Unlike in English, you don't have to change the forms of adjectives and adverbs in order to compare things and people in Japanese. To say "*A is more . . . than B,*" you just add a short phrase that means "*than B,*" which is B より **B yori** in Japanese. For example:

> デイビッドさんは親切です。
> **Deibiddo-san wa shinsetsu desu.**
> *David is kind.*

> デイビッドさんはエドワードさんより親切です。
> **Deibiddo-san wa Edowādo-san yori shinsetsu desu.**
> *David is kinder than Edward.*

Say that you want to ask a question that involves comparing two items, X and Y, as in, *Which is more . . . , X or Y?* To do this, you place X と Y と **X to Y to** at the beginning of the sentence and use どちらの方 **dochira no hō** (*which one*) to create a question sentence. For example:

> ライオンとトラと、どちらの方が速く走れますか。
> **Raion to tora to, dochira no hō ga hayaku hashiremasu ka.**
> *Which can run faster, lions or tigers?*

You can use どっちの方 **dotchi no hō**, or simply どちら **dochira** or どっち **dotchi**, instead of どちらの方 **dochira no hō**. For example:

> 刺し身とすしと、どっちの方が好きですか。
> **Sashimi to sushi to, dotchi no hō ga suki desu ka.**
> *Which do you like better, sashimi or sushi?*

> 漢字とカタカナと、どちらが難しいですか。
> **Kanji to katakana to, dochira ga muzukashii desu ka.**
> *Which is more difficult, kanji or katakana?*

Answers to such questions usually start with . . . の方が . . . **no hō ga**, as in:

> 九州と四国と、どちらの方が広いですか。
> **Kyūshū to Shikoku to, dochira no hō ga hiroi desu ka.**
> *Which is larger, Kyushu or Shikoku?*

> 九州の方が広いです。
> **Kyūshū no hō ga hiroi desu.**
> *Kyushu is larger.*

EXERCISE
8·10

Ask the following questions in Japanese.

1. *Which is larger, Canada or the United States?* (*Canada*: カナダ **Kanada**)

   _____

2. *Which is easier, Chinese or Korean?* (*Chinese language*: 中国語 **Chūgokugo**; *Korean*: 韓国語 **Kankokugo**)

   _____

3. *Which are more convenient, trains or planes?* (*trains*: 電車 **densha**; *airplanes*: 飛行機 **hikōki**; *convenient*: 便利な **benri na**)

   _____

4. *Who works harder, the Japanese or the Chinese?* (*work hard*: よく働く **yoku hataraku**)

   _____

5. *Which is colder, New York or Chicago?* (*cold*: 寒い **samui**)

   _____

Answer the following questions in Japanese.

1. ケーキとクッキーと、どちらの方が好きですか。

   Kēki to kukkī to, dochira no hō ga sukidesu ka.

   Which do you like more, cakes or cookies?

   _____

2. お父さんとお母さんと、どちらの方が厳しいですか。

   Otōsan to okāsan to, dochira no hō ga kibishii desu ka.

   Who is stricter, your father or your mother?

   _____

3. 犬と猫と、どちらが好きですか。

   Inu to neko to, dochira ga suki desu ka.

   Which do you like better, dogs or cats?

   _____

Equivalent-degree comparison

Use the phrase 同じぐらい **onaji gurai** to express the equivalence of two items in terms of the degree of some property in an affirmative sentence. For example:

> ねこは犬と同じぐらいかわいいです。
> **Neko wa inu to onaji gurai kawaii desu.**
> *Cats are as cute as dogs.*

By contrast, to express non-equivalence, use the particle ほど **hodo** along with a negative adjective or verb. For example:

> 猫は犬ほどかわいくありません。
> **Neko wa inu hodo kawaiku arimasen.**
> *Cats are not as cute as dogs.*

Translate the following sentences into English.

1. 私はあなたほど頭がよくありません。

   Watashi wa anata hodo atama ga yoku arimasen.

   _____

2. 期末テストは中間テストと同じぐらい難しかったです。

   Kimatsu tesuto wa chūkan tesuto to onaji gurai muzukashikatta desu.

   _____

3. 母は父ほどやさしくありません。

Haha wa chichi hodo yasashiku arimasen.

_____

4. 今年は去年ほど雪が降りませんでした。

Kotoshi wa kyonen hodo yuki ga furimasendeshita.

_____

5. 電話はメールほど便利じゃありません。

Denwa wa mēru hodo benri ja arimasen.

_____

Comparing activities

You can compare different activities by using a verb as a noun. To use a verb as a noun, you need to add the noun-maker particle の **no** after the verb. Then you can use the verb as a noun before a particle such as が **ga**, と **to**, は **wa**, or で **de**. However, の **no** is not needed when you have a verb before より **yori** or ほど **hodo**. For example:

> 寝るのと食べるのと、どちらの方が好きですか。
> **Neru no to taberu no to, dochira no hō ga suki desu ka.**
> _Which do you like better, sleeping or eating?_

> 私は寝る方が食べるより好きです。
> **Watashi wa neru hō ga taberu yori suki desu.**
> _I like sleeping better than eating._

> レポートを書くのは試験を受けるほど難しくありません。
> **Repōto o kaku no wa shiken o ukeru hodo muzukashiku arimasen.**
> _Writing a report is not as hard as taking an exam._

EXERCISE 8·13

Translate the following sentences into English.

1. 教えるのと習うのと、どちらの方が好きですか。

Oshieru no to narau no to, dochira no hō ga suki desu ka. (教える **oshieru**: _to teach_; 習う **narau**: _to learn_)

_____

2. 教えるのは習うより難しいです。

Oshieru no wa narau yori muzukashii desu.

_____

3. 習うのは教えるほど難しくありません。

Narau no wa oshieru hodo muzukashiku arimasen.

_____

4. 映画を見るのは本を読むのと同じぐらい好きです。

Eiga o miru no wa hon o yomu no to onaji gurai suki desu.

_____

EXERCISE
8·14

Translate the following sentences into Japanese.

1. _I eat as much as my older brother does._

_____

2. _America is larger than Japan._

_____

3. _Dogs can run faster than cats._

_____

4. _Reading kanji is not as difficult as writing kanji._

_____

5. _Is this book more expensive than that book?_

_____

Superlative comparison

You can express the superlative comparison by using the adverb 一番 **ichiban**, which literally means _the first_, _the best_, or _the most_. For example:

母が一番優しいです。
Haha ga ichiban yasashii desu.
My mom is the kindest.

In a formal context or in written forms, you can use 最も **mottomo** instead of 一番 **ichiban**. The basis of superlative comparison can be a list of items or a class of items. If it is a list of items, list the items in the form X と Y と Z の中で **X to Y to Z no naka de** or X と Y と Z とで **X to Y to Z to de**. If it is a class of items, add の中で **no naka de** after the name of the class. All such phrases may be followed by は **wa**. For example:

猫と犬と兎の中で（は）猫が一番好きです。
Neko to inu to usagi no naka de (wa) neko ga ichiban suki desu.
Among cats, dogs, and rabbits, I like cats the best.

動物の中で (は) 猫が一番好きです。
Dōbutsu no naka de (wa) neko ga ichiban suki desu.
Among animals, I like cats the best.

For superlative questions, never use どちら **dochira** because どちら **dochira** is used only for two-item comparisons. Instead, use question words appropriate for the type of items, such as だれ **dare** for people, どこ **doko** for locations, いつ **itsu** for time, and 何 **nani** for other kinds of items. Note that 何 **nani** is replaced with どれ **dore** if the question is based on a list of items. For example:

果物の中で何が一番好きですか。
Kudamono no naka de nani ga ichiban suki desu ka.
Among fruit, what do you like the best?

桃と苺とりんごの中でどれが一番好きですか。
Momo to ichigo to ringo no naka de dore ga ichiban suki desu ka.
Among peaches, strawberries, and apples, which do you like the best?

うちではだれが一番 背が高いですか。
Uchi de wa dare ga ichiban se ga takai desu ka.
Who is the tallest in your home?

足立さんと谷さんと森さんの中で、 だれが一番背が高いですか。
Adachi-san to Tani-san to Mori-san no naka de, dare ga ichiban se ga takai desu ka.
Who is the tallest, Ms. Adachi, Ms. Tani, or Ms. Mori?

日本ではどこが一番人口が多いですか。
Nihon de wa doko ga ichiban jinkō ga ōi desu ka.
In Japan, which place has the largest population?

季節ではいつが一番好きですか。
Kisetsu de wa itsu ga ichiban suki desu ka.
Which season do you like the best?

EXERCISE
8·15

For each of the following, choose the appropriate answer from the options in the parentheses.

1. クラスの中で(どちら, だれ, どれ)が一番背が高いですか。

   Kurasu no naka de (dochira, dare, dore) ga ichiban se ga takai desu ka.

   Who is the tallest in class?

2. 動物では(どれ, 何)が 一番好きですか。

   Dōbutsu de wa (dore, nani) ga ichiban suki desu ka.

   What do you like the best among animals?

3. 韓国語と日本語と中国語の中で(どれ, 何)が一番難しいですか。

   Kankokugo to Nihongo to Chūgokugo no naka de (dore, nani) ga ichiban muzukashii desu ka.

   Which is most difficult, Korean, Japanese, or Chinese?

4. 本州と北海道と九州の中では(どちら, どこ, どれ)が一番広いですか。

Honshū to Hokkaidō to Kyūshū no naka de wa (dochira, doko, dore) ga ichiban hiroi desu ka.

Which is most spacious, Honshu, Hokkaido, or Kyushu?

5. 寝るのと食べるのと遊ぶのとでは(どれ, 何)が一番今したいですか。

Neru no to taberu no to asobu no to de wa (dore, nani) ga ichiban ima shitai desu ka.

Which do you want to do the most now, sleeping, eating, or playing?

Sentence types

In this chapter, you will learn a variety of sentence types, including statements, questions, suggestions, requests, and commands.

Statements

A statement sentence expresses a fact. It ends with a predicate, which can be a verb, an adjective, or a copular verb, that is either affirmative or negative, in non-past or past tense, and in plain or informal style. For example:

> 私はあしたボストンに行きます。
> **Watashi wa ashita Bosuton ni ikimasu.**
> *I will go to Boston.*

> 父はカナダの会社の社長だった。
> **Chichi wa Kanada no kaisha no shachō datta.**
> *My father was the president of a company in Canada.*

Questions

Question sentences can be either yes/no questions, for which agreement or disagreement is an answer, or content questions, for which the answer must provide some information. In either case, question sentences end in the question particle か **ka** in Japanese. A question mark (?) is not formally needed, but it is actually frequently used in personal letters and many literary works. Unlike in English, there is no need to invert the subject and the verb or to place a question word at the beginning of a question sentence in Japanese. Japanese question sentences maintain the word order in the statement sentences, and question words are placed where the answers would be placed in a statement. For example:

> あしたはボストンに行きますか。
> **Ashita wa Bosuton ni ikimasu ka.**
> *Will you go to Boston tomorrow?* (yes/no question)

> あしたはどこに行きますか。
> **Ashita wa doko ni ikimasu ka.**
> *Where will you go to tomorrow?* (content question)

Question words

The following table shows basic question words in Japanese along with examples of their usage:

Meaning	Question Word	Usage Examples
who	だれ **dare**	あの人はだれですか。 **Ano hito wa dare desu ka.** *Who is that person over there?*
what	何 **nani**	何を食べましたか。 **Nani o tabemashita ka.** *What did you eat?*
where	どこ **doko**	どこに行きましたか。 **Doko ni ikimashita ka.** *Where did you go?*
when	いつ **itsu**	いつ卒業しましたか。 **Itsu sotsugyō shimashita ka.** *When did you graduate?*
why	どうして **dōshite**	どうして帰るんですか。 **Dōshite kaeru n desu ka.** *Why are you going home?*
how	どう **dō**	新しいアパートはどうですか。 **Atarashii apāto wa dō desu ka.** *How is the new apartment?*

The following are some additional question words:

- どなた **donata**: *who* (polite version)
- なぜ **naze**: *why* (formal version)
- どれ **dore**: *which one*
- どの **dono**: *which*
- どちら **dochira**: *which one of the two, which way*, or *who/where* (honorific)
- どんな **donna**: *what kind of*
- 何時 **nan-ji**: *what time* (o'clock)
- 何人 **nan-nin**: *how many* (people)
- いくら **ikura**: *how much* (price)
- いくつ **ikutsu**: *how many* (things)
- どのくらい **dono kurai**: *approximately how much*

EXERCISE 9·1

For each of the following, choose the appropriate answer from the options in the parentheses. For a greater challenge, cover the English translations as you work on this exercise.

1. 昨日は（だれ, どこ, 何）に行きましたか。

   Kinō wa (dare, doko, nani) ni ikimashita ka.

   Where did you go?

2. パーティーには（だれ, どこ, 何）が来ましたか。

   Pātī ni wa (dare, doko, nani) ga kimashita ka.

   Who came to the party?

3. 今朝は（だれ, どこ, 何）を食べましたか。

   Kesa wa (dare, doko, nani) o tabemashita ka.

   What did you eat this morning?

4. 新しい車は（だれ, いつ, どう）ですか。

   Atarashii kuruma wa (dare, itsu, dō) desu ka.

   How is your new car?

5. デイビッドさんは（だれ, いつ, どう）中国に行ったんですか。

   Deibiddo-san wa (dare, itsu, dō) Chūgoku ni itta n desu ka.

   When did David go to China?

Sometimes a question is embedded in a sentence. In the following examples, the parts marked by the brackets are questions embedded in a sentence:

> マイクさんは[トムさんが来るか（どうか）]知りません。
> **Maiku-san wa [Tomu-san ga kuru ka (dō ka)] shirimasen.**
> *Mike does not know [whether Tom will come].*

> マイクさんは[だれが来るか]知りません。
> **Maiku-san wa [dare ga kuru ka] shirimasen.**
> *Mike does not know [who will come].*

See Chapter 11 for question clauses that are complements of a verb.

Sentences with indefinite pronouns

Indefinite pronouns are pronouns that do not have a definite reference but mean, for example, *someone, anybody, no one, anywhere,* and so on. By using them, you can make a statement or a question without a specific reference item. In Japanese, you create an indefinite pronoun by adding a particle at the end of a question word.

Existential pronouns (*someone, anyone,* etc.)

By adding the particle か **ka** at the end of a question word, you can create an existential pronoun that expresses the existence of some item. It is useful when you know there is someone, but don't know who—for example, *there was someone at the counter.* It is also useful when you ask a general question, such as *Was there anyone at the counter?* In English, existential pronouns are *someone* or *something* or *anyone* or *anything,* depending on whether the sentence is a statement or a question. On the other hand, the existential pronoun remains the same in Japanese in both questions and statements. For example:

> カウンターにはだれかいました。
> **Kauntā ni wa dareka imashita.**
> *There was someone at the counter.*

> カウンターにはだれかいましたか。
> **Kauntā ni wa dareka imashita ka.**
> *Was there anyone at the counter?*

The subject particle が **ga** and the direct object particle を **o** are usually dropped when they occur after an existential pronoun, but other particles remain. For example:

ブライアンさんはどこかに行きました。
Buraian-san wa dokoka ni ikimashita.
Brian went somewhere.

夏休みはどこかに行きましたか。
Natsuyasumi wa dokoka ni ikimashita ka.
Did you go anywhere during summer vacation?

昨日はだれか来ましたよ。
Kinō wa dareka kimashita yo.
Someone came yesterday.

何か食べましょうよ。
Nanika tabemashō yo.
Let's eat something!

この事をだれかと話しましたか。
Kono koto o dareka to hanashimashita ka.
Did you talk with anyone about this matter?

EXERCISE
9·2

Translate the following sentences into English.

1. あの部屋にだれかいますよ。

   Ano heya ni dare ka imasu yo.

   _____

2. この箱の中に何かあります。

   Kono hako no naka ni nanika arimasu.

   _____

3. 犯人はこの建物の中のどこかにいます。

   Hannin wa kono tatemono no naka no dokoka ni imasu.

   _____

4. 新しい車はいつか買います。

   Atarashii kuruma wa itsuka kaimasu.

   _____

Negative pronouns (*no one*, etc.)

A negative pronoun negates the existence of some kind of item. You create a negative pronoun by adding the particle も **mo** after a question word and its associated structural particle and placing it in a negative sentence. Note that the particles が **ga** and を **o** must be deleted if they are followed by も **mo**, as discussed in Chapter 7. For example:

夏休みはどこにも行きませんでした。
Natsu-yasumi wa doko ni mo ikimasen deshita.
I did not go anywhere during summer vacation.

昨日はだれも来ませんでした。
Kinō wa dare mo kimasendeshita.
No one came yesterday.

EXERCISE
9·3

Translate the following sentences into English.

1. 私は何も知りません。

   Watashi wa nani mo shirimasen.

   _____

2. 私は何もほしくありません。

   Watashi wa nani mo hoshiku arimasen.

   _____

3. 私はだれにも会いたくありません。

   Watashi wa dare ni mo aitaku arimasen.

   _____

EXERCISE
9·4

Complete the following sentences.

1. A: 夏休みは _____ 行きましたか。

   Natsu-Yasumi wa _____ ikimashita ka.

   Did you go somewhere during summer vacation?

   B: いいえ、_____ 行きませんでした。

   Īe, _____ ikimasendeshita.

   No, I did not go anywhere.

2. A: 今朝は _____ 食べましたか。

   Kesa wa _____ tabemashita ka.

   Did you eat anything this morning?

   B: いいえ、_____ 食べませんでした。

   Īe, _____ tabemasendeshita.

   No, I did not eat anything.

Universal pronouns (*everyone*, etc.)

By adding the particle も **mo** at the end of a question word and using it in an affirmative sentence, you can create a universal pronoun that refers to all of some kind of items. For example:

会社のだれもが反対しました。
Kaisha no dare mo ga hantai shimashita.
Everyone in the company disagreed.

山田さんはいつもネックレスをしています。
Yamada-san wa itsumo nekkuresu o shite imasu.
Ms. Yamada is always wearing a necklace.

EXERCISE

9·5

Translate the following sentences into English.

1. この大学ではどの学生も寮に住んでいます。

   Kono daigaku de wa dono gakusei mo ryō ni sunde imasu.

   _____

2. どの会社もパソコンを使っています。

   Dono kaisha mo pasokon o tsukatte imasu.

   _____

3. コンビニはどの町にもあります。

   Konbini wa dono machi ni mo arimasu.

   _____

4. 宇多田のCDはどれも買いました。

   Utada no CD wa dore mo kaimashita.

   _____

Free choice (*any*)

By adding the particle でも **demo** after a question word plus its associated particle, you can create a free-choice indefinite pronoun that indicates *any*. When you use the particle でも **demo**, you must be sure to delete the relevant particles が **ga** and を **o**. For example:

東京ではコンビニはどこにでもありますよ。
Tōkyō de wa konbini wa doko ni demo arimasu yo.
You can find a convenience store in anywhere in Tokyo.

そんなことはだれでも知っていますよ。
Sonna koto wa dare demo shitte imasu yo.
Anyone knows such a thing.

To negate a statement with these phrases, you do not just negate the predicate; rather, you use わけではありません **wake de wa arimasen**. The following examples show the use of a free-choice indefinite pronoun and how to negate it:

> だれでもできます。
> **Dare demo dekimasu.**
> *Anyone can do it.*

> だれでもできるわけではありません。
> **Dare demo dekiru wake de wa arimasen.**
> *It is not the case that anyone can do it.*

EXERCISE
9·6

Translate the following sentences into Japanese.

1. *I will do anything.*

   _____

2. *I will go anywhere.*

   _____

3. *I will buy anything.*

   _____

Enriching statements

There are some elements you can use at the end of a sentence to express your certainty, intention, and feelings about the statement. In this section, you'll learn some of these sentence-ending elements. Most of them follow a sentence that ends in verbs and adjectives in the plain form, but there are some exceptions. It is a good idea to summarize the plain forms of verbs and adjectives, as shown in this table:

	Plain Forms of Verbs and Adjectives			
	Non-past		**Past**	
	Affirmative	**Negative**	**Affirmative**	**Negative**
Verb	食べる **taberu**	食べない **tabenai**	食べた **tabeta**	食べなかった **tabenakatta**
Noun + copula	犬だ **inu da**	犬じゃない **inu ja nai**	犬だった **inu datta**	犬じゃなかった **inu ja nakatta**
Na adjective	高価だ **kōka da**	高価じゃない **kōka ja nai**	高価だった **kōka datta**	高価じゃなかった **kōka ja nakatta**
I adjective	高い **takai**	高くない **takaku nai**	高かった **takakatta**	高くなかった **takaku nakatta**

Convert the following polite-form words into the plain form.

1. 安いです **yasui desu** _____

2. 日本人です **Nihonjin desu** _____

3. ねませんでした **nemasendeshita** _____

4. よくありませんでした **yoku arimasendeshita** _____

5. 見ました **mimashita** _____

6. 来ません **kimasen** _____

7. おもしろかったです **omoshirokatta desu** _____

8. きれいでした **kirei deshita** _____

. . . そうです **sō desu** (*hear/say*)

そうです **sō desu** or its plain counterpart そうだ **sō da** is added at the end of a sentence in the plain form, regardless of whether it is affirmative or negative, non-past or past. It shows that the content of the sentence is the report of what the speaker heard or read. For example:

東京で地震があったそうです。
Tōkyō de jishin ga atta sō desu.
I heard that there was an earthquake in Tokyo.

渡辺さんは歌が上手だそうです。
Watanabe-san wa uta ga jōzu da sō desu.
They say that Mr. Watanabe is good at singing.

来月、駅の近くにイタリア料理のレストランがオープンするそうです。
Raigetsu, eki no chikaku ni Itaria ryōri no resutoran ga ōpun suru sō desu.
I heard that an Italian restaurant will open near the train station next month.

EXERCISE
9·8

Rephrase these sentences using そうです *sō desu.*

1. 石田さんの奥さんは中国人です。

   Ishida-san no oku-san wa Chūgokujin desu.

   Mr. Ishida's wife is Chinese.

   _____

2. 日本の牛肉は高いです。

   Nihon no gyūniku wa takai desu.

   Beef in Japan is expensive.

   _____

3. 高橋さんはイタリア人と結婚しました。

Takahashi-san wa Itariajin to kekkon shimashita.

Ms. Takahashi is married to an Italian.

_____

4. 砂糖は健康によくありません。

Satō wa kenkō ni yoku arimasen.

Sugar is not good for a person's health.

_____

Share two things that you have heard or read about Japan.

1. _____

2. _____

...でしょう deshō (probability)

でしょう **deshō** or its plain counterpart だろう **darō** can be placed at the end of a sentence and shows that the situation stated in the statement is probably true. For example:

> あしたは雨が降るでしょう。
> **Ashita wa ame ga furu deshō.**
> *I guess it will rain tomorrow.*

The predicate of the sentence must be in the plain form, but the non-past affirmative copula in the form of だ **da** must be absent, regardless of whether it is after a noun or a **na** adjective stem. For example, if you want to say *I guess Mike is serious*, it is ungrammatical to say:

> マイクさんはまじめだでしょう。
> **Maiku-san wa majime da deshō.**

Instead, you should say:

> マイクさんはまじめでしょう。
> **Maiku-san wa majime deshō.**

The following are some more examples:

> あの人はスパイでしょう。
> **Ano hito wa supai deshō.**
> *I guess that person is a spy.*

> 陽子さんと武さんは結婚しないでしょう。
> **Yōko-san to Takeshi-san wa kekkon shinai deshō.**
> *I guess Yoko and Takeshi won't get married.*

田中さんがいなかったら、大変だったでしょう。
Tanaka-san ga inakattara, taihen datta deshō.
If Ms. Tanaka had not been there, we would have had a hard time.

あしたはたぶん さむくないでしょう。
Ashita wa tabun samuku nai deshō.
It will probably not be cold tomorrow.

When でしょう **deshō** is used with a question word and/or the question particle か **ka**, as in どうでしょうか **dō deshō ka**, どうでしょう **dō deshō**, or 来るでしょうか **kuru deshō ka**, it shows that the speaker wonders about something and wants to hear what the listener thinks. For example:

あしたの天気はどうでしょうか。or あしたの天気はどうでしょう。
Ashita no tenki wa dō deshō ka. or Ashita no tenki wa dō deshō.
I wonder how tomorrow's weather will be. What do you think?

今日は雪が降るでしょうか。
Kyō wa yuki ga furu deshō ka.
I wonder whether it will snow today. What do you think?

In an informal speech context, use だろう **darō** instead of でしょう **deshō**. For example:

たぶん雨が降るだろう。
Tabun ame ga furu darō.
It will probably rain.

EXERCISE
9·10

Rephrase the following sentences using でしょう *deshō*.

1. あしたは寒いです。

   Ashita wa samui desu.

   It will be cold tomorrow.

   _____

2. あさっては寒くありません。

   Asatte wa samuku arimasen.

   It will not be cold the day after tomorrow.

   _____

3. 今年は雪が降りません。

   Kotoshi wa yuki ga furimasen.

   It will not snow this year.

   _____

4. あしたのサッカーの試合はありません。

   Ashita no sakkā no shiai wa arimasen.

   There will not be a soccer game tomorrow.

   _____

5. あの人は韓国人です。

Ano hito wa kankokujin desu.

That person is Korean.

. . . かもしれません **kamoshiremasen** (possibility)

You add かもしれません **kamoshiremasen** or its plain counterpart かもしれない **kamoshire-nai** at the end of a sentence to show that the situation stated in the sentence is possible. The predicate of the sentence must be in the plain form, but the non-past affirmative copula in the form of だ **da** must be absent, regardless of whether it is after a noun or a **na** adjective stem, as with でしょう **deshō**, discussed earlier in this chapter. For example:

風邪かもしれません。でも、風邪じゃないかもしれません。
Kaze kamoshiremasen. Demo, kaze ja nai kamoshiremasen.
It may be a cold. However, it may not be a cold.

頭が痛いんです。仕事に 行けないかもしれません。
Atama ga itai n desu. Shigoto ni ikenai kamoshiremasen.
I have a headache. I may not be able to go to work.

だれかが家に入ったかもしれない。
Dareka ga ie ni haitta kamoshirenai.
It's possible that someone entered the house.

EXERCISE
9·11

Rephrase the following sentences using かもしれません *kamoshiremasen.*

1. 仕事を変えます。

Shigoto o kaemasu.

I will change my job.

2. あの人は親切じゃありません。

Ano hito wa shinsetsu ja arimasen.

That person is not kind.

3. 大学に行きません。

Daigaku ni ikimasen.

I will not go to college.

4. 薬がありません。

Kusuri ga arimasen.

I don't have medicine.

_____

5. この車は古いです。

Kono kuruma wa furui desu.

This car is old.

_____

. . . つもりです tsumori desu (*plan*)

When you plan to do something or not to do something—and that plan could change in the future—add つもりです **tsumori desu** after a verb in the plain form. For example:

来週の水曜日は休暇をとるつもりです。
Raishū no Suiyōbi wa kyūka o toru tsumori desu.
I plan to take a day off on Wednesday next week.

武さんはお兄さんを結婚式に招待しないつもりです。
Takeshi-san wa onīsan o kekkonshiki ni shōtai shinai tsumori desu.
Takeshi plans not to invite his older brother to his wedding.

EXERCISE

9·12

Rephrase the following sentences using つもりです *tsumori desu.*

1. 帰りに買い物をします。

Kaeri ni kaimono o shimasu.

I will go shopping on the way home.

_____

2. アトランタの友達のうちに寄ります。

Atoranta no tomodachi no uchi ni yorimasu.

I will stop by at my friend's house in Atlanta.

_____

3. 新しい車は買いません。

Atarashii kuruma wa kaimasen.

I will not buy a new car.

_____

4. 銀行には就職しません。

Ginkō ni wa shūshoku shimasen.

I will not work for a bank.

. . . はずです **hazu desu** (objective conclusion)

はず **hazu** is an abstract noun that means something like *normal expectation* or *objective conclusion*. By adding はず **hazu** and the copula です **desu** or だ **da** at the end of a sentence, you can show that the statement's content is what is objectively expected or concluded in the given circumstance. はず **hazu** usually refers to what you as the speaker expect of other people or things, not of yourself. The sentence before はずです **hazu desu** should be in the plain form, except that the non-past affirmative copula in the form of だ **da** must be な **na** if preceded by a **na** adjective stem, and it must be の **no** if preceded by a noun. For example:

この店は返品ができるはずです。
Kono mise wa henpin ga dekiru hazu desu.
I suppose this store allows returns.

森さんはよく居酒屋に行きますから，お酒が好きなはずです。
Mori-san wa yoku izakaya ni ikimasu kara, o-sake ga suki na hazu desu.
Mr. Mori often goes to izakaya bars, so he must like liquor.

今，1ドルは98円のはずです。
Ima, ichi-doru wa 98-en no hazu desu.
I suppose a dollar is 98 yen now.

うちの息子はそんな大金はないはずです。
Uchi no musuko wa sonna taikin wa nai hazu desu.
I suppose that my son does not have such a big amount of money.

You can negate the copula after はず **hazu**. For example:

うちの息子はそんな大金があるはずはありません。
Uchi no musuko wa sonna taikin ga aru hazu wa arimasen.
It cannot be true that my son has such a big amount of money.

EXERCISE
9·13

Rephrase the following using はずです *hazu desu.*

1. 田中さんは昨日ここに来ました。

Tanaka-san wa kinō koko ni kimashita.

Mr. Tanaka came here yesterday.

2. この本は簡単です。

Kono hon wa kantan desu.

This book is easy.

_____

3. あしたは山田さんの誕生日です。

Ashita wa Yamada-san no tanjōbi desu.

Tomorrow is Ms. Yamada's birthday.

_____

4. 手紙はあした着きます。

Tegami wa ashita tsukimasu.

The letter will arrive tomorrow.

_____

. . . べきです **beki desu** (subjective opinion)

You use べきです **beki desu** or べきだ **beki da** only following the dictionary form of a verb, to express your subjective opinion about what should be the case. For example:

> 早く寝て早く起きるべきです。
> **Hayaku nete hayaku okiru beki desu.**
> *One should go to bed early and wake up early.*

する **suru** (*to do*) is often contracted to す **su** before べき **beki**, as in 勉強すべきです **benkyō subeki desu**. For example:

> 学生はもっと勉強す(る)べきです。
> **Gakusei wa motto benkyō su(ru) beki desu.**
> *Students should study more.*

> 教師は 学生に厳しくす(る)べきです。
> **Kyōshi wa gakusei ni kibishiku su(ru) beki desu.**
> *Teachers should be strict with the students.*

To express what should not be the case, the negative element usually appears after べき **beki**, as in:

> うそをつくべきじゃありません。
> **Uso o tsuku beki ja arimasen.**
> *One should not tell a lie.*

To express what should have be done, make the copula after べき **beki** past tense. For example:

> 予約を確認するべきでした。
> **Yoyaku o kakunin suru beki deshita.**
> *(I) should have confirmed the reservation.*

Fill in each blank with either はず *hazu or* べき *beki.*

1. あなたは 学生ですから、もっと勉強する _____ です。

   Anata wa gakusei desu kara, motto benkyō suru _____ desu.

   You are a student, so you should study more.

2. 昨日送りましたから、あした着く _____ です。

   Kinō okurimashita kara, ashita tsuku _____ desu.

   I sent it yesterday, so it should arrive tomorrow.

3. へんですね。ここに おいた _____ ですが、ありませんね。

   Hen desu ne. Koko ni oita _____ desu ga, arimasen ne.

   It's weird. I suppose I put it here, but it's not here.

4. 人の悪口を言う _____ じゃありません。

   Hito no waruguchi o iu _____ ja arimasen.

   You shouldn't say ill of others.

5. 日本は今冬ですから、オーストラリアは今夏の _____ です。

   Nihon wa ima fuyu desu kara, Ōsutoraria wa ima natsu no _____ desu.

   It is winter now in Japan, so it should be summer now in Australia.

. . . らしいです rashii desu (objective conjecture)

You add らしいです **rashii desu** or its plain counterpart らしい **rashii** at the end of a sentence to show that the fact you're expressing is your objective, logical, careful, and non-intuitive conjecture, based on what you heard, saw, or read. The predicate of the sentence must be in the plain form, but the non-past affirmative copula in the form of だ **da** must be absent, regardless of whether it is after a noun or a **na** adjective stem, as is the case with でしょう **deshō** and かもしれません **kamoshiremasen**, discussed earlier in this chapter. For example:

> 谷川さんのお宅で何かあったらしいですよ。
> **Tanikawa-san no otaku de nanika atta rashii desu yo.**
> *It seems that something has happened at Ms. Tanikawa's house.*

> 今度の部長は大川さんらしいです。
> **Kondo no buchō wa Ōkawa-san rashii desu.**
> *The new division head seems to be Mr. Okawa.*

> 大川さんはカラオケが好きらしいです。
> **Ōkawa-san wa karaoke ga suki rashii desu.**
> *Mr. Okawa seems to like karaoke.*

Rephrase the following sentences using らしいです *rashii desu.*

1. 中国では飲料水が足りません。

   Chūgoku de wa inryōsui ga tarimasen.

   Drinking water is in shortage in China.

   _____

2. 日本の円が安くなりました。

   Nihon no en ga yasuku narimashita.

   The Japanese yen became cheaper.

   _____

3. この機械は操作が簡単です。

   Kono kikai wa sōsa ga kantan desu.

   This machine is easy to operate.

   _____

. . . ようです yō desu (general conjecture)

You add ようです **yō desu** or its plain counterpart ようだ**yō da** at the end of a sentence to show that the fact you're expressing is your conjecture, which can be any sort of conjecture, including intuitive or objective conjectures. Therefore, the sentences that end in らしいです **rashii desu** discussed above can be rephrased with ようです **yō desu**, but not vice versa. However, note that the forms you need before ようです **yō desu** and らしいです **rashii desu** are different. The sentence before ようです **yō desu** should be in the plain form, but the non-past affirmative copula in the form of だ **da** must be な **na** if preceded by a **na** adjective stem, and it must be の **no** if preceded by a noun, as is the case with はずです **hazu desu**, discussed earlier in this chapter. For example:

> 日本の円が安くなったようですよ。
> **Nihon no en ga yasuku natta yō desu yo.**
> *It seems that the Japan yen became cheaper.*

> 大山さんは中田さんが嫌いなようです。
> **Ōyama-san wa Nakada-san ga kirai na yō desu.**
> *Ms. Oyama seems to dislike Ms. Nakada.*

> 留守のようですね。帰りましょう。
> **Rusu no yō desu ne. Kaerimashō.**
> *It appears that there's no one here. Let's go home.*

> 林さんは何も知らなかったようです。
> **Hayashi-san wa nani mo shiranakatta yō desu.**
> *It seems that Mr. Hayashi did not know anything about it.*

> あの人は何か困っているようですね。
> **Ano hito wa nani ka komatte iru yō desu ne.**
> *That person seems to be having some trouble.*

Complete each of the following sentences with either よう **yō** or らしい **rashii**, and do not add anything else.

1. 山田さんのお姉さんは看護師の ＿＿＿＿＿＿＿＿＿＿＿ です。

   Yamada-san no onēsan wa kangoshi no ＿＿＿＿＿＿＿＿＿ desu.

   Ms. Yamada's older sister seems to be a nurse.

2. あのバンドは下手 ＿＿＿＿＿＿＿＿＿＿＿ です。

   Ano bando wa heta ＿＿＿＿＿＿＿＿＿ desu.

   That band seems to be unskilled.

3. 順子さんはマイクさんが好きな ＿＿＿＿＿＿＿＿＿＿ です。

   Junko-san wa Maiku-san ga suki na ＿＿＿＿＿＿＿＿＿ desu.

   Junko seems to like Mike.

4. でも、マイクさんは恵子さんが好き ＿＿＿＿＿＿＿＿＿＿ ですよ。

   Demo, Maiku-san wa Keiko-san ga suki ＿＿＿＿＿＿＿＿＿ desu yo.

   However, Mike seems to like Keiko.

...の/ん です no/n desu (explanatory predicate)

The abstract noun の **no**, or its contracted version ん **n**, followed by the copula です **desu** or だ **da**, makes a special expression that literally means *It is a fact that . . .* Its function is to make a conversation more interactive. When you use this construction, you connect your statement to the conversational context and show that your statement is to provide an explanation for something in the context or to elicit response to the statement. You also use it to soften the tone of your expression when requesting, suggesting, or demanding. So its hidden meanings are *that's why* or *but what do you think?* The statement sentence must end in the plain form, but the non-past affirmative copula in the form of だ **da** must appear as な **na**, regardless of whether it is after a noun or a **na** adjective stem. The following conversations provide examples:

> A: あれ？もう帰る？ **Are? Mō kaeru?**
> *Oh. Are you leaving already?*

> B: はい。今日はピアノのレッスンがあるんです。
> **Hai. Kyō wa piano no ressun ga aru n desu.**
> *Yes. I have a piano lesson today. (That's why.)*

> A: あのう、実は来月結婚するんです。
> **Anō, jitsu wa raigetsu kekkon suru n desu.**
> *Umm, as a matter of fact, I'm going to get married next month. (What do you think?)*

> B: え？本当ですか？
> **E? Hontō desu ka?**
> *What? Is it true?*

んです **n desu** is very commonly used when the sentence is not completed but left dangling with a particle like が **ga** (*but*). For example:

> A: 社長。あした会社を休みたいんですが。
> **Shachō. Ashita kaisha o yasumi-tai n desu ga.**
> *President. I'd like to take a day off tomorrow, but . . . (Is it okay? Please say something . . .)*

> B: ああ。
> **Ā.**
> *Oh.*

When you ask a confirmation question, use んですか **n desu ka**. For example, suppose your friend suddenly started smoking in front of you, and you did not know that he was a smoker. To confirm that he is a smoker, you can ask him:

> タバコをすうんですか。
> **Tabako o suu n desu ka.**
> *Is it true that you smoke?*

In this context, if you don't use んですか **n desu ka**, but say the following, you sound like you are somehow unable to see anything:

> タバコをすいますか。
> **Tabako o suimasu ka.**
> *Do you smoke?*

EXERCISE
9·17

Complete the following sentences.

1. あれ?ポールさんはタバコを ＿＿＿＿＿＿＿＿＿＿ んですか。

   Are? Pōru-san wa tabako o ＿＿＿＿＿＿＿＿＿＿ n desu ka.

2. 実は昨日新しい車を ＿＿＿＿＿＿＿＿＿＿ んです。

   Jitsu wa kinō atarashii kuruma o ＿＿＿＿＿＿＿＿＿＿ n desu.

3. あのう、ねこはあまり好きじゃ ＿＿＿＿＿＿＿＿＿＿ んです。

   Anō, neko wa amari suki ja ＿＿＿＿＿＿＿＿＿＿ n desu.

4. 私の母は中国人 ＿＿＿＿＿＿＿＿＿＿ んです。

   Watashi no haha wa Chūgokujin ＿＿＿＿＿＿＿＿＿＿ n desu.

5. おくれて、すみません。ちょっと寝坊 ＿＿＿＿＿＿＿＿＿＿ んです。

   Okurete, sumimasen. Chotto nebō ＿＿＿＿＿＿＿＿＿＿ n desu.

. . . ね **ne** (agreement) and . . . よ **yo** (emphasis)

Some sentence-ending particles show the function of the sentence. For example, you can convert a statement sentence into a question sentence by adding the particle か **ka**, as discussed earlier in this chapter. For example:

> メアリーさんはアメリカ人ですか。
> **Mearī-san wa Amerika-jin desu ka.**
> *Is Mary an American?*

By adding the particle ね **ne** to a statement sentence, you can create a tag question, as in the following example:

> メアリーさんはアメリカ人ですね。
> **Mearī-san wa Amerika-jin desu ne.**
> *Mary is an American, isn't she?*

By adding the particle よ **yo**, you can emphasize the statement. For example:

> メアリーさんはアメリカ人ですよ。
> **Mearī-san wa Amerika-jin desu yo.**
> *Mary is an American, I tell you!*

EXERCISE 9·18

In the following short dialogues, complete the sentences with appropriate particles.

1. A: 今日はいい天気です＿＿＿。

   Kyō wa ii tenki desu ＿＿＿.

   It is a nice day, isn't it?

   B: ええ、そうですね。

   Ē, sō desu ne.

   Yes, it is.

2. A: それはカメラです ＿＿＿。

   Sore wa kamera desu ＿＿＿.

   Is that a camera?

   B: いいえ、これは携帯です。

   Īe, kore wa keitai desu. (携帯 **keitai**: *cell phone*)

   No, it's a cell phone.

3. A: 日本語はむずかしいですね。

   Nihongo wa muzukashii desu ne.

   Japanese is difficult, isn't it?

   B: いいえ、日本語はとても簡単です ＿＿＿。

   Īe, Nihongo wa totemo kantan desu ＿＿＿.

   No, it's very easy!

Suggestions, requests, and commands

. . . ませんか masen ka (suggestion)

In order to make a suggestion, you can ask a negative question. You do not need to have a subject noun. The following are some examples:

週末いっしょに映画を見ませんか。
Shūmatsu isshoni eiga o mimasen ka.
Why don't we watch a movie together this weekend? (polite/neutral speech style)

いっしょに飲まないか。
Isshoni nomanai ka.
Why don't we drink together? (plain/informal speech style)

**EXERCISE
9·19**

What would you say to politely suggest that your friend do the following?

1. To go to a restaurant together (レストランに行く **resutoran ni iku**: *to go to a restaurant*)

_____

2. To do homework together (宿題をする **shukudai o suru**: *to do one's homework*)

_____

3. To drink coffee together (コーヒーを飲む **kōhī o nomu**: *to drink coffee*)

_____

4. To play tennis together (テニスをする **tenisu o suru**: *to play tennis*)

_____

. . . ましょう mashō (*let's do . . .*)

You use ましょう **mashō** following a verb in the stem form to enthusiastically invite your conversational partner to some activity. For example:

美術館に行きましょう。
Bijutsukan ni ikimashō.
Let's go to an art museum!

In this case, the speaker necessarily intends to be involved in the same activity. If the question particle **ka** is added, as in ましょうか **mashō ka**, it expresses a suggestion rather than an enthusiastic invitation. For example:

デパートに行きましょうか。
Depāto ni ikimashō ka.
Shall we go to a department store?

ちょっと休みましょうか。
Chotto yasumimashō ka.
Shall we take a rest?

You can use ましょうか **mashō ka** to offer help. In this case, it is best to add 私が **watashi ga**. For example:

私が料理しましょうか。
Watashi ga ryōri shimashō ka.
Shall I cook?

EXERCISE
9·20

You would like to offer help in doing the following. What would you say in each case?

1. Cleaning (掃除する **sōji suru**)

   _____

2. Writing (書く **kaku**)

   _____

3. Carrying (運ぶ **hakobu**)

   _____

4. Driving (運転する **unten suru**)

   _____

5. Washing dishes (皿を洗う **sara o arau**)

   _____

. . . よう **(y)ō (volitional form)**

The plain version of ましょう **mashō** discussed earlier is actually the volitional form of verbs. It expresses one's volition or will. For example, the volitional form of 行く **iku** is 行こう **ikō**. Instead of saying 行きましょう **ikimashō**, you can say 行こう **ikō** in an informal context to mean *Let's go!* You can create a volitional form by removing the ending **ru** or **u** in the dictionary form and adding **yō** or **ō**. To conjugate a verb, look at the following table and follow the pattern of a verb with the same ending and in the same category:

	Ending	Dictionary Form	Volitional Form
Ru verbs	-える -eru	かえる **kaeru** (*change*)	かえよう **kaeyō**
	-いる -iru	きる **kiru** (*wear*)	きよう **kiyō**
U verbs	-す -su	はなす **hanasu** (*speak*)	はなそう **hanasō**
	-く -ku	かく **kaku** (*write*)	かこう **kakō**
	-ぐ -gu	およぐ **oyogu** (*swim*)	およごう **oyogō**
	-む -mu	よむ **yomu** (*read*)	よもう **yomō**
	-ぬ -nu	しぬ **shinu** (*die*)	しのう **shinō**
	-ぶ -bu	とぶ **tobu** (*jump*)	とぼう **tobō**
	-う -(w)u	かう **kau** (*buy*)	かおう **kaō**
	-る -ru	きる **kiru** (*cut*)	きろう **kirō**
	-つ -tsu	まつ **matsu** (*wait*)	まとう **matō**
Irregular verbs		くる **kuru** (*come*)	こよう **koyō**
		する **suru** (*do*)	しよう **shiyō**

EXERCISE

9·21

Convert each of the following into the plain form.

1. 行きましょう。 **Ikimashō.**

_____

2. 食べましょう。 **Tabemashō.**

_____

3. 飲みましょう。 **Nomimashō.**

_____

4. 帰りましょう。 **Kaerimashō.**

_____

5. しましょう。 **Shimashō.**

_____

6. 見ましょう。 **Mimashō.**

_____

7. がんばりましょう。 **Ganbarimashō.**

_____

. . . てください te kudasai (request)

To request a service of someone else, add ください **kudasai** at the end of a verb in the **te** form. ください **kudasai** literally means *give (it to me please)*. (See Chapter 5 for verbs of giving and receiving.) The combination of a verb in the **te** form and ください **kudasai** means *Do such and such and give me that (as a service)* or *(Please) do . . . .* To ask someone not to do something, use the **nai** form plus で **de** and ください **kudasai**. For example:

> 会議に出てください。
> **Kaigi ni dete kudasai.**
> *Please attend the meeting.*

> 会議に出ないでください。
> **Kaigi ni denai de kudasai.**
> *Please do not attend the meeting.*

To make your request polite, add ませんか **masen ka** to this form and say it with a rising intonation. For example:

> 会議に出てくださいませんか。
> **Kaigi ni dete kudasaimasen ka.**
> *Could you please attend the meeting, please?*

> 会議に出ないでくださいませんか。
> **Kaigi ni denai de kudasaimasen ka.**
> *Could you please not attend the meeting, please?*

EXERCISE 9·22

Request the following actions, using ください *kudasai.*

1. ちょっと待つ **chotto matsu** (*to wait a little bit*)

   _____

2. 入る **hairu** (*to enter*)

   _____

3. ここに座る **koko ni suwaru** (*to sit here*)

   _____

4. 住所を書く **jūsho o kaku** (*to write your address*)

   _____

5. 静かにする **shizuka ni suru** (*to be quiet*)

   _____

. . . なさい nasai (polite command)

なさい **nasai** follows a verb in the stem form and expresses a polite command. Although なさい **nasai** is not as harsh as the plain command, which is discussed in the following section, it is still a command and is not usually used in conversations. However, it is frequently used by parents to children or in written instructions on exams and tests. For example:

早く食べなさい。
Hayaku tabenasai.
Eat quickly.

しずかにしなさい。
Shizukani shinasai.
Be quiet.

括弧の中から正しい漢字を選びなさい。
kakko no naka kara tadashii kanji o erabinasai.
Choose the correct kanji in the parentheses.

なさい **nasai** does not have a negative form. You express the negative polite command by actually saying *Stop doing . . .* or *You are not allowed to do . . . .* For example:

しゃべるのをやめなさい。
Shaberu no o yamenasai.
Stop eating.

しゃべってはいけません。
Shabette wa ikemasen.
You must not eat.

EXERCISE

9·23

Complete the following requests from a mother to her son.

朝おきたら、「おはようございます。」と ＿＿＿＿＿＿＿＿＿＿ なさい。食べる前には手を ＿＿＿＿＿＿＿＿＿＿ なさい。毎日、2時間勉強 ＿＿＿＿＿＿＿＿＿＿ なさい。寝る前には歯を ＿＿＿＿＿＿＿＿＿＿ なさい。

Asa okitara, "Ohayō gozaimasu." to ＿＿＿＿＿＿＿＿＿＿ nasai. Taberu mae ni wa te

o ＿＿＿＿＿＿＿＿＿＿ nasai. Mainichi, ni-jikan benkyō ＿＿＿＿＿＿＿＿＿＿ nasai.

Neru mae ni wa ha o ＿＿＿＿＿＿＿＿＿＿ nasai.

After you wake up, say "Good morning." Wash your hands before eating. Study for two hours every day. Brush your teeth before going to bed.

. . . ろ ro (plain command)

You can create a plain command form by removing the final **ru** or **u** in the dictionary form and adding **ro** or **e**. The negative counterpart is in fact a dictionary form followed by な **na**. To conjugate a verb, look at the following table and follow the pattern of the verb with the same ending and in the same category:

	Ending	Dictionary Form	Plain Command Form (Affirmative)	Plain Command Form (Negative)
Ru verbs	-eる -eru	かえる kaeru (*change*)	かえろ kaero	かえるな kaeruna
	-iる -iru	きる kiru (*wear*)	きろ kiro	きるな kiruna
U verbs	-す -su	はなす hanasu (*speak*)	はなせ hanase	はなすな hanasuna
	-く -ku	かく kaku (*write*)	かけ kake	かくな kakuna
	-ぐ -gu	およぐ oyogu (*swim*)	およげ oyoge	およぐな oyoguna
	-む -mu	よむ yomu (*read*)	よめ yome	よむな yomuna
	-ぬ -nu	しぬ shinu (*die*)	しね shine	しぬな shinuna
	-ぶ -bu	とぶ tobu (*jump*)	とべ tobe	とぶな tobuna
	-う -(w)u	かう kau (*buy*)	かえ kae	かうな kauna
	-る -ru	きる kiru (*cut*)	きれ kire	きるな kiruna
	-つ -tsu	まつ matsu (*wait*)	まて mate	まつな matsuna
Irregular verbs		くる kuru (*come*)	こい koi	くるな kuruna
		する suru (*do*)	しろ shiro	するな suruna

Plain command forms sound extremely blunt and rough, except when they are used in embedded sentences, as in the following examples:

ボタンを押せと説明書に書いてあります。
Botan o ose to setsumeisho ni kaite arimasu.
The instruction manual says to press the button. (Literally: It is written to press the button in the instruction manual.)

このボタンは押すなと注意しました。
Kono botan wa osu na to chūi shimashita.
I warned them not to press this button.

Conjugate the following verbs into plain commands.

1. 書く **kaku** (*to write*) _____

2. 飲む **nomu** (*to drink*) _____

3. 頑張る **ganbaru** (*to try one's best*) _____

4. 立つ **tatsu** (*to stand up*) _____

5. 行く **iku** (*to go*) _____

6. 持つ **motsu** (*to hold*) _____

What would you say in the following situations? Consider the appropriate sentence ending in each case.

1. You want to ask your teacher to lend you her book. (本を貸す **hon o kasu**: *to lend a book*)

   _____

2. You want to ask your student to hand in homework. (宿題を出す **shukudai o dasu**: *to hand in homework*)

   _____

3. Someone tries to park his car in front of your garage, and you want to ask him not to do so. (ここに車をとめる **koko ni kuruma o tomeru**: *to park a car here*)

   _____

4. You want to tell your child to brush his teeth. (歯をみがく **ha o migaku**: *to brush one's teeth*)

   _____

Complex words and phrases

·10·

You can create some words and phrases by adding elements at the end of a word. This chapter shows how to use some of these complex words and phrases that are useful in daily life conversations.

. . . すぎる **sugiru,** etc. (verbal compound)

In Japanese, you can form verbal compounds by following a verb in the stem form with another verb. The outcome is a verb that you can conjugate just as you do other verbs. Many of these verbal compounds express the extent of the action or the aspect of the action. Therefore, some consider them to be auxiliary verbs that follow the stem form. (See Chapter 6 for auxiliary verbs that follow **te** forms.) The following table lists just a few of them:

Verbal Compound	Sentence Examples
. . . すぎる **sugiru** (*to overdo . . .*) すぎる **sugiru** may also follow an adjective in the stem form.	昨日は飲みすぎました。 **Kinō wa nomi-sugimashita.** *(I) drank too much yesterday.* この車は高すぎます。 **Kono kuruma wa taka-sugimasu.** *This car is too expensive.*
. . . はじめる **hajimeru** (*to start . . .*)	仕事を探しはじめました。 **Shigoto o sagashi-hajimemashita.** *(I) started to look for a job.*
. . . おわる **owaru** (*to finish . . .*)	この本は読みおわりました。 **Kono hon wa yomi-owarimashita.** *I finished reading this book.*
. . . つづける **tsuzukeru** (*to continue . . .*)	日本語を勉強しつづけます。 **Nihongo o benkyō-shi-tsuzukemasu.** *(I) will continue to study Japanese.*
. . . わすれる **wasureru** (*to forget to do . . .*)	ドアの鍵をかけわすれました。 **Doa no kagi o kake-wasuremashita.** *I forgot to lock the door.*
. . . そこねる **sokoneru** (*to miss . . .*)	すしを食べそこねました。 **Sushi o tabe-sokonemashita.** *I missed to eat the sushi.*
. . . かける **kakeru** (*to do . . . a little bit, to be about to do . . .*)	ワインを飲みかけました。 **Wain o nomi-kakemashita.** *I drank wine a bit.* or *I was about to drink wine.*

Translate each of the following sentences into English.

1. 面白い映画を見そこねました。

   Omoshiroi eiga o mi-sokonemashita.

   _____

2. お酒を飲みすぎたかもしれません。

   Osake o nomi-sugita kamoshiremasen.

   _____

3. 早く食べおわりなさい。

   Hayaku tabe-owarinasai.

   _____

4. 薬をのみわすれないでください。

   Kusuri o nomi-wasurenai de kudasai.

   _____

. . . やすい yasui / . . . にくい nikui (toughness)

にくい **nikui** and やすい **yasui** follow a verb in the stem form and show that the action is difficult to perform or easy to perform. For example:

すしは食べやすいですが、ロブスターは食べにくいです。
Sushi wa tabe-yasui desu ga, robusutā wa tabe-nikui desu.
Sushi is easy to eat, but lobsters are difficult to eat.

片仮名は書きやすいですが、平仮名はちょっと書きにくいです。
Katakana wa kaki-yasui desu ga, hiragana wa chotto kaki-nikui desu.
Katakana is easy to write, but hiragana is a bit difficult to write.

高橋さんは話しやすくて 親切です。
Takahashi-san wa hanashi-yasukute shinsetsu desu.
Ms. Takahashi is easy to talk to and kind.

着物は着にくくて 歩きにくいですが、大好きです。
Kimono wa ki-nikukute aruki-nikui desu ga, daisuki desu.
A kimono is difficult to put on and difficult to walk in, but I love it.

Complete the following sentences.

1. 大きい車は ＿＿＿＿＿＿＿＿＿ にくいです。

   Ōkii kuruma wa ＿＿＿＿＿＿＿＿＿ nikui desu.

   A big car is difficult to drive.

2. このバッグは軽くて ＿＿＿＿＿＿＿＿＿ やすいです。

   Kono baggu wa karukute ＿＿＿＿＿＿＿＿＿ yasui desu.

   This bag is light and easy to hold.

3. この辞書はとても ＿＿＿＿＿＿＿＿＿ やすいです。

   Kono jisho wa totemo ＿＿＿＿＿＿＿＿＿ yasui desu.

   This dictionary is very easy to use.

4. この漢字はとても ＿＿＿＿＿＿＿＿＿ にくいです。

   Kono kanji wa totemo ＿＿＿＿＿＿＿＿＿ nikui desu.

   This kanji is very difficult to write.

. . . たい tai (*to want to do . . .*)

You express the desire to obtain something by using the adjective ほしい **hoshii**, as in this example:

> 私は本がほしいです。
> **Watashi wa hon ga hoshii desu.**
> *I want a book.*

However, you must express the desire to do something by using the suffix たい **tai** but not ほしい **hoshii**. たい **tai** follows a verb in the stem form. For example:

> 私はうちで 寝たいです。
> **Watashi wa uchi de ne-tai desu.**
> *I want to sleep at home.*

> 祖母に会いたいです。
> **Sobo ni ai-tai desu.**
> *I want to see my grandmother.*

> 大学院に行きたいですか。
> **Daigakuin ni iki-tai desu ka.**
> *Do you want to go to graduate school?*

The direct object of a verb may be marked by が **ga** or を **o**, as in the following two sentences, which have slightly different nuances:

> 私はてんぷらを食べたいです。
> **Watashi wa tenpura o tabetai desu.**
> *I want to eat tempura. (What I want to do is eat tempura.)*

> 私はてんぷらが食べたいです。
> **Watashi wa tenpura ga tabetai desu.**
> *I want to eat tempura. (What I want to eat is tempura.)*

Note that you can use both たい **tai** and ほしい **hoshii** to express the desire of the first person or ask the desire of the second person, but not to express or ask the desire of the third person. (See the following section for がる **garu** in this chapter.)

EXERCISE
10·3

Translate the following sentences into Japanese.

1. *I want to go to Canada.*

_____

2. *I want a new car.*

_____

3. *Do you want to meet Mr. Tanaka?*

_____

4. *I want to see a Japanese movie.*

_____

...がる **garu** (*to show the signs of...*)

がる **garu** follows an adjective in the stem form and creates a verb that means *to show the signs of...*. It is used to describe a third person's certain kinds of psychological/physiological perception, such as 怖い **kowai** (*scared*), 暑い **atsui** (*hot*), and 嫌な **iya na** (*unpleasant*).

兄は犬を怖がります。
Ani wa inu o kowa-garimasu.
My big brother is scared of dogs.

子供が暑がっています。
Kodomo ga atsugatte imasu.
My child is feeling hot.

野菜は嫌がらないで食べなさい。
Yasai wa iyagaranai de tabenasai.
Don't hate vegetables. Eat them.

がる **garu** is also needed for describing the third person's desire. The direct object should be marked by the particle を **o** rather than the particle が **ga** because がる **garu** creates a verb. For example:

スティーブさんは車をほしがっています。
Sutību-san wa kuruma o hoshi-gatte imasu.
Steve wants a car.

スティーブさんは映画を見たがっています。
Sutību-san wa eiga o mi-ta-gatte imasu.
Steve wants to see a movie.

10·4

Translate the following into Japanese.

1. *Don't be scared of dogs.*

_____

2. *I want a new computer.*

_____

3. *My older brother wants a new car.*

_____

4. *I want to play the piano.*

_____

5. *My father wants to play golf.*

_____

Noun + らしい **rashii** (*typical*)

らしい **rashii** follows a noun and creates a complex i adjective that means *like the ideal model of* or *stereotypical . . . .* For example, 男らしい男の人 **otoko-rashii otoko no hito** means *a manly man.* らしい **rashii** does not create a simile, so do not use it for a noun that does not qualify a person. (To create a simile, use のような **no yō na** or みたいな **mitai na**, discussed later in this chapter.) For example:

> 私の彼氏は勇気があってとても男らしいんです。
> **Watashi no kareshi wa yūki ga atte totemo otoko-rashii n desu.**
> *My boyfriend is courageous and very manly.*

> あの人は日本人なのにぜんぜん日本人らしくありません。
> **Ano hito wa Nihonjin na noni zenzen Nihonjin rashiku arimasen.**
> *That person is Japanese but is not like a typical Japanese person at all.*

> もっと女らしくしなさい。
> **Motto onna-rashiku shinasai.**
> *Act more like a woman (because you are).*

> 日本人らしい日本人とはどんな人ですか。
> **Nihonjin-rashii Nihonjin to wa donna hito desu ka.**
> *What kind person is a typical Japanese person?*

> 陽子さんは今日静かですね。いつもの陽子さんらしくありません。
> **Yōko-san wa kyō shizuka desu ne. Itsumo no Yōko-san rashiku arimasen.**
> *Yoko is quiet today. She is not like herself.*

らしい **rashii** expresses conjecture if it follows a statement, as discussed in Chapter 9. For example:

> 日本の円は高くなったらしいです。
> **Nihon no en wa takaku natta rashii desu.**
> *It seems that the Japanese yen became expensive.*

In this case, the plain non-past affirmative copula だ **da** cannot be present. Accordingly, when らしい **rashii** follows a noun, it can either indicate conjecture or description. For example, the following sentence is ambiguous:

あの人は日本人らしいです。
Ano hito wa Nihonjin rashii desu.
That person seems to be Japanese. (conjecture)
That person is a typical ideal model of Japanese. (describing/typicality)

EXERCISE 10·5

Indicate the meaning of each of the following sentences. If a sentence is ambiguous, provide two meanings.

1. 私の兄はとても男らしいです。

   Watashi no ani wa totemo otoko-rashii desu.

   _____

2. 山口さんはカラオケが好きらしいです。

   Yamaguchi-san wa karaoke ga suki-rashii desu.

   _____

3. もう少し学生らしくしなさい。

   Mō sukoshi gakusei-rashiku shinasai.

   _____

4. 私の母は母親らしくありませんでした。

   Watashi no haha wa hahaoya rashiku arimasendeshita.

   _____

5. あの人は学生らしいです。

   Ano hito wa gakusei rashii desu.

   _____

Noun + のような **no yō na** (simile)

よう **yō** literally means *appearance*. When it occurs in the construction . . . のような **no yō na**, following a noun, it creates a complex **na** adjective that describes things and people in terms of similarities and resemblances. For example, 天使のような人 means *a person who is just like an angel*. Unlike らしい **rashii**, which expresses typicality (see the preceding section in this chapter), . . . のような **no yō na** cannot be used for something that is equal to what it is. So you cannot say 母は女のような人です **Haha wa onna no yō na hito desu** (*My mother is a person who is just* *like a woman*), but you can say 母は女らしい人です **Haha wa onna-rashii hito desu** (*My mother is a person who is a typical woman*). For example:

> 先生は神さまのような人です。
> **Sensei wa kami-sama no yō na hito desu.**
> *The teacher is a person who is like a god.*

> 先生は私の母のようです。
> **Sensei wa watashino haha no yō desu.**
> *My teacher acts as if she were my mother.* or *My teacher resembles my mother.*

> お好み焼きはパンケーキのようなものです。
> **Okonomiyaki wa pankēki no yō na mono desu.**
> *Okonomiyaki is something like a pancake.*

> 父は子供のようです。一人で何もできません。
> **Chichi wa kodomo no yō desu. Hitori de nani mo dekimasen.**
> *My father is just like a child. He cannot do anything by himself.*

ようです **yō desu** expresses a conjecture if it follows a statement, as discussed in Chapter 9. For example:

> 日本の円は高くなったようです。
> **Nihon no en wa takaku natta yō desu.**
> *It seems that the Japanese yen became expensive.*

In this case, the non-past affirmative copula だ **da** that follows a noun changes to の **no**. Accordingly, when のようです **no yō desu** follows a noun, it can indicate either conjecture or simile. The following sentence is ambiguous:

> あの人は日本人のようです。
> **Ano hito wa Nihonjin no yō desu.**
> *That person seems to be Japanese.* (conjecture)
> *That person is just like a Japanese person.* (describing/simile)

EXERCISE 10·6

Indicate the meaning of each of the following sentences. If a sentence is ambiguous, provide two meanings.

1. 私の兄はスーパーマンのようです。

   Watashi no ani wa sūpāman no yō desu.

   _____

2. 川口さんの奥さんはファッションモデルのようです。

   Kawaguchi-san no okusan wa fasshon moderu no yō desu.

   _____

3. 田中さんは私の父のような人です。

   Tanaka-san wa watashi no chichi no yō na hito desu.

   _____

4. イルカのように泳ぎたいです。

   Iruka no yō ni oyogi-tai desu. (イルカ **iruka**: *dolphin*)

Noun + みたいな **mitai na** (simile)

みたいな **mitai na** follows a noun and forms a complex **na** adjective that means *just like* . . . . みたいな **mitai na** expresses a simile, just like のような **no yō na** discussed in the preceding section, and they are often used interchangeably. However, みたいな **mitai na** is more colloquial than のような **no yō na**.

EXERCISE 10·7

For each of the following, choose the appropriate answer from the options in the parentheses. There can be more than one appropriate option in a sentence.

1. この犬は熊 (らしい, みたい, のよう) です。

   Kono inu wa kuma (rashii, mitai, no yō) desu. (熊 **kuma**: *bear*)

   This dog is like a bear.

2. 母は女 (らしい, みたいな, のような) 人です。

   Haha wa onna (rashii, mitai na, no yō na) hito desu.

   My mother is a typical woman.

3. 兄はスーパーマン (らしい, みたいな, のような) 人です。

   Ani wa sūpāman (rashii, mitai na, no yō na) hito desu.

   My older brother is like a superman.

4. この犬は人間 (らしい, みたい, のよう) です。

   Kono inu wa ningen (rashii, mitai, no yō) desu. (人間 **ningen**: *human*)

   This dog is like a human being.

5. 父は子供 (らしい, みたいな, のような) 人です。

   Chichi wa kodomo (rashii, mitai na, no yō na) hito desu.

   My father is like a child.

Stem form + そうな **sō na** (appearance)

そうな **sō na** follows an adjective or a verb in the stem form and creates a new na adjective. When it follows an adjective, it expresses the speaker's intuitive guess about the internal character of a person or thing, based on its appearance. For example:

あの人はまじめそうな人ですね。
Ano hito wa majime-sō na hito desu ne.
That person appears to be a serious person, doesn't he?

これは難しそうな問題ですね。
Kore wa muzukashi-sō na mondai desu ne.
This question appears difficult, doesn't it?

この映画はおもしろそうですね。
Kono eiga wa omoshiro-sō desu ne.
This movie appears interesting, doesn't it?

あの人はやさしそうです。
Ano hito wa yasashi-sō desu.
That person looks kind.

The adjective いい **ii** becomes よさそうな **yosasō na**, as in 頭がよさそうな人 **atama ga yosasō na hito** (*a person who looks smart*). You can create a negative version by replacing ない **nai** in the **nai** form with なさそうな **nasasō na**, as in まじめじゃなさそうな人 **majime ja nasasō na hito** (*a person who does not look serious*) and やさしくなさそうな人 **yasashikunasasō na hito** (*a person who does not look kind*). Since そうな **sō na** expresses the speaker's conjecture based on the appearance, it cannot be used for a visually evident physical property, such as color, size, or shape. So, you cannot say きれいそうな人 **kirei sō na hito** (*a person who looks pretty*) or 背がひくそうな人 **se ga hikusō na hito** (*a person who looks short*) when you are actually seeing the person.

When そうな **sō na** follows a verb, it expresses the speaker's intuitive conjecture about what will happen or what has happened. For example:

この車は壊れそうです。
Kono kuruma wa koware-sōdesu.
This car is about to break down.

この車は壊れていそうです。
Kono kuruma wa kowarete i-sō desu.
This car looks like broken.

ころびそうになりましたが、大丈夫でした。
Korobi-sō ni narimashita ga, daijōbu deshita.
I almost fell, but I was okay.

EXERCISE
10·8

Complete the following sentences.

1. この映画は _____ そうですね。見ましょう。

   Kono eiga wa _____ sō desu ne. Mimashō.

   This movie looks interesting. Let's watch it.

2. この映画は _____ そうですね。他のを見ましょう。

   Kono eiga wa _____ sō desu ne. Hoka no o mimashō.

   This movie does not look interesting. Let's watch another one.

3. あれ。くもが たくさん ありますよ。雨が _____ そうですね。

   Are. Kumo ga takusan arimasu yo. Ame ga _____ sō desu ne.

   Oh. There are a lot of clouds. It looks like it's going to rain.

4. あの人は _____ そうですよ。あの人に聞きましょう。

Ano hito wa _____ sō desu yo. Ano hito ni kikimashō.

That person looks kind. Let's ask that person.

5. _____ そうになりましたが、泣きませんでした。

_____ **sō ni narimashita ga, nakimasendeshita.**

I was about to cry, but I didn't.

Volitional form + と思う **to omou** (intention)

Verbs in the volitional form, such as 行こう **ikō** and 食べよう **tabeyō** (see Chapter 9), can be used with a verb that expresses thinking, such as 思う **omou** (*to think*) and 考える **kangaeru** (*to consider*), to express one's intention. Make sure you add the quotation particle と **to.** (See Chapter 11 for the quotation particle と **to.**) For example, 行こうと思います **ikō to omoimasu** means *I'm thinking of going.* The verb of thinking is often in the **te iru** form, and it must be in the **te iru** form if the thinker is a third person. The following are examples of this construction:

北京に留学しようと思っています。
Pekin ni ryūgaku shiyō to omotte imasu.
I'm thinking of studying abroad in Beijing.

今度スカイダイビングをしてみようと思います。
Kondo sukaidaibingu o shite miyō to omoimasu.
I'm thinking of trying skydiving next time.

前の試験は悪かったので、今度の試験は頑張ろうと考えています。
Mae no shiken wa warukatta node, kondo no shiken wa ganbarō to kangaete imasu.
The previous exam was bad, so I am thinking of trying my best for the next one.

弟はバイトをしようと思っています。
Otōto wa baito o shiyō to omotte imasu.
My younger brother is thinking of doing a part-time job.

If you use a dictionary form instead of a volitional form, you are merely expressing what you think will happen in the future. For example, compare the following two sentences:

私は今月でこの仕事を辞めようと思います。
Watashi wa kongetsu de kono shigoto o yameyō to omoimasu.
I'm thinking of quitting this job by the end of this month. (intention)

私はこの仕事をいつか辞めると思います。
Watashi wa kono shigoto o itsuka yameru to omoimasu.
I think I will quit this job someday. (future event)

Complete the following sentences appropriately.

1. カウンセラーと ＿＿＿＿＿＿＿＿ 思います。

   Kaunserā to ＿＿＿＿＿＿＿＿ omoimasu.

   I'm thinking of talking with a counselor.

2. 経済学を ＿＿＿＿＿＿＿＿ 思っています。

   Keizaigaku o ＿＿＿＿＿＿＿＿ omotte imasu.

   I'm thinking of studying economics.

3. 姉は田中さんと結婚 ＿＿＿＿＿＿＿＿。

   Ane wa Tanaka-san to kekkon ＿＿＿＿＿＿＿＿.

   My older sister is thinking of getting married to Mr. Tanaka.

4. ２年で卒業 ＿＿＿＿＿＿＿＿ 思います。

   Ni-nen de sotsugyō ＿＿＿＿＿＿＿＿ omoimasu.

   I think I can graduate in two years.

5. コンピューターゲームがいつか嫌いに ＿＿＿＿＿＿＿＿。

   Konpyūtāgēmu ga itsuka kirai ni ＿＿＿＿＿＿＿＿.

   I think I will start hating computer games someday.

Volitional form + とする **to suru** (attempt)

Verbs in the volitional form can be followed by the particle と **to** and the verb する **suru** to express a momentum act of attempting. You often use such a phrase when you could not achieve something after an attempt. Depending on the context, either the act of attempt or the time of the attempt is emphasized. For example:

> 納豆を食べようとしましたが、くさくて食べられませんでした。
> **Nattō o tabeyō to shimashita ga, kusakute taberaremasendeshita.**
> *I tried to eat fermented soybean, but it was smelly, and I couldn't eat (it).* (act of attempt)

> 晩ご飯を食べようとした時に電話が来ました。
> **Bangohan o tabeyō to shita toki ni denwa ga kimashita.**
> *When I tried to have dinner, the phone rang.* (time of attempt)

To express your intention rather than attempt, use the verb 思う **omou** instead of する **suru**. For example, 日本に行ったら、歌舞伎を見ようと思います **Nihon ni ittara kabuki o mi-yō to omoimasu** expresses intention and means *I am thinking of seeing a kabuki play when I go to Japan*. See the previous section in this chapter for this construction.

Translate each of the following sentences into English.

1. うそをつこうとしましたが、つけませんでした。

   Uso o tsukō to shimashita ga, tsukemasendeshita.

   _____

2. 夏はハワイに行こうと思います。

   Natsu wa Hawai ni ikō to omoimasu.

   _____

3. 出かけようとしたとき田中さんが来ました。

   Dekakeyō to shita toki Tanaka-san ga kimashita.

   _____

4. 泣きそうになりましたが、泣きませんでした。

   Nakisō ni narimashita ga, nakimasendeshita.

   _____

... ように + する /なる yō ni suru/naru (change)

ようにする **yō ni suru** follows a verb in the plain non-past form and means to make some kind of change. You can use it to express your willingness to make an effort to change your behavior. For example:

> 毎日運動をするようにしています。
> **Mainichi undō o suru yō ni shite imasu.**
> *I'm trying to do exercise every day.*

> あまり甘いものを食べないようにしています。
> **Amari amai mono o tabenai yō ni shite imasu.**
> *I'm trying not to eat sweet things so much.*

You can also use this construction to express an arrangement that you can make to change the state of something or someone. For example:

> 一つのテーブルに10人座れるようにしましょう。
> **Hitotsu no tēburu ni jū-nin suwareru yō ni shimashō.**
> *Let's make it so ten people can sit at one table.*

> この窓は開かないようにしました。
> **Kono mado wa akanai yōni shimashita.**
> *I made it so this window will not open.*

When the verb する **suru** in this construction is replaced with なる **naru**, as in ようになる **yō ni naru**, it expresses what change has taken place, without showing the person's conscious effort. Note the contrast between the two sentences that follow:

私は早く起きるようにしました。
Watashi wa hayaku okiru yō ni shimashita.
I tried to wake up early. (conscious effort)

私は早く起きるようになりました。
Watashi wa hayaku okiru yō ni narimashita.
I wake up early (now). (change)

ようになる **yō ni naru** is often used with a potential form to mean *to become able to do something.* (See Chapter 4 for potential forms.) For example:

私は早く起きられるようになりました。
Watashi wa hayaku okirareru yō ni narimashita.
I became able to wake up early.

ないようになる **nai yō ni naru** is often contracted to なくなる **naku naru**. For example, the following two sentences can be used interchangeably:

私の弟は最近マンガを読まないようになりました。
Watashi no otōto wa saikin manga o yomanai yō ni narimashita.

私の弟は最近マンガを読まなくなりました。
Watashi no otōto wa saikin manga o yomanaku narimashita.
My younger brother recently stopped reading comic books.

EXERCISE
10·11

For each of the following, choose the appropriate answer from the options in the parentheses. For a greater challenge, cover the English translations as you work on this exercise.

1. 頑張ってもっと早く起きるように（します, なります）。

   Ganbatte motto hayaku okiru yō ni (shimasu, narimasu).

   I'll try my best, and try to wake up much earlier.

2. 変ですね。マイクさんは最近あまり話さなく（しましたね, なりましたね）。

   Hen desu ne. Maiku-san wa saikin amari hanasanaku (shimashita ne, narimashita ne).

   It's weird. Mike recently stopped talking much.

3. たくさん勉強して漢字が（読める, 読む）ようになりました。

   Takusan benkyō shite kanji ga (yomeru, yomu) yō ni narimashita.

   I studied hard, and I became able to read kanji.

4. 健康のために毎日8時間は寝るように（なって, して）います。

   Kenkō no tame ni mainichi hachi-jikan wa neru yō ni (natte, shite) imasu.

   I'm trying to sleep eight hours a day for my health.

. . . ことに + する /なる **koto ni + suru/naru** (decision)

When a verb in the plain non-past form is followed by ことにする **koto ni suru** or ことになる **koto ni naru**, it expresses decision making. The difference between the two is that the former shows the decision maker's intention, whereas the latter does not. Note the difference between the two sentences that follow:

兄は日本に行くことにしました。
Ani wa Nihon ni iku koto ni shimashita.
My older brother has decided to go to Japan.

兄は日本に行くことになりました。
Ani wa Nihon ni iku koto ni narimashita.
It has been decided that my older brother will go to Japan.

**EXERCISE
10·12**

Translate the following sentences into English.

1. 私は試験を受けないことにしました。

   Watashi wa shiken o ukenai koto ni shimashita.

   _____

2. 私は試験を受けないことになりました。

   Watashi wa shiken o ukenai koto ni narimashita.

   _____

3. この美術館には学生は無料で入れることになりました。

   Kono bijutsukan ni wa gakusei wa muryō de haireru koto ni narimashita. (無料 **muryō**: *free of charge*)

   _____

4. この建物ではタバコがすえないことになりました。

   Kono tatemono de wa tabako ga suenai koto ni narimashita.

   _____

. . . ことができる **koto ga dekiru** (potential)

To express your potential or ability, you can use a verb in the potential form, as discussed in Chapter 4, and you can also do so by using the construction . . . ことができる **koto ga dekiru**. For example:

この漢字を読むことができますか。
Kono kanji o yomu koto ga dekimasu ka.
Can you read this kanji?

耳を動かすことができますか。
Mimi o ugokasu koto ga dekimasu ka?
Can you wiggle your ears?

あなたのためなら死ぬこともできます。
Anata no tame nara shinu koto mo dekimasu.
If it is for you, I can even die.

EXERCISE 10·13

Translate the following into Japanese using the construction . . . ことができる **koto ga dekiru.**

1. *Can you read katakana?*

   _____

2. *Can you eat with chopsticks?* (*chopsticks*: 箸 **hashi**)

   _____

3. *Can you greet in Japanese?* (*to greet*: 挨拶をする **aisatsu o suru**)

   _____

4. *Can you read a Japanese newspaper?* (*newspaper*: 新聞 **shinbun**)

   _____

EXERCISE 10·14

Answer the above questions in Japanese, based on your situation.

1. _____

2. _____

3. _____

4. _____

. . . ことがある **koto ga aru** (experience)

To tell someone what experience you have had, do not just use a simple past tense like うなぎを食べました **Unagi o tabemashita** (*I ate eel*). Instead, use the verb ある **aru** (*to exist, to have*) in the non-past tense. Then combine a verb in the **ta** form (plain past affirmative form; see Chapter 4), the abstract noun こと **koto**, the particle が **ga**, and ある **aru**, in this order. For example:

うなぎを食べたことがあります。
Unagi o tabeta koto ga arimasu.
I have eaten eel.

The simple past sentence うなぎを食べました **Unagi o tabemashita** (*I ate eel*) necessarily implies *at that time*, or at some specific time in the past. When discussing experiences, it does not matter whether one performed the action or not on a specific day at a specific time. What matters is whether you have an experience of doing it at any time during your lifetime. This is why you use . . . ことがある **koto ga aru** to express your experiences.

If you want to say that you have never done something, just negate the verb ある **aru**, as shown in this example:

私はうなぎを食べたことがありません。
Watashi wa unagi o tabeta koto ga arimasen.
I have never eaten eel (in my life).

EXERCISE
10·15

Translate the following into Japanese.

1. *Have you ever been to Iceland? (Iceland:* アイスランド **Aisurando**)

   _____

2. *Have you ever eaten fermented soybean? (fermented soybean:* 納豆 **nattō**)

   _____

3. *Have you ever seen Kurosawa's movies? (Kurosawa:* 黒澤 **Kurosawa** [the famous Japanese movie director Akira Kurosawa])

   _____

4. *Have you ever taken Shinkansen? (Shinkansen:* 新幹線 **Shinkansen** [bullet train])

   _____

EXERCISE
10·16

Answer the above questions in Japanese, based on your situation.

1. _____
2. _____
3. _____
4. _____

If a non-past verb is used in this construction, it means *to have occasions to do* . . . . For example:

香港に行くことがよくあります。
Honkon ni iku koto ga yoku arimasu.
I often have occasions to go to Hong Kong. or *I often go to Hong Kong.*

Clauses

A clause has a subject and a predicate along with tense specification, and it is part of a main sentence. A clause is used for modifying or completing a part of the main sentence. For example, a clause can serve as the direct object of a main verb (verb complement clause), an adverb of the main sentence (adverbial clause), or a modifier of a noun (noun modifier clause).

... と **to** and ... か **ka** (verb complement clause)

Verbs such as *to eat* and *to buy* take nouns as their direct objects (e.g., *eats sushi, bought a bag*). However, certain verbs take a clause as their direct object. For example, verbs such as *to think* require a statement clause, as in *He thinks that she will come*, and verbs such as *to ask* require a question clause, as in *He asked who will come*. In Japanese, statement clauses are marked by the particle と **to**, whereas question clauses are marked by the particle か **ka**, and the predicate in either type of clause must be in the plain form unless it is in a direct quotation. For example:

> ビルさんは日本語は簡単だと言いました。
> **Biru-san wa Nihongo wa kantan da to iimashita.**
> *Bill said that Japanese is easy.*

> マイクさんはだれが来るか知りません。
> **Maiku-san wa dare ga kuru ka shirimasen.**
> *Mike does not know who will come.*

> ビルさんは韓国語は難しいか聞きました。
> **Biru-san wa Kankokugo wa muzukashii ka kikimashita.**
> *Bill asked whether Korean is difficult.*

If the question clause expresses a yes/no question, the particle か **ka** may be followed by どうか **dō ka**. If it is a content question, it can't. In either case, remember that the non-past affirmative copula in the form of だ **da** is usually absent when followed by か **ka**, regardless of whether it is after a noun or a **na** adjective stem. For example:

> ビルさんは韓国語は簡単 (だ) か (どうか) 聞きました。
> **Biru-san wa Kankokugo wa kantan (da) ka (dō ka) kikimashita.**
> *Bill asked whether Korean is easy.*

In a direct quotation, you use a pair of quotation marks (「 and 」) and add the quotation particle と **to**. For example:

ビルさんは「日本語は難しいです。」と言いました。
Biru-san wa "Nihongo wa muzukashii desu." to ii mashita.
Bill said, "Japanese is difficult."

ビルさんは「韓国語は難しいですか。」と聞きました。
Biru-san wa "Kankokugo wa muzukashii desu ka." to kikimashita.
Bill asked, "Is Korean difficult?"

EXERCISE
11·1

Choose the correct answer or answers from the options in parentheses.

1. どのレストランがいい(か, かどうか, と)知っていますか。

   Dono resutoran ga ii (ka, ka dō ka, to) shitte imasu ka.

   Do you know which restaurant is good?

2. せまいアパートでもいい(か, かどうか, と)聞いてください。

   Semai apāto de mo ii (ka, ka dō ka, to) kiite kudasai.

   Please ask (him) whether small apartment is acceptable.

3. いつ来られる(か, かどうか, と)教えてください。

   Itsu korareru (ka, ka dō ka, to) oshiete kudasai.

   Please let me know when you can come.

4. このレストランが一番おいしい(か, かどうか, と)思います。

   Kono resutoran ga ichiban oishii (ka, ka dō ka, to) omoimasu.

   I think this restaurant is most delicious.

5. このレストランが一番おいしい(か, かどうか, と)思いますか。

   Kono resutoran ga ichiban oishii (ka, ka dō ka, to) omoimasu ka.

   Do you think this restaurant is most delicious?

6. このパソコンは便利(だと, と, ですと)思います。

   Kono pasokon wa benri (da to, to, desu to) omoimasu.

   I think this computer is convenient.

7. どのパソコンが便利(だと, か, ですか)聞いてみます。

   Dono pasokon ga benri (da to, ka, desu ka) kiite mimasu.

   I will try asking which computer is convenient.

. . . 前に **mae ni** (adverbial clause *before* . . .) and . . . 後に **ato ni** (adverbial clause *after* . . .)

To indicate *before*, use a verb in the plain non-past form followed by . . . 前に **mae ni** and place the entire sequence at the position where you usually place a time adverb such as 昨日 **kinō** (*yesterday*) or 7時に **shichi-ji ni** (*at 7 o'clock*) in a sentence. Remember that the verb before 前 **mae** must be in the non-past form, regardless of the actual time of the action, even if the action took place in the past. For example:

> 私はクラスが始まる前に携帯をサイレントモードにします。
> **Watashi wa kurasu ga hajimaru mae ni keitai o sairento-mōdo ni shimasu.**
> *I make my cell phone silent before classes start.*

> 私はクラスが始まる前に携帯をサイレントモードにしました。
> **Watashi wa kurasu ga hajimaru mae ni keitai o sairento-mōdo ni shimashita.**
> *I made my cell phone silent before the class started.*

By contrast, to indicate *after*, use a verb in the plain past form followed by . . . 後に **ato ni**. Remember that the verb before 後 **ato** must be in the past form, regardless of the actual time of the action, even if the action is taking place in the future. For example:

> 何でも母に相談した後に決めます。
> **Nan demo haha ni sōdan shita ato ni kimemasu.**
> *I always make my decision after consulting with my mother.*

> 大学の専攻は父に相談した後に決めました。
> **Daigaku no senkō wa chichi ni sōdan shita ato ni kimemashita.**
> *I decided on my major after having consulted with my father.*

EXERCISE
11·2

Choose the correct answer from the options in parentheses.

1. 映画を見る（前, 後）に本を読みます。

   Eiga o miru (mae, ato) ni hon o yomimasu.

   Before watching a movie, I read the book (about it).

2. 食べた（前, 後）に歯をみがきます。

   Tabeta (mae, ato) ni ha o migakimasu.

   I brush my teeth after eating.

3. （おきる, おきた）後にシャワーをあびます。

   (Okiru, Okita) ato ni shawā o abimasu.

   I take a shower after I wake up.

4. 日本に（行く, 行った）後に日本の地図を買うつもりです。

   Nihon ni (iku, itta) ato ni Nihon no chizu o kau tsumori desu.

   I plan to buy a Japanese map after I go to Japan.

. . . 間に **aida ni** (adverbial clause *during/while* . . .)

To indicate *during* or *while*, you can use 間に **aida ni**, which can follow a verb in the progressive form. For example:

> 昨日は母が寝ている間に朝ごはんを作りました。
> **Kino wa haha ga nete iru aida ni asa-gohan o tsukurimashita.**
> *I made breakfast while my mother was sleeping yesterday.*

> 先生が話している間にしゃべってはいけませんよ。
> **Sensei ga hanashite iru aida ni shabette wa ikemasen yo.**
> *It is not good to chat while the teacher is talking.*

If a verb expresses a state, you do not need to put it in the progressive form. For example:

> お金がある間に家のリフォームをします。
> **Okane ga aru aida ni ie no rifōmu o shimasu.**
> *I'll do home improvement while I have money.*

間に **aida ni** can also follow an adjective or a noun, but remember to use な **na** after a **na** adjective stem and の **no** after a noun. This is because 間 **aida** is a noun. For example:

> 勉強がきらいな間は何を言っても無駄です。
> **Benkyō ga kirai na aida wa nani o itte mo muda desu.**
> *No matter what you tell him, it is no use while he hates studying.*

> 学生の間は勉強だけしなさい。
> **Gakusei no aida wa benkyō dake shinasai.**
> *While you are a student, just study.*

> 利息が高い間は銀行からお金を借りません。
> **Risoku ga takai aida wa ginkō kara o-kane o karimasen.**
> *While the interest rate is high, I won't borrow money from a bank.*

. . . うちに **uchi ni** (adverbial clause *during/while/ before* . . .)

うちに **uchi ni** is very similar to 間に **aida ni** in that it follows the same form of verbs and adjectives and refers to a certain period of time. For example:

> その話を聞いている間／うちに気持ちが悪くなりました。
> **Sono hanashi o kiite iru aida/uchi ni kimochi ga waruku narimashita.**
> *I became nauseated while listening to that story.*

However, when the main verb expresses some controllable action, うちに **uchi ni** additionally implies that there is a special benefit in doing the action during the specified time and that failing to do so will result in a negative consequence. For example:

> お金があるうちに家のリフォームをします。
> **Okane ga aru uch ni ie no rifōmu o shimasu.**
> *I'll do home improvement while I have money.*

> TA がいるうちに宿題をおわります。
> **TA ga iru uchi ni shukudai o owarimasu.**
> *I'll finish my homework while my TA is here.*

> ピザが熱いうちに食べましょう。
> **Piza ga atsui uchi ni tabemashō.**
> *Let's eat pizza while it's hot.*

若くて元気なうちにしっかり働きなさい。
Wakakute genki na uchi ni shikkari hataraki-nasai.
Work hard while you are young and healthy.

うちに **uchi ni** often follows a verb in the **nai** form (plain negative non-past) to provide the meaning *before . . . .* For example:

手遅れにならないうちに手術をした方がいいですよ。
Teokure ni naranai uchi ni shujutsu o shita hō ga ii desu yo.
It's better to have surgery before it is too late.

EXERCISE
11·3

Complete the following sentences creatively.

1. 夏休みの間に _____○

   Natsu-yasumi no aida ni _____.

2. 朝、涼しいうちに _____○

   Asa, suzushii uchi ni _____.

3. 道が混まないうちに _____○

   Michi ga komanai uchi ni _____.

4. 忘れないうちに _____○

   Wasurenai uchi ni _____.

5. 赤ちゃんが寝ている間に _____○

   Akachan ga nete iru aida ni _____.

. . . ときに **toki ni** (adverbial clause *at the time when . . .*)

To express *at the time when . . .* , use a verb in the plain form and ときに **toki ni**. Depending on the tense and the aspect of the verb, such a phrase means *right before . . .* , *right after . . .* , or *at the time of doing . . . .* For example:

日本に着いたときに電話しますね。
Nihon ni tsuita toki ni denwa shimasu ne.
I'll call you when (right after) I arrive in Japan.

新幹線に乗るときにホームで駅弁を買います。
Shinkansen ni noru toki ni hōmu de ekiben o kaimasu.
When (right before) I get on Shinkansen [a bullet train in Japan], I'll buy a train station boxed lunch on the platform.

勉強しているときには音楽はききません。
Benkyō shite iru toki ni wa ongaku wa kikimasen.
I don't listen to music when studying.

口の中に食べ物があるときにしゃべってはいけません。
Kuchi no naka ni tabemono ga aru toki ni shabette wa ikemasen.
You should not talk while you have food in your mouth.

Remember that the non-past affirmative copula in the form of だ **da** is replaced by the particle の **no** or な **na** when followed by とき **toki**: の **no** after a noun, or な **na** after a **na** adjective stem. This is because 時 **toki** is a noun. For example:

これは必要なときに使ってください。
Kore wa hitsuyō na toki ni tsukatte kudasai.
Please use this when you need it.

津波のときにはすぐに高いところに行ってください。
Tsunami no toki ni wa sugu ni takai tokoro ni itte kudasai.
Please go to a higher location during a tsunami (warning).

暑いときはエアコンをつけます。
Atsui toki wa eakon o tsukemasu.
I turn on the air conditioning when it is hot.

EXERCISE
11·4

Complete the following sentences appropriately.

1. _____ ときに遊びに来てください。

   _____ **toki ni asobi ni kite kudasai.**

   Please come to visit me when you are free.

2. _____ ときに電話をください。

   _____ **toki ni denwa o kudasai.**

   Please give me a phone call when you are coming to Tokyo.

3. _____ ときにピアノを習いました。

   _____ **toki ni piano o naraimashita.**

   I took piano lessons when I was a high school student.

4. _____ ときに本を読みます。

   _____ **toki ni hon o yomimasu.**

   I read a book when my child is quiet.

5. _____ ときにラジオをききます。

   _____ **toki ni rajio o kikimasu.**

   I listen to a radio when I'm driving.

...ながら nagara (adverbial clause *simultaneously*)

ながら **nagara** can follow a verb in the stem form and shows the action that takes place simultaneously with the action expressed by the main verb. For example:

いつも音楽をききながら勉強します。
Itsumo ongaku o kiki-nagara benkyō shimasu.
I always study while listening to music.

運転しながら朝ごはんを食べます。
Unten shi-nagara asa-gohan o tabemasu.
I eat breakfast while driving.

EXERCISE
11·5

Complete the sentence creatively, based on your own situation.

私はよく ＿＿＿＿＿＿＿＿＿ ながら ＿＿＿＿＿＿＿＿＿ ます。

Watashi wa yoku ＿＿＿＿＿＿＿ nagara ＿＿＿＿＿＿＿ masu.

ながら **nagara** can also express some contrasting state or facts. In this case, it can follow not only verbs but also adjectives. For example:

口ではいいことを言いながら、ずるいことばかりしている。
Kuchi de wa ii koto o ii nagara, zurui koto bakari shite iru.
While saying fair things, he does only sneaky things.

この機械は小さいながら性能がいい。
Kono kikai wa chīsai nagara seinō ga ii.
This machine performs very well despite its small size.

EXERCISE
11·6

Choose the correct answer from the options in parentheses.

1. 大学生（だ, の, な）間に旅行をたくさんするつもりです。

   Daigakusei (da, no, na) aida ni ryokō o takusan suru tsumori desu.

   I plan to make a lot of trips while I'm a college student.

2. 元気（だ, の, な）うちに働きなさい。

   Genki (da, no, na) uchi ni hataraki-nasai.

   Work while you are healthy.

3. いつも（食べ, 食べる, 食べている）ながら話します。

   Itsumo (tabe, taberu, tabete iru) nagara hanashimasu.

   I always talk while eating.

4. いつも（食べ, 食べて, 食べている）ときに話します。

Itsumo (tabe, tabete, tabete iru) toki ni hanashimasu.

I always talk when I'm eating.

5. いつも（食べ, 食べる, 食べている）間に話します。

Itsumo (tabe, taberu, tabete iru) aida ni hanashimasu.

I always talk during the time I'm eating.

...から **kara** and ... ので **node** (adverbial clause *because*...)

You use both から **kara** and ので **node** to create an adverbial clause that shows the reason or cause for the facts expressed by the main sentence. However, the usage of から **kara** is broader than that of ので **node**. The reasoning expressed by ので **node** needs to be objective, while から **kara** can accommodate a vague subjective reasoning. With から **kara**, you need to be sure to use the same form for the predicate in the **kara** clause and the predicate in the main clause: both plain forms or both polite forms. If the **kara** clause is in the plain form while the main predicate is in the polite form, the entire sentence gives the impression that the speaker's reasoning is insistent or emotional. For example, the following sentences both mean *As I will not tell anyone, please tell me about it*, but the first one sounds insistent, and the second one does not:

だれにも言わないから話してください。
Dare nimo iwanai kara hanashite kudasai.

だれにも言いませんから話してください。
Dare nimo iimasen kara hanashite kudasai.

ので **node** usually follows a predicate in the plain form, but remember that the plain affirmative non-past copula だ **da** must be changed to な **na** when it occurs before ので **node**. For example:

明日はテストなので今日は勉強します。
Ashita wa tesuto na node kyō wa benkyō shimasu.
Because we have a test tomorrow, I'll study today.

図書館は静かなので勉強しやすい。
Toshokan wa shizuka na node benkyō shi-yasui.
Because the library is quiet, it is easy to study.

このバイトは時給が安いので辞めました。
Kono baito wa jikyū ga yasui node yamemashita.
I quit this part-time job because the hourly pay is so low.

兄が辞めたので私も辞めました。
Ani ga yameta node watashi mo yamemashita.
Because my older brother quit, I also quit.

In a very polite context, ので **node** often follows a polite form. For example:

ちょっと今日は時間がございませんので、明日にいたします。
Chotto kyō wa jikan ga gozaimasen node, asu ni itashimasu.
Because we don't have enough time today, we'll do it tomorrow.

*Recast the following sentences using ので **node**. Use a predicate in the plain form before* ので **node**.

1. あしたは車がありますから心配しないでください。

   Ashita wa kuruma ga arimasu kara shinpai shinai de kudasai.

   We'll have a car tomorrow, so please don't worry about it.

   _____

2. まだ子供ですから分からないと思います。

   Mada kodomo desu kara wakaranai to omoimasu.

   Because he is still a child, I think he won't understand it.

   _____

3. あしたはテストがありませんから今日は勉強しません。

   Ashita wa tesuto ga arimasen kara kyō wa benkyō shimasen.

   We don't have a test tomorrow, so I will not study today.

   _____

4. 弟はまじめですから宿題は忘れないと思います。

   Otōto wa majime desu kara shukudai wa wasurenai to omoimasu.

   My younger brother is serious, so I don't think he'll forget his homework.

   _____

. . . が ga and . . . のに noni (adverbial clause although . . .)

が **ga** and のに **noni** both follow a clause, creating an adverbial clause that shows a conflict or contradiction. For example, the following sentences both express the conflict *My brother is going to a party even though he has a test tomorrow*:

> 兄はあした試験がありますが、今晩はパーティーにいきます。
> **Ani wa ashita shiken ga arimasu ga, konban wa pātī ni ikimasu.**

> 兄はあした試験があるのに、今晩はパーティーにいきます。
> **Ani wa ashita shiken ga aru noni, konban wa pātī ni ikimasu.**

However, the usage of が **ga** is much broader than the usage of のに **noni**. First, のに **noni** cannot be used when the main sentence expresses the speaker's controllable act, intention, suggestion, or request, but が **ga** can. So, the following sentences both mean *I will go to the party tonight although I have a test tomorrow*, but only the sentence with が **ga** is appropriate:

私はあした試験がありますが、今晩はパーティーに行きます。 (appropriate)
Watashi wa ashita shiken ga arimasu ga, konban wa pātī ni ikimasu.

私はあした試験があるのに、今晩はパーティーに行きます。 (not appropriate)
Watashi wa ashita shiken ga aru noni, konban wa pātī ni ikimasu.

Second, が **ga** can be used not only for conflict or contradiction but also for simple contrast, which does not necessarily involve surprise. However, のに **noni** cannot be used if there is no strong unexpectedness, surprise, or contradiction associated with the contrast. So the following two sentences both mean *My sister eats meat but does not eat vegetables*, but only the sentence with が **ga** is appropriate:

姉は肉は食べますが、野菜は食べません。(appropriate)
Ane wa niku wa tabemasu ga, yasai wa tabemasen.

姉は肉は食べるのに、野菜は食べません。(not appropriate)
Ane wa niku wa taberu noni, yasai wa tabemasen.

Third, が **ga** can be used even when there is no contrast or conflict. It can simply connect two sentences when there is a temporal or logical transition. For example, the following sentences are all natural and appropriate, but のに **noni** cannot be used instead of が **ga** in these sentences:

佐藤と申しますが、社長にお会いできますか。
Satō to mōshimasu ga, shachō ni o-ai dekimasu ka.
My name is Sato. Could I see the president of your company?

これは日本で買ったんですが、とても便利ですよ。
Kore wa Nihon de katta n desu ga, totemo benri desu yo.
I bought this one in Japan, and it is very convenient!

これは終わりましたが、次は何をしましょうか。
Kore wa owarimashita ga, tsugi wa nani o shimashō ka.
I finished this one. What shall I do next?

When you use が **ga**, make sure to use the same form for the predicate in the **ga** clause and the predicate in the main clause: both plain forms or both polite forms. By contrast, のに **noni** usually follows a plain form, but remember that the plain affirmative non-past copula だ **da** must be changed to な **na**, as is the case with ので **node**. For example:

便利なのにだれも使いません。
Benri na noni dare mo tsukaimasen.
Although it is convenient, no one uses it.

日本人なのに日本語がうまく話せません。
Nihonjin na noni Nihongo ga umaku hanasemasen.
Although he is Japanese, he cannot speak Japanese well.

Choose the appropriate answer or answers from the options in parentheses.

1. あまりおいしくありません（が, のに）食べてください。

   Amari oishiku arimasen (ga, noni) tabete kudasai.

   It's not very delicious, but please eat it.

2. もしもし。山田と申します（が, のに）陽子さんはいらっしゃいますか。

   Moshimoshi. Yamada to mōshimasu (ga, noni) Yoko-san wa irasshaimasu ka.

   Hello. This is Mr. Yamada. Is Yoko in?

3. 勉強した（が, のに）テストはできなかった。

   Benkyō shita (ga, noni) tesuto wa dekinakatta.

   I studied, but I couldn't do well on the test.

4. 勉強した（が, のに）テストはできませんでした。

   Benkyō shita (ga, noni) tesuto wa dekimasendeshita.

   I studied, but I couldn't do well on the test.

5. これはとても安いです（が, のに）とてもいいですよ。

   Kore wa totemo yasui desu (ga, noni) totemo ii desu yo.

   It is very cheap, but very good.

Complete each of the following sentences with から **kara**, ので **node**, が **ga**, *or* のに **noni**.

1. 来年日本に行く＿＿＿＿＿ 今日本語を勉強しています。

   Rainen Nihon ni iku ＿＿＿＿＿ ima Nihongo o benkyō shite imasu.

   Because I'm going to Japan next year, I'm studying Japanese now.

2. 今日は雨がふる ＿＿＿＿＿ 兄は傘を持っていきませんでした。

   Kyō wa ame ga furu ＿＿＿＿＿ ani wa kasa o motte ikimasendeshita.

   Although it will rain today, my brother didn't bring an umbrella (with him).

3. これはちょっと高すぎます ＿＿＿＿＿ 買えません。

   Kore wa chotto taka-sugimasu ＿＿＿＿＿ kaemasen.

   This one is a bit too expensive, so I cannot buy it.

4. ここは静かな ＿＿＿＿＿ 勉強しやすいです。

   Koko wa shizuka na ＿＿＿＿＿ benkyō shiyasui desu.

   It is quiet here, so it's easy to study (here).

Noun modifier clauses (*which/that . . .*)

A clause can modify a noun. In English, you place a noun modifier clause after the noun it modifies, and such a clause is introduced with a word like *which* or *that*. For example, each of the following sentences has a noun modifier clause, marked by a pair of brackets, right after the underlined noun:

> *The movie [that I saw <gap> with Mary yesterday] was scary.*
>
> *Tom did not see the notice [that students are not allowed to use the bathroom on the second floor].*

The noun modifier clause in the first sentence has a gap, which is indicated by <gap>: there should be a noun after the verb *saw*, but it is missing, and the gap in fact corresponds to the noun being modified (*the movie*). Such a noun modifier clause with a gap is called a *relative clause*. The function of a relative clause is to qualify a noun.

In contrast, such a gap does not exist in the noun modifier clause in the second sentence above, but the information expressed in that noun modifier clause is absolutely needed to complete the meaning of the noun (*the notice*). Such gapless clauses are called *noun complement clauses*.

In Japanese, both kinds of noun modifier clauses are placed before a noun. Relative clauses do not need to include a word like *which* or *that*. Noun complement clauses may include という **to iu**, which is a combination of the quotation particle と **to** and the verb 言う **iu** (*to say*). Now consider the Japanese counterparts of the earlier sentences:

> [昨日私がメアリーと<gap>見た]映画は怖かった。
> **[Kinō watashi ga Mearī to <gap> mita] eiga wa kowakatta.**
> *The movie [that I saw <gap> with Mary yesterday] was scary.*
>
> トムは[学生は2階のトイレを使ってはいけない]という知らせを見なかった。
> **Tomu wa [gakusei wa 2-kai no toire o tsukatte wa ikenai] to iu shirase o minakatta.**
> *Tom did not see the notice [that students are not allowed to use the bathroom on the second floor].*

It is possible to use an abstract noun こと **koto** or の **no** as the modified noun. They do not have a concrete meaning, but their meaning is close to *fact*, *matter*, or *occasion*. For example:

> [僕がレストランで働いている](という) ことは誰にも言わないでください。
> **[Boku ga resutoran de hataraite iru] (to iu) koto wa dare ni mo iwanai de kudasai.**
> *Please do not tell anyone (the fact) that I'm working at a restaurant.*
>
> [だれとでも話せる]というのはいいことです。
> **[Dare to demo hanaseru] (to iu) no wa ii koto desu.**
> *Being able to talk with anyone is a good thing.*

EXERCISE
11·10

Translate the following sentences into English.

1. あの人は昨日田中さんと歩いていた人です。

   Ano hito wa kinō Tanaka-san to aruite ita hito desu.

2. あの建物にはだれも住んだことがなかった（という）可能性があります。

   Ano tatemono ni wa dare mo sunda koto ga nakatta (to iu) kanōsei ga arimasu.

   _____

3. 武さんがお父さんに手紙を書いているということはお金がないということです。

   Takeshi-san ga otōsan ni tegami o kaite iru to iu koto wa o-kane ga nai to iu koto desu.

   _____

4. 私がはじめてふぐを食べたレストランはあれです。

   Watashi ga hajimete fugu o tabeta resutoran wa are desu.

   _____

5. 私の趣味はインターネットで買い物をすることです。

   Watashi no shumi wa intānetto de kaimono o suru koto desu.

   _____

という **to iu** is a convenient phrase to use for introducing a specific item that the listener may have never heard of. You combine its proper name and common name by using という **to iu**, as in the following examples:

> 筑波という所で研究をしました。
> **Tsukuba to iu tokoro de kenkyū o shimashita.**
> _I conducted research in a place called Tsukuba._

> ふぐいちというレストランに行きました。
> **Fuguichi to iu resutoran ni ikimashita.**
> _I went to a restaurant called Fuguichi._

> 尾崎聡さんという方をご存知ですか。
> **Ozaki Satoshi-san to iu kata o go-zonji desu ka?**
> _Do you know the person called Satoshi Ozaki?_

EXERCISE
11·11

Translate the following sentences into Japanese.

1. _Do you know a Japanese singer called Utada?_ (singer: 歌手 **kashu**)

   _____

2. _I went to a place called Yokkaichi._

   _____

3. _Do you know the Japanese test called JLPT?_

   _____

Conjunctions

In this chapter, you will learn how to list nouns, verbs, and adjectives in a sentence. In addition, you will learn a variety of conjunctions that show relationships between sentences.

Listing nouns with と to (exhaustive), や ya (partial), か ka (disjunctive), and も mo (addition)

Use the particle と to for listing two or more items exhaustively, as in *A, B, and C*. Place the particle after each noun you want to list, except the very last one. For example:

> メアリーさんとエミリーさんが来ました。
> **Mearī-san to Emirī-san ga kimashita.**
> *Mary and Emily came.*

> テレビとパソコンとカメラを買いました。
> **Terebi to, pasokon to, kamera o kaimashita.**
> *I bought a TV, a PC, and a camera.*

Use the particle や ya for listing two or more items just as examples, as in *A, B, C, and so on*. With や ya, you can imply that there are more items in addition to the listed items. For example:

> 私はビールやワインを 飲みました。
> **Watashi wa bīru ya wain o nomimashita.**
> *I drank beer, wine, etc.*

> 中国や韓国やシンガポールに行きました。
> **Chūgoku ya Kankoku ya Singapōru ni ikimashita.**
> *(I) went to China, Korea, Singapore, etc.*

Use the particle か ka for listing two or more nouns disjunctively, as in *A, B, or C*. For example:

> このネクタイは父か兄か叔父にあげます。
> **Kono nekutai wa chichi ka ani ka oji ni agemasu.**
> *I will give this tie to my father, my older brother, or my uncle.*

> あの人は中国人か日本人です。
> **Ano hito wa Chūgokujin ka Nihonjin desu.**
> *That person is Chinese or Japanese.*

165

For listing items as additions, as in *A, B, and C, too,* use も **mo.** (See Chapter 7 for more about も **mo.**) In this case, the particles が **ga** and を **o** are completely dropped, and other particles such as に **ni** and で **de** are repeated after each noun. For example:

兄は東京にも大阪にも住んだことがあります。
Ani wa Tōkyō ni mo Ōsaka ni mo sunda koto ga arimasu.
My older brother has lived in Tokyo and Osaka, too.

僕はチョコレートもクッキーもケーキも好きです。
Boku wa chokorēto mo kukkī mo kēki mo suki desu.
I like chocolate, cookies, and cakes, too.

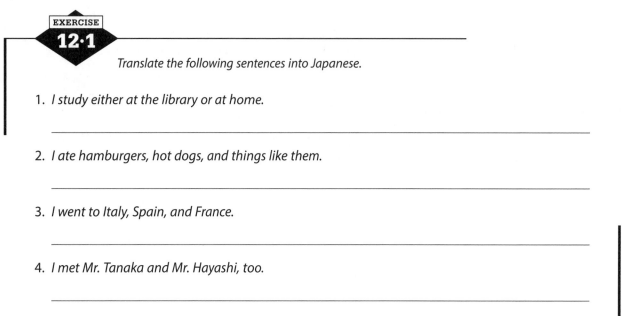

EXERCISE
12·1

Translate the following sentences into Japanese.

1. *I study either at the library or at home.*

   _____

2. *I ate hamburgers, hot dogs, and things like them.*

   _____

3. *I went to Italy, Spain, and France.*

   _____

4. *I met Mr. Tanaka and Mr. Hayashi, too.*

   _____

Listing verbs with **te** forms

In order to list two or more verbs in the same sentence, you need to convert them to **te** forms, except the last verb in the sentence. (Remember that the particle と **to** can list only nouns; it cannot list verbs.) How to make the **te** form of a verb is discussed in Chapter 4.

Depending on the context, a list of two or more verbs in the same sentence may be random, temporally ordered, or in a cause-and-effect relationship. For example:

週末は買い物をして料理をして洗濯をします。
Shūmatsu wa kaimono o shite ryōri o shite sentaku o shimasu.
I go shopping, cook, and do laundry on weekends.

昨日はテレビを見て宿題をして寝ました。
Kinō wa terebi o mite shukudai o shite nemashita.
(I) watched TV, did (my) homework, and slept yesterday.

宿題をして疲れました。
Shukudai o shite tsukaremashita.
(I) did my homework and got tired.

*Translate the following sentences into Japanese, using **te** forms.*

1. *I brush my teeth, wash my face, and have breakfast every day.*

   _____

2. *I practice kanji, listen to a CD, and study grammar. (grammar: 文法 **bunpō**)*

   _____

3. *My mother makes breakfast, cleans, and watches TV.*

   _____

4. *My father drove for five hours and got very tired yesterday.*

   _____

There are two kinds of negative **te** forms for verbs: One kind ends in なくて **nakute**, and the other ends in ないで **nai de** (see Chapter 4). The former is used to express a cause-and-effect relationship, as in *not do . . . and so . . . .* The latter is used to mean *not do . . . and then . . .* (*without doing . . .*) or *not do . . . but do . . .* (*instead of doing . . .*). For example:

子供がご飯を食べなくて困っています。
Kodomo ga gohan o tabenakute komatte imasu.
I'm in trouble because my child does not eat.

朝ご飯を食べないで仕事に行きました。
Asa-gohan o tabenai de shigoto ni ikimashita.
I did not have breakfast, and then went to work. or *I went to work without having had breakfast.*

ご飯を食べないでパンを食べました。
Gohan o tabenai de pan o tabemashita.
I did not eat rice, but ate bread. or *I ate bread instead of eating rice.*

EXERCISE
12·3

*Translate the following sentences into Japanese, using **te** forms.*

1. *I took a test without studying.*

   _____

2. *I ate without washing my hands.*

   _____

3. *I walked without wearing shoes.*

   _____

4. *I had a problem last month because my cold didn't get better. (a cold does not get better:* 風邪が治らない **kaze ga naoranai**)

_____

5. *I watched a movie instead of reading a book.*

_____

Although it is not common in conversation, it is also possible to list verbs by using stem forms. For example:

だれもが生まれ育ち死ぬのです。
Dare mo ga umare sodachi shinu no desu.
Everyone is born, grows up, and dies.

Listing adjectives with **te** forms

For listing two or more adjectives in the same sentence, you can use their **te** forms. (For forming the **te** forms of adjectives, both affirmative and negative, see Chapter 8.) The following examples show multiple-adjective sentences:

このラーメンは安くておいしいです。
Kono rāmen wa yasukute oishii desu.
This ramen noodle is cheap and delicious.

このラーメンはあまり高くなくておいしいです。
Kono rāmen wa amari takaku nakute oishii desu.
This ramen noodle is not very expensive and delicious.

田中さんのお姉さんはきれいで優しいです。
Tanaka-san no onēsan wa kirei de yasashii desu.
Mr. Tanaka's older sister is pretty and kind.

EXERCISE
12·4

*Translate the following into Japanese using **te** forms.*

1. *This course is easy, has little homework, and is fun.*

_____

2. *This restaurant's food is expensive and not delicious.*

_____

3. *Tom is smart, good-looking, and a nice person.*

_____

See Chapter 8 for more usage examples of the **te** form of adjectives.

Listing verbs and adjectives as examples using the tari form

To list actions and states randomly in a sentence, as examples, use the **tari** forms for all the verbs and adjectives in the sentence and add the verb する **suru** in the proper tense. You make the **tari** form by just adding り **ri** at the end of the **ta** form (plain past affirmative). (See Chapter 4 for the **ta** form of verbs and Chapter 8 for the **ta** form of adjectives.) For example:

昨日はコンピューターゲームをしたり漫画を読んだりテレビを見たりしました。
Kinō wa konpyūtā gēmu o shitari manga o yondari terebi o mitari shimashita.
I played computer games, read comic books, watched TV, and so on yesterday.

あしたは勉強したり仕事をしたりします。
Ashita wa benkyō shitari shigoto o shitari shimasu.
I will study, work, and so on tomorrow.

このクラスは宿題が多かったり試験が難しかったりします。
Kono kurasu wa shukudai ga ōkattari shiken ga muzukashikattari shimasu.
This course sometimes has a lot of homework, and its exams are sometimes difficult.

この犬は静かだったりうるさかったりします。
Kono inu wa shizuka dattari urusakattari shimasu.
This dog is sometimes quiet and sometimes noisy.

EXERCISE
12·5

*Convert each of the following verbs into the **tari** form.*

1. 買う **kau** (*buy*) _____

2. 食べる **taberu** (*eat*) _____

3. 飲む **nomu** (*drink*) _____

4. 寝る **neru** (*sleep*) _____

5. する **suru** (*do*) _____

6. 作る **tsukuru** (*make*) _____

7. 書く **kaku** (*write*) _____

8. 行く **iku** (*go*) _____

EXERCISE
12·6

*Convert each of the following adjectives into the **tari** form.*

1. 古い **furui** (*old*) _____

2. 便利な **benri na** (*convenient*) _____

3. 楽しい **tanoshii** (*fun*) _____

4. ひどい **hidoi** (*terrible*) _____

5. 楽な **raku na** (*easy*) _____

6. 優しい **yasashii** (*kind*) _____

7. 厳しい **kibishii** (*strict*) _____

8. いい **ii** (*good*) _____

*Translate the following sentences into Japanese, using the **tari** form.*

1. *I did things like check email and watch movies yesterday.* (*to check email:* メールをチェックする **mēru o chekku suru**)

   _____

2. *I will clean the room and things like that tomorrow.*

   _____

3. *My younger brother is doing things like watch anime and read comic books every day.*

   _____

4. *My teacher is sometimes kind and sometimes strict.*

   _____

5. *Email is sometimes convenient and sometimes inconvenient.*

   _____

Listing verbs and adjectives emphatically using し shi

For listing actions and states emphatically, use verbs and adjectives in the plain form and add し **shi** after each of them. For example:

> 宿題はしたし、あしたのテストの準備もしたし、もうねてもいいですね。
> **Shukudai wa shita shi, ashita no tesuto no junbi mo shita shi, mō nete mo ii desu ne.**
> *Not only did I do my homework, but I also prepared for tomorrow's test, so I can go to bed, right?*

> 山田さんはきれいだし、頭もいい。
> **Yamada-san wa kirei da shi, atama mo ii.**
> *Ms. Yamada is pretty, and she is also smart.*

It is very common to end a sentence with し **shi**. For example:

> 宿題はしたし、あしたのテストの準備もしたし。
> **Shukudai wa shita shi, ashita no tesuto no junbi mo shita shi.**
> *Not only did I do my homework, but I also prepared for tomorrow's test.*

> 山田さんはきれいだし、頭もいいし。
> **Yamada-san wa kirei da shi, atama mo ii shi.**
> *Ms. Yamada is pretty, and she is smart.*

EXERCISE
12·8

Connect the following sentences using し *shi.*

1. 武さんは意地悪です。かっこよくありません。

   Takeshi-san wa ijiwaru desu. Kakkoyoku arimasen.

   Takeshi is mean. (He) is not good looking.

   _____

2. 掃除をしました。買い物もしました。洗濯もしました。

   Sōji o shimashita. Kaimono mo shimashita. Sentaku mo shimashita.

   I cleaned (the rooms). I also went to shopping. I also did laundry.

   _____

3. 真さんは勇気があります。男らしいです。親切です。

   Makoto-san wa yūki ga arimasu. Otoko rashii desu. Shinsetsu desu.

   Makoto has courage. (He) is manly. (He) is kind.

   _____

EXERCISE
12·9

Who do you admire the most? Describe him/her in Japanese using し *shi to make it clear why you admire that person.*

_____

_____

Sentence conjunctions

Many words are used to begin a sentence and show the relationship between the sentence and the preceding sentence or the existing context.

それから **sorekara,** それに **soreni,** and そして **soshite** (*and*)

それから **sorekara** connects sentences that express temporally ordered events or randomly listed events or states. For example:

今日はまずテニスをします。それから、友達に手紙を書きます。
Kyō wa mazu tenisu o shimasu. Sorekara, tomodachi ni tegami o kakimasu.
Today, I will play tennis first. And then I will write a letter to my friends.

週末はよくテニスをします。それから、友達に手紙を 書きます。
Shūmatsu wa yoku tenisu o shimasu. Sorekara, tomodachi ni tegami o kakimasu.
On weekends, (I) often play tennis. In addition, I write letters to my friends.

村上さんはきれいです。それから、センスがいいです。
Murakami-san wa kirei desu. Sorekara, sensu ga ii desu.
Ms. Murakami is pretty. In addition, she has a good taste.

それに **soreni** shows that a sentence expresses information that is additional to the information expressed by the preceding sentence. Two sentences connected by それに **soreni** must make the same point in the context. For example:

この部屋は明るいです。それに、きれいです。
Kono heya wa akarui desu. Soreni, kirei desu.
This room is bright. In addition, it is clean/pretty. (all favorable properties)

この部屋は暗いです。それに、きたないです。
Kono heya wa kurai desu. Soreni, kitanai desu.
This room is dark. In addition, it is dirty. (all unfavorable properties)

そして **soshite** can replace それから **sorekara** or それに **soreni**. However, そして **soshite** is a better choice than それから **sorekara** when the following event has some logical connection to the preceding event. For example:

姉はボストンの大学に入りました。そして、人類学を専攻しました。
Ane wa Bosuton no daigaku ni hairimashita. Soshite, jinruigaku o senkō shimashita.
My older sister was admitted to a university in Boston. Then she majored in anthropology.

EXERCISE
12·10

Complete the following sentences creatively.

1. 昨日は朝買い物をしました。それから、＿＿＿＿＿＿＿＿＿＿＿＿＿＿＿＿＿。

   Kinō wa asa kaimono o shimashita. Sorekara, ＿＿＿＿＿＿＿＿＿＿＿＿＿.

2. 日曜日はよく買い物をします。それから、＿＿＿＿＿＿＿＿＿＿＿＿＿＿＿。

   Nichiyōbi wa yoku kaimono o shimasu. Sorekara, ＿＿＿＿＿＿＿＿＿＿＿＿.

3. このクラスは難しいです。それに、＿＿＿＿＿＿＿＿＿＿＿＿＿＿＿＿＿＿。

   Kono kurasu wa muzukashii desu. Soreni, ＿＿＿＿＿＿＿＿＿＿＿＿＿＿.

4. 兄は去年卒業しました。そして、＿＿＿＿＿＿＿＿＿＿＿＿＿＿＿＿＿＿。

   Ani wa kyonen sotsugyō shimashita. Soshite, ＿＿＿＿＿＿＿＿＿＿＿＿＿.

そうすると sōsuruto (*then*)

そうすると **sōsuruto** shows automatic results or unexpected results depending on the tense of the sentence. So it should not be used to express the speaker's controllable actions, requests, suggestions, conjectures, or the speaker's volition. If the sentence is in the non-past tense,

そうすると **sōsuruto** shows an automatic result or something that always happens. For example:

> このボタンを押してください。そうすると、お釣りが出ます。
> **Kono botan o oshite kudasai. Sōsuruto, otsuri ga demasu.**
> *Please press this button. Then you'll get the change.*

> 酢を入れてください。そうすると、色が変わります。
> **Su o irete kudasai. Sōsuruto, iro ga kawarimasu.**
> *Please add vinegar. Then the color will change.*

If the sentence is in the past tense, そうすると **sōsuruto** shows what happened after some action. In this case, the result should not be what the speaker expected or something the speaker had a control over. It does not have to be an exciting surprise, but the event should not be something expected. For example:

> 箱を開けました。そうすると、中から煙が出て来ました。
> **Hako o akemashita. Sōsuruto, naka kara kemuri ga dete kimashita.**
> *I opened the box. Then smoke came out from inside.*

See Chapter 13 to see the similarity between そうすると **sōsuruto** and the conditional clause with と **to**.

EXERCISE 12·11

State whether each of the following is grammatical or not grammatical.

1. この道をまっすぐ行ってください。そうすると、橋が見えます。

   Kono michi o massugu itte kudasai. Sōsuruto, hashi ga miemasu.

2. この道をまっすぐ行ってください。そうすると、次の交差点で右に曲がってください。

   Kono michi o massugu itte kudasai. Sōsuruto, tsugi no kōsaten de migi ni magatte kudasai.

3. 昨日渋谷に行きました。そうすると、雨が降ってきました。

   Kinō Shibuya ni ikimashita. Sōsuruto, ame ga futte kimashita.

4. 昨日渋谷に行きました。そうすると、ジャケットを買いました。

   Kinō Shibuya ni ikimashita. Sōsuruto, jaketto o kaimashita.

EXERCISE 12·12

The following sentences provide directions to someone's house. Complete each with either それから *sorekara or* そうすると *sōsuruto.*

この道をまっすぐ行ってください。＿＿＿＿＿＿＿＿＿＿、一つ目の交差点を右に曲がってくださ

い。＿＿＿＿＿＿＿＿＿＿、橋があります。その橋を渡ってください。＿＿＿＿＿＿＿＿＿＿、

次の交差点を左に曲がってください。＿＿＿＿＿＿＿＿＿＿、左に私の家があります。

Kono michi o massugu itte kudasai. _____, **hitotsu-me no kōsaten o migi**

ni magatte kudasai. _____, **hashi ga arimasu. Sono hashi o watatte**

kudasai. _____, **tsugi no kōsaten o hidari ni magatte**

kudasai. _____, **hidari ni watashi no ie ga arimasu.**

それで **sorede** (*and so*)

それで **sorede** shows a conclusion or an expected result. Unlike そうすると **sōsuruto**, it should not be used for something that is not expected. However, like そうすると **sōsuruto**, it should not be used to express commands, requests, suggestions, invitations, conjectures, or the speaker's volition. However, because it shows conclusion, it is fine to express the speaker's action or decision that has already been performed or made based on valid reasoning. For example:

> 円が高くなりました。それで、今年は日本に行かないことにしました。
> **En ga takaku narimashita. Sorede, kotoshi wa Nihon ni ikanai koto ni shimashita.**
> *The Japanese yen became expensive. As a result, I decided not to go to Japan this year.*

> あまり勉強しませんでした。それで、いい成績はもらえませんでした。
> **Amari benkyō shimasendeshita. Sorede, ii seiseki wa moraemasendeshita.**
> *I did not study much. So I could not get a good grade.*

> よく勉強しました。それで、いい成績をもらいました。
> **Yoku benkyō shimashita. Sorede, ii seiseki o moraimashita.**
> *I studied very well. So I got a good grade.*

EXERCISE
12·13

State whether each of the following is grammatical or not grammatical.

1. 寝坊しました。それで、クラスに遅れました。

   Nebō shimashita. Sorede, kurasu ni okuremashita.

2. 父が病気になりました。それで、大学に行かないで働くことにしました。

   Chichi ga byōki ni narimashita. Sorede, daigaku ni ikanai de hataraku koto ni shimashita.

3. 昨日渋谷に行きました。それで、雨が降ってきました。

   Kinō Shibuya ni ikimashita. Sorede, ame ga futte kimashita.

4. 昨日渋谷に行きました。それで、ジャケットを買いました。

   Kinō Shibuya ni ikimashita. Sorede, jaketto o kaimashita.

ですから desukara (*therefore*) and でも demo (*however*)

ですから **desukara** shows that a sentence expresses a conclusion or a consequence with respect to what is expressed in the preceding sentence. In an informal speech context or in plain written form, だから **dakara** is used instead of ですから **desukara**. For example:

父は日本人です。ですから、うちで日本語を話します。
Chichi wa Nihonjin desu. Desukara, uchi de Nihongo o hanashimasu.
My father is Japanese. So he speaks Japanese at home. (polite style)

父は日本人だ。だから、うちで日本語を話す。
Chichi wa Nihonjin da. Dakara, uchi de Nihongo o hanasu.
My father is Japanese. So he speaks Japanese at home. (plain style)

Both だから **dakara** and ですから **desukara** can be used for commands, requests, suggestions, invitations, conjectures, volitions, etc., as long as there is a logical reasoning for the use. For example:

今日は雨が降ります。ですから、傘を持っていってください。
Kyō wa ame ga furimasu. Desukara, kasa o motte itte kudasai.
It will rain today. So please bring an umbrella.

See Chapter 11 for から **kara**, which connects clauses rather than sentences in a similar manner.

In contrast to だから **dakara** and ですから **desukara**, でも **demo** shows that a sentence expresses conflicts or contrasts with respect to what is stated in the preceding sentence. In a formal speech context or in written forms, しかし **shikashi** is often used instead of でも **demo**. For example:

兄の専攻は数学です。でも、私の専攻は文学です。
Ani no senkō wa sūgaku desu. Demo, watashino senkō wa bungaku desu.
My older brother's major is mathematics. However, my major is literature. (contrast)

兄の車は高いです。でも、よくこわれます。
Ani no kuruma wa takai desu. Demo, yoku kowaremasu.
My older brother's car is expensive. However, it often breaks down. (conflict)

兄の専攻は数学だ。しかし、私の専攻は文学だ。
Ani no senkō wa sūgaku da. Shikashi, watashino senkō wa bungaku da.
My older brother's major is mathematics. However, my major is literature. (contrast)

兄の車は高い。しかし、よくこわれる。
Ani no kuruma wa takai. Shikashi, yoku kowareru.
My older brother's car is expensive. However, it often breaks down. (contrast)

See Chapter 11 for が **ga**, which connects clauses rather than sentences in a similar manner.

EXERCISE

12·14

Complete the following sentences creatively.

1. 私は猫が好きです。でも、＿＿＿＿＿＿＿＿＿＿。

   Watashi wa neko ga suki desu. Demo, ＿＿＿＿＿＿＿＿＿＿.

2. 妹はアイスクリームが好きです。ですから、＿＿＿＿＿＿＿＿＿＿。

   Imōto wa aisukurīmu ga suki desu. Desukara, ＿＿＿＿＿＿＿＿＿＿.

3. あしたは台風が来るようです。ですから、_____。(台風 **taifū**: *typhoon*)

Ashita wa taifū ga kuru yō desu. Desukara, _____.

4. 昨日 _____。でも、だれもけがをしませんでした。

Kinō _____. Demo, dare mo kega o shimasendeshita. (けが **kega**: *injury*)

EXERCISE
12·15

In each of the following, choose the correct answer or answers from the options in the parentheses.

1. ドアをあけました。(そうすると, それで, ですから)、犬がいました。

Doa o akemashita. (Sōsuruto, Sorede, Desukara), inu ga imashita.

2. 財布を忘れてしまいました。(そうすると, それで, ですから)、田中さんにお金を借りました。

Saifu o wasurete shimaimashita. (Sōsuruto, Sorede, Desukara), Tanaka-san ni o-kane o karimashita.

3. あしたはデパートでセールがあります。(そうすると, それで, ですから)、いっしょに買い物に行きませんか。

Ashita wa depāto de sēru ga arimasu. (Sōsuruto, Sorede, Desukara), isshoni kaimono ni ikimasen ka.

それか soreka (*or*) and それとも soretomo (*or*)

To list statement sentences as alternatives, use それか **soreka**. To list question sentences as alternatives, use それとも **soretomo**. For example:

うちでは英語を話します。それか、フランス語を話します。
Uchi de wa eigo o hanashimasu. Soreka, Furansu-go o hanashimasu.
I speak English at home. Or I speak French.

英語を話しますか。それとも、フランス語を話しますか。
Eigo o hanashimasu ka. Soretomo, Furansugo o hanashimasu ka.
Do you speak English? Or do you speak French?

EXERCISE
12·16

Complete each of the following sentences with それか **soreka** or それとも **soretomo**.

1. バスで行きます。_____、車で行きます。

Basu de ikimasu. _____, kuruma de ikimasu.

2. バスで行きますか。_____、車で行きますか。

Basu de ikimasu ka. _____, kuruma de ikimasu ka.

3. タブレットを買いますか。_____、ノートパソコンを買いますか。

Taburetto o kaimasu ka. _____, nōto pasokon o kaimasu ka.

Conditionals

Many situations in our lives hold only in some cases or only under some condition. This chapter introduces frequently used conditional clauses that express such situations and shows exactly when and how you can use each conditional clause.

...たら **tara** (*whenever, when, if*)

You can create the **tara** form of verbs and adjectives just by adding ら **ra** at the end of the **ta** form (plain past affirmative form). It is very similar to the **tari** form discussed in Chapter 12. For example, the **ta** form of 行く **iku** (*to go*) is 行った **itta**, and its **tara** form is 行ったら **ittara**.

EXERCISE

13·1

*Convert each of the following verbs and adjectives in the dictionary form into its **tara** form, following the example.*

EXAMPLE   食べる **taberu** (*to eat*)   →   食べたら **tabetara**

1. 読む **yomu** (*to read*)   → _____

2. 来る **kuru** (*to come*)   → _____

3. 買う **kau** (*to buy*)   → _____

4. する **suru** (*to do*)   → _____

5. 書く **kaku** (*to write*)   → _____

6. 書かない **kakanai** (*not to write*)   → _____

7. 安い **yasui** (*to be cheap*)   → _____

8. 静かだ **shizuka da** (*to be quiet*)   → _____

9. 学生だ **gakusei da** (*to be a student*)   → _____

The clause that ends in たら **tara** (called the **tara** clause) is interpreted differently depending on the tense of the main clause, but it always requires that the situation in the **tara** clause precede the situation in the main clause. When the main clause is in the non-past tense, the **tara** clause expresses a generic condition or a non-generic condition.

Generic condition

Some events or situations almost always cause some result due to generic facts in nature, mathematics, society, family, and so on. When a **tara** clause expresses such a generic condition, the main clause expresses what is predicted to happen whenever the condition is met. Accordingly, the main clause does not express the speaker's controllable act, requests, suggestions, etc. The following are some examples of sentences that express generic conditions:

春になったら、雪はとけます。
Haru ni nattara, yuki wa tokemasu.
The snow will melt when the spring comes.

5時になったら、父が帰ります。
Go-ji ni nattara, chichi ga kaerimasu.
When it's five o'clock, my father comes home.

風邪をひいたら、くしゃみが出ます。
Kaze o hiitara, kushami ga demasu.
Whenever I catch a cold, I sneeze.

3に2をたしたら、5になります。
San ni ni o tashitara, go ni narimasu.
If you add 2 to 3, you'll get 5.

試験を受けなかったら、成績が下がります。
Shiken o ukenakattara, seiseki ga sagarimasu.
If you do not take the exam, your grades will go down.

山田さんが来たら楽しいでしょう。
Yamada-san ga kitara tanoshii deshō.
It will probably be fun if Ms. Yamada comes.

安かったら、よく売れます。
Yasukattara, yoku uremasu.
If they are cheap, things sell well.

この会社の社員だったら、あのレストランで割引がもらえます。
Kono kaisha no shain dattara, ano resutoran de waribiki ga moraemasu.
If you are an employee of this company, you can get a discount at that restaurant.

Non-generic condition

An event or a situation can serve as the condition for someone to act in a certain way after it is met. In this case, the main clause can express the speaker's controllable act, suggestions, requests, etc. Such non-generic condition can be temporal or hypothetical, depending on how likely it is that the condition will be met. For example:

林さんが来たら、私は帰ります。
Hayashi-san ga kitara, watashi wa kaerimasu.
I'll go home when Mr. Hayashi comes. (temporal condition)
I'll go home if Mr. Hayashi comes. (hypothetical condition)

The adverb もし **moshi** (*if*) is often used for hypothetical conditions. Additional examples of non-generic conditions are:

5時になったら、電話しますね。
Go-ji ni nattara, denwa shimasu ne.
I'll call you when it's 5 o'clock. (or *I'll call you at 5 o'clock.*) (temporal condition)

もし病気が治ったら、また働きます。

Moshi byōki ga naottara, mata hatarakimasu.

If my illness is cured, I'll work again. (hypothetical condition)

もし病気が治らなかったら、働きません。

Moshi byōki ga naoranakattara, hatarakimasen.

If my illness is not cured, I will not work. (hypothetical condition)

安かったら、買いましょう。

Yasukattara, kaimashō.

Let's buy it if it is inexpensive. (hypothetical condition)

暇だったら、来てください。

Hima dattara, kite kudasai.

If you are free, please come over. (hypothetical condition)

もし私があなただったら、あんなことは言いません。

Moshi watashi ga anata dattara, anna koto wa iimasen.

If I were you, I wouldn't say that kind of thing. (hypothetical condition)

もしもう一度生まれることができたら、また私と結婚しますか。

Moshi mō ichi-do umareru koto ga dekitara, mata watashi to kekkon shimasu ka.

If you could be born again, would you marry me again? (hypothetical condition)

EXERCISE 13·2

*In the following, form **tara** clauses creatively, to make sensible sentences.*

1. _____ ら、雪がとけます。

_____ **ra, yuki ga tokemasu.**

2. _____ ら、電話します。

_____ **ra, denwa shimasu.**

3. _____ ら、公園に行きませんか。

_____ **ra, kōen ni ikimasen ka.**

4. _____ ら、私はとても幸せでしょう。

_____ **ra, watashi wa totemo shiawase deshō.** (幸せ **shiawase**: *happy*)

When the main clause is in the past tense, a sentence with a **tara** clause expresses what happened after doing something. For example:

ドアを開けたら、犬が外に出ました。

Doa o aketara, inu ga soto ni demashita.

When I opened the door, the dog went out.

Do not use a **tara** clause if two actions were intentionally performed by the same person when the main clause is in the past tense. In that case, use the **te** form to connect the actions. For example:

ドアを開けて、犬を外に出しました。

Doa o akete, inu o soto ni dashimashita.

I opened the door and let the dog go out.

Complete each of the sentences with one of the following phrases.

a. まあまあおいしかったです **māmā oishikatta desu** (*it was relatively delicious*)

b. 鳥が入って来ました **tori ga haitte kimashita** (*a bird came in*)

c. 気分がよくなりました **kibun ga yoku narimnashita** (*I started to feel better*)

d. 石田さんに会いました **Ishida-san ni aimashita** (*I met Mr. Ishida*)

e. 頭が痛くなりました **atama ga itaku narimashita** (*I started to have a headache*)

1. 窓を開けたら、＿＿＿＿。

   Mado o aketara, ＿＿＿＿.

2. 食べてみたら、＿＿＿＿。

   Tabete mitara, ＿＿＿＿.

3. 音楽を聞いたら、＿＿＿＿。

   Ongaku o kiitara, ＿＿＿＿.

4. スーパーに行ったら、＿＿＿＿。

   Sūpā ni ittara, ＿＿＿＿.

5. お酒を飲んだら、＿＿＿＿。

   O-sake o nondara, ＿＿＿＿.

. . . ば **ba** (*whenever, when, if*)

You create the **ba** form of verbs and adjectives as follows:

- **Ru** verbs: Replace **ru** at the end of the dictionary form with **reba** (e.g., 食べる **taberu** (*to eat*) → 食べれば **tabereba**).
- **U** verbs: Replace **ru** at the end of the potential form (see Chapter 4 for potential forms) with **ba** (e.g., 書く **kaku** (*to write*) → 書ける **kakeru** (*to be able to write*) → 書けば **kakeba**).
- Irregular verbs: する **suru** → すれば **sureba**; くる **kuru** → くれば **kureba**.
- **I** adjectives: Add **kereba** after the stem (e.g., 高い **takai** (*expensive*) → 高ければ **takakereba**). The **ba** form of いい **ii** is よければ **yokereba**.
- **Na** adjectives: Add であれば **de areba** after the stem (e.g., 静かな **shizuka na** → 静かであれば **shizuka de areba**).
- Copular verb: Replace だ **da** or です **desu** with であれば **de areba** (e.g., 学生だ **gakusei da** → 学生であれば **gakusei de areba**).
- Negative forms of verbs and adjectives: Create the **nai** form and treat it as if it is an **i** adjective, regardless of whether it is a verb or an adjective (e.g., 食べない **tabenai** (*not to eat*) → 食べなければ **tabenakereba**; 高くない **takaku nai** (*not expensive*) → 高くなければ **takaku nakereba**; 静かじゃない **shizuka ja nai** (*not quiet*) → 静かじゃなければ **shizuka ja nakereba**; 学生じゃない **gakusei ja nai** (*not to be a student*) → 学生じゃなければ **gakusei ja nakereba**).

*Convert the following verbs and adjectives in the plain form into their **ba** form.*

EXAMPLE 食べる **taberu** (*to eat*)   →   食べれば **tabereba**

1. 書く **kaku** (*to write*)   →   _____

2. 飲む **nomu** (*to drink*)   →   _____

3. 来る **kuru** (*to come*)   →   _____

4. 来ない **konai** (*not to come*)   →   _____

5. ある **aru** (*to exist*)   →   _____

6. ない **nai** (*not to exist*)   →   _____

7. する **suru** (*to do*)   →   _____

8. いない **inai** (*not to exist*)   →   _____

9. 安い **yasui** (*to be cheap*)   →   _____

10. いい **ii** (*to be good*)   →   _____

11. よくない **yokunai** (*not to be good*)   →   _____

12. 静かだ **shizuka da** (*to be quiet*)   →   _____

13. まじめじゃない **majime ja nai** (*not serious*)   →   _____

14. 学生じゃない **gakusei ja nai** (*not student*)   →   _____

The clauses that end with ば **ba** (called **ba** clauses) express all kinds of conditionals that the **tara** clauses can express, except the main clause cannot express a command, request, suggestion, etc. if the predicate in the **ba** clause denotes an action or event. See the contrast among the following sentences:

山田さんが来たら、いっしょにテニスをしましせんか。
Yamada-san ga kitara, isshoni tenisu o shimasen ka.
How about playing tennis together if (when) Ms. Yamada comes?

✗山田さんが来れば、いっしょにテニスをしませんか。(ungrammatical)
Yamada-san ga kureba, isshoni tenisu o shimasen ka.
(Intended: *How about playing tennis together if (when) Ms. Yamada comes?*)

山田さんが来れば、楽しいでしょう。
Yamada-san ga kureba, tanoshii deshō.
If Ms. Yamada comes, it would be fun.

あした天気がよければ、いっしょにテニスをしませんか。
Ashita tenki ga yokereba, isshoni tenisu o shimasen ka.
How about playing tennis together if the weather is nice tomorrow?

Unlike **tara** clauses, **ba** clauses cannot be used to express two sequentially ordered events that took place in the past. For example:

ドアを開けたら、犬が外に出ました。
Doa o aketara, inu ga soto ni demashita.
When I opened the door, the dog went out.

✗ドアを開ければ、犬が外にでました。(ungrammatical)
Doa o akereba, inu ga soto ni demashita.
(Intended: *When I opened the door, the dog went out.*)

The following are additional examples of conditionals with a **ba** clause:

押せば開きます。
Oseba akimasu.
Once you push it, it will open.

7時になれば父が帰ります。
Shichi-ji ni nareba chichi ga kaerimasu.
My father will get home at 7 o'clock.

勉強すればAがもらえますよ。
Benkyō sureba ē ga moraemasu yo.
If you study, you'll be able to get an A.

犬と話せれば楽しいでしょう。
Inu to hanasereba tanoshii deshō.
If I could talk with a dog, it would be enjoyable.

高ければ買わないでください。
Takakereba kawanai de kudasai.
If it is expensive, please do not buy it.

高くなければ買った方がいいですよ。
Takaku nakereba katta hō ga ii desu yo.
If not expensive, it's better to buy it.

The ba clause is preferably used for expressing one's wishes and regrets, describing what should be or should have been the desired situation. In this case, the main clause often ends in んです **n desu** (*it is the case that . . .*) or のに **no ni** (*but . . .*). For example:

私がすれば良かったんです。
Watashi ga sureba yokatta ndesu.
I should have done it (instead of him).

もっと勉強すればいいのに。
Motto benkyō sureba ii noni.
You should study harder, but . . .

EXERCISE
13·5

Complete each of the following sentences creatively to express a possible regret and then translate each sentence into English.

1. 小さいときに _____ ば良かった。

   Chīsai toki ni _____ ba yokatta.

_____

2. 高校生のときに ＿＿＿＿＿＿＿＿＿＿＿ば良かった。

   Kōkōsei no toki ni ＿＿＿＿＿＿＿＿＿＿＿ ba yokatta.

   _____

3. 母が生きているときに ＿＿＿＿＿＿＿＿＿＿＿ば良かったと思います。

   Haha ga ikite iru toki ni ＿＿＿＿＿＿＿＿＿＿＿ ba yokatta to omoimasu.

   _____

4. 日本にいる間に ＿＿＿＿＿＿＿＿＿＿＿ば良かった。

   Nihon ni iru aida ni ＿＿＿＿＿＿＿＿＿＿＿ ba yokatta.

   _____

5. 車を買うときに ＿＿＿＿＿＿＿＿＿＿＿ば良かったのに。

   Kuruma o kau toki ni ＿＿＿＿＿＿＿＿＿＿＿ ba yokatta no ni.

   _____

... と to (*whenever, when*)

The particle と **to** follows verbs and adjectives in the plain non-past form. If the main clause is in the non-past tense, the clause with と **to** only describes generic condition. Accordingly, the main clause cannot express the speaker's controllable action, requests, suggestions, permissions, commands, desires, etc. For example:

> ニューヨークでは冬になると雪が降ります。
> **Nyūyōku de wa fuyu ni naru to yuki ga furimasu.**
> *When it is winter, it snows in New York.*

> 需要が多いと値段が上がります。
> **Juyō ga ōi to nedan ga agarimasu.**
> *When the demand is great, the price goes up.*

> 60歳以上だと家賃が安くなります。
> **Rokujus-sai ijō da to yachin ga yasuku narimasu.**
> *The rent is reduced for those who are 60 years old or older.*

> 薬を飲まないとよくなりませんよ。
> **Kusuri o nomanai to yoku narimasen yo.**
> *If you don't take medicine, you will not get better.*

> 父はお酒を飲むとよくしゃべります。
> **Chichi wa o-sake o nomu to yoku shaberimasu.**
> *My father starts speaking a lot when he drinks sake.*

When the main clause is in the past tense, a sentence with と **to** expresses what happened after doing something, just like a sentence with a **tara** clause. Thus, the two sentences below are synonymous:

> ドアを開けると犬が外に出ました。
> **Doa o akeru to inu ga soto ni demashita.**

> ドアを開けたら犬が外に出ました。
> **Doa o aketara inu ga soto ni demashita.**
> *I opened the door and then the dog went out.* (or *When I opened the door, the dog went out.*)

Complete the following sentences by using some of these phrases.

a. 私は寝ます **watashi wa nemasu** (*I will go to bed*)

b. 太ります **futorimasu** (*gain weight*)

c. 売れます **uremasu** (*sell well*)

d. 売れません **uremasen** (*not sell well*)

e. 復習しましょう **fukushū shimashō** (*let's review it*)

f. 暗くなります **kuraku narimasu** (*get dark*)

g. 100点がとれるかもしれません **hyaku-ten ga toreru kamoshiremasen** (*may be able to get a 100*)

h. 100点はとれません **hyaku-ten wa toremasen** (*cannot get a 100*)

1. たくさん食べると ＿＿＿＿＿。

   Takusan taberu to ＿＿＿＿＿.

2. よく勉強しないと ＿＿＿＿＿。

   Yoku benkyō shinai to ＿＿＿＿＿.

3. よく勉強すると ＿＿＿＿＿。

   Yoku benkyō suru to ＿＿＿＿＿.

4. ５時になると ＿＿＿＿＿。

   Go-ji ni naru to ＿＿＿＿＿.

5. 安くないと ＿＿＿＿＿。

   Yasuku nai to ＿＿＿＿＿.

Complete each sentence appropriately.

1. 漢字はときどき ＿＿＿＿＿＿＿＿＿＿＿ と、忘れますよ。

   Kanji wa tokidoki ＿＿＿＿＿＿＿＿＿＿ to, wasuremasu yo.

   If you don't write kanji sometimes, you'll easily forget them.

2. 父はお酒を ＿＿＿＿＿＿＿＿＿＿＿ と、すぐ寝ます。

   Chichi wa o-sake o ＿＿＿＿＿＿＿＿＿＿ to, sugu nemasu.

   My father falls asleep whenever he drinks sake.

3. 2に3を _____ と、5になります。

Ni ni san o _____ to, go ni narimasu.

Two plus three equals five. (*to add*: 足す **tasu**)

4. マイケルはメアリーを _____ と、赤くなります。

Maikeru wa Mearī o _____ to, akaku narimasu.

Michael blushes whenever he sees Mary.

5. 母は _____ と、何でも買います。

Haha wa _____ to, nan demo kaimasu.

My mother buys whatever is cheap.

EXERCISE
13·8

Explain why each of the following sentences is ungrammatical.

1. ✗冬になるとスキーをしませんか。

Fuyu ni naru to sukī o shimasen ka.

(Intended meaning: *Why don't we ski in winter?*)

_____

2. ✗ビールを飲んだと眠くなりました。

Bīru o nonda to nemuku narimashita.

(Intended meaning: *After having beer, I became sleepy.*)

_____

3. ✗勉強すると復習しました。

Benkyō suru to fukushū shimashita.

(Intended meaning: *I studied and then reviewed.*)

_____

4. ✗いびきをかくと寝ます。

Ibiki o kaku to nemasu.

(Intended meaning: *Whenever I sleep, I snore.*)

_____

...なら nara (*if it is the case that...*)

なら **nara** can follow verbs and adjectives in the plain form to create a conditional clause (called a **nara** clause). Note that the non-past affirmative copula だ **da** must be deleted, and plain past forms are commonly followed by の **no** when they occur right before なら **nara**. A **nara** clause defines the basis of a statement, meaning *if it is the case that...* or *if you are talking about....* For example:

> 京都に行くなら新幹線がいいですよ。北海道に行くなら飛行機がいいですよ。
> **Kyōto ni iku nara Shinkansen ga ii desu yo. Hokkaidō ni iku nara hikōki ga ii desu yo.**
> *If you are going to Kyoto, it is better to take the bullet train. If you are going to Hokkaido, an airplane is better.*

> 去年北海道に行った (の) なら、今年は九州に行きましょう。
> **Kyonen Hokkaidō ni itta (no) nara, kotoshi wa kyūshū ni ikimashō.**
> *If you went to Hokkaidō last year, let's go to Kyūshū this year.*

> 好きなら好きだと言った方がいいですよ。
> **Suki nara suki da to itta hō ga ii desu yo.**
> *If you like (her), it's better to say that you like (her).*

> カメラなら秋葉原がいいですよ。
> **Kamera nara Akihabara ga ii desu yo.**
> *For (If you are talking about) cameras, Akihabara is good.*

> 田中さんなら1時間前にここにいましたよ。
> **Tanaka-san nara ichi-jikan mae ni koko ni imashita yo.**
> *If you are looking for Mr. Tanaka, he was here one hour ago.*

Unlike clauses with **tara**, **ba**, and **to**, a **nara** clause does not impose a restriction in terms of the relative temporal order of the actions in the clauses in a sentence. The action expressed in a **nara** clause may take place either before or after the action expressed in the main clause. For example:

> 中国に行くなら、万里の長城を見てください。
> **Chūgoku ni iku nara, Banri no Chōjō o mite kudasai.**
> *If you are going to China, please see the Great Wall (after you get there).*

> 中国に行くなら、ビザをとってください。
> **Chūgoku ni iku nara, biza o totte kudasai.**
> *If you are going to China, please get a visa (before you get there).*

Expectedly, a **nara** clause cannot be used for a temporal condition or a generic condition that expresses what is predicted to happen after some event. Similarly, a **nara** clause cannot express two sequentially ordered events that happened in the past. However, a **nara** clause is most convenient for evaluating facts or expressing intentions, conjectures, suggestions, and requests based on some assumption. For example:

> あなたが行くなら私も行きます。
> **Anata ga iku nara watashi mo ikimasu.**
> *If you are going (there), I'll go (there), too.*

> 新車なら高いでしょう。
> **Shinsha nara takai deshō.**
> *If (you are interested in) a brand new car, it will be expensive.*

> 林さんが来ないなら帰りませんか。
> **Hayashi-san ga konai nara kaerimasen ka.**
> *If Ms. Hayashi is not coming, why don't we go home?*

郵便局に行くなら６０円の切手を５枚買って来てください。

Yūbinkyoku ni iku nara rokujū-en no kitte o go-mai katte kite kudasai.

If you are going to the post office, please buy five 60-yen stamps.

前の試験が難しかった (の) なら今度の試験も難しいかもしれません。

Mae no shiken ga muzukashikatta (no) nara kondo no shiken mo muzukashii kamoshiremasen.

If the previous test was hard, the next test may also be hard.

もし私が男ならフットボールをするでしょう。

Moshi watashi ga otoko nara futtobōru o suru deshō.

If I were a male, I would play football.

EXERCISE 13·9

In each of the following sentences, choose the correct answer from the options in parentheses.

1. 日本に（行く, 行った）なら日本のタクシーを見ましたね。

   Nihon ni (iku, itta) nara Nihon no takushī o mimashita ne.

   If you had been to Japan, you saw Japanese taxies, right?

2. 日本に（行く, 行った）なら京都に必ず行ってください。

   Nihon ni (iku, itta) nara Kyōto ni kanarazu itte kudasai. (必ず **kanarazu**: *without fail*)

   If you are going to Japan, please visit Kyoto without fail.

3. （暑い, 暑かった）なら窓を開けてもいいですよ。

   (Atsui, Atsukatta) nara mado o akete mo ii desu yo. (開けてもいい **akete mo ii**: *it is okay to open (it)*)

   If you feel hot, you can open the window.

4. （聞きたい, 聞きたくない）なら聞かなくてもいいですよ。

   (Kiki-tai, Kikitaku nai) nara kikanaku te mo ii desu yo. (聞かなくてもいい **kikanakute mo ii**: *it is okay not to listen*)

   If you don't want to listen, you don't have to listen.

5. （食べる, 食べない）なら注文しないでください。

   (Taberu, Tabenai) nara chūmon shinai de kudasai. (注文する **chūmon suru**: *to order*)

   If you are not goint to eat (it), please do not order (it).

Complete the following sentences creatively.

1. 日本語を勉強したいなら、_____ 方がいいですよ。

   Nihon-go o benkyō shitai nara, _____ **hō ga ii desu yo. (Ta** form of a verb + 方がいい **hō ga ii:** *It is better to . . .*)

2. スーパーに行くなら、_____ ください。

   Sūpā ni iku nara, _____ **kudasai.**

3. 漢字をたくさん勉強したなら、_____ はずですね。

   Kanji o takusan benkyō shita nara, _____ **hazu desu ne.**

4. _____ なら、食べなくてもいいですよ。

   _____ **nara, tabenakute mo ii desu yo.** (食べなくてもいい **tabenakute mo ii:** *no need to eat (it)*)

5. _____ なら、買いません。

   _____ **nara, kaimasen.**

EXERCISE
13·11

The following table summarizes the availability of the four conditional clauses discussed in this chapter, using examples. ✗ indicates that a sentence is ungrammatical. For each of the numbered sentences, explain why it is ungrammatical.

	Intended Reading	たら	ば	と	なら
Generic condition	*If you push it, it will open.*	押したら開きます。 **Oshitara akimasu.**	押せば開きます。 **Oseba akimasu.**	押すと開きます。 **Osu to akimasu.**	1. ✗押すなら開きます。 **Osu nara akimasu.**
	If cheap, things sell well.	安かったら売れます。 **Yasukattara uremasu.**	安ければ売れます。 **Yasukereba uremasu.**	安いと売れます。 **Yasui to uremasu.**	安いなら売れます。 **Yasui nara uremasu.**
Non-generic condition	*Why don't we go home at 5 o'clock?*	5時になったら帰りませんか。 **Go-ji ni nattara kaerimasen ka.**	✗5時になれば帰りませんか。 **Go-ji ni nareba kaerimasen ka.**	✗5時になると帰りませんか。 **Go-ji ni naru to kaerimasen ka.**	2. ✗5時になるなら帰りませんか。 **Go-ji ni naru nara kaerimasen ka.**
	Why don't we go home if Mr. Hayashi comes?	林さんが来たら帰りませんか。 **Hayashi-san ga kitara kaerimasen ka.**	✗林さんが来れば帰りませんか。 **Hayashi-san ga kureba kaerimasen ka.**	3. ✗林さんが来ると帰りませんか。 **Hayashi-san ga kuru to kaerimasen ka.**	林さんが来るなら帰りませんか。 **Hayashi-san ga kuru nara kaerimasen ka.**
	If you are going to China, get a visa (before going there).	4. ✗中国に行ったらビザをとってください。 **Chūgoku ni ittara biza o totte kudasai.**	✗中国に行けばビザをとってください。 **Chūgoku ni ikeba biza o totte kudasai.**	✗中国に行くとビザをとってください。 **Chūgoku ni iku to biza o totte kudasai.**	中国に行くならビザをとってください。 **Chūgoku ni iku nara biza o totte kudasai.**
	Why don't we buy it if it's cheap?	安かったら買いませんか。 **Yasukattara kaimasen ka.**	安ければ買いませんか。 **Yasukereba kaimasen ka.**	✗安いと買いませんか。 **Yasui to kaimasen ka.**	安いなら買いませんか。 **Yasui nara kaimasen ka.**
Two past events	*When I pushed it, it opened.*	押したら開きました。 **Oshitara akimashita.**	5. ✗押せば開きました。 **Oseba akimashita.**	押すと開きました。 **Osu to akimashita.**	✗押すなら開きました。 **Osu nara akimashita.**

1. _____

2. _____

3. _____

4. _____

5. _____

EXERCISE
13·12

In each of the following sentences, choose the correct answer or answers from the options in parentheses.

1. このドアは（押したら, 押すと, 押せば, 押すなら）開きます。

   Kono doa wa (oshitara, osu to, oseba, osu nara) akimasu.

   This door opens if you push it.

2. ７時に（なったら, なると, なれば, なるなら）父が帰ります。

   Shichi-ji ni (nattara, naru to, nareba, naru nara) chichi ga kaerimasu.

   My father comes home at 7 o'clock.

3. ７時に（なったら, なると, なれば, なるなら）帰りましょう。

   Shichi-ji ni (nattara, naru to, nareba, naru nara) kaerimashō.

   Let's go home at 7 o'clock.

4. このドアが（開いたら, 開くと, 開けば, 開くなら）入りませんか。

   Kono doa ga (aitara, aku to, akeba, aku nara) hairimasen ka.

   Why don't we enter if this door opens?

5. （寒かったら, 寒いと, 寒ければ, 寒いなら）入りませんか。

   (Samukattara, Samui to, Samukereba, Samui nara) hairimasen ka.

   If you feel cold, why don't you come in?

6. （安かったら, 安いと, 安ければ, 安いなら）売れます。

   (Yasukattara, Yasui to, Yasukereba, Yasui nara) uremasu.

   If things are cheap, they sell well.

7. （安かったら, 安いと, 安ければ, 安いなら）買いませんか。

   (Yasukattara, Yasui to, Yasukereba, Yasui nara) kaimasen ka.

   If it is cheap, why don't we buy it?

8. 中国に（行ったら，行くと，行けば，行くなら）ビザを取らなくてはいけません。

   Chūgoku ni (ittara, iku to, ikeba, iku nara) biza o toranakute wa ikemasen.

   If you are going to China, you need to get a visa.

9. 窓を（開けたら，開けると，開ければ，開けるなら）鳥が入って来ました。

   Mado o (aketara, akeru to, akereba, akeru nara) tori ga haitte kimashita.

   When I opened the window, a bird came in.

...ても **te mo** (*even if/though, no matter...*)

A clause that ends in a verb or an adjective in the **te** form plus the particle も **mo** forms a concessive clause that means *even if...* or *even though....* For example:

> いっしょうけんめい勉強しても100点は取れませんでした。
> **Isshōkenmei benkyō shite mo 100-ten wa toremasendeshita.**
> *I couldn't get 100 even though I studied very hard.*

> いい本なら高くても買います。
> **Ii hon nara takakute mo kaimasu.**
> *If it is a good book, I will buy it even if it is expensive.*

> 高いなら便利でも買いません。
> **Takai nara benri demo kaimasen.**
> *If it is expensive, I will not buy it even if it is convenient.*

When such a clause contains a question word, it means *no matter....* For example:

> どこを探しても見つかりませんでした。
> **Doko o sagashite mo mitsukarimasendeshita.**
> *No matter where I searched, I could not find (it).*

> 姉は何を食べても太りません。
> **Ane wa nani o tabete mo futorimasen.**
> *My older sister does not gain weight no matter what she eats.*

> いくら がんばってもできません。
> **Ikura ganbatte mo dekimasen.**
> *No matter how much effort I make, I cannot do (it).*

EXERCISE
13·13

Translate the following sentences into English.

1. 兄はどんな映画でも見ます。

   Ani wa donna eiga demo mimasu.

   _____

2. 私はどこで寝てもよく眠れます。

   Watashi wa doko de nete mo yoku nemuremasu.

   _____

3. 私の弟はだれが話しても聞きません。

Watashi no otōto wa dare ga hanashite mo kikimasen.

_____

4. おいしいものならいくら高くても買います。

Oishii mono nara ikura takakute mo kaimasu.

_____

Permission and prohibition

You can express permission by combining a conditional phrase in the form . . . ても **te mo** (_even if . . ._) and an agreement phrase such as いいです **ii desu** (_it is fine_). For example, 帰ってもいいです **Kaette mo ii desu** literally means _even if you go home, it is fine_, which actually means _you may go home._

On the other hand, you express prohibition by combining a conditional phrase in the form . . . ては **te wa** (_if . . ._) and a disagreement phrase such as いけません **ikemasen** (_it is bad_). For example, 帰ってはいけません **Kaette wa ikemasen** literally means _if you go home, it is bad_, which actually means _you may not go home_. Permission sentences are often followed by the emphasis particle よ **yo** to show helpfulness or kindness.

EXERCISE

13·14

In Japanese, ask whether the following are permitted.

1. じしょを見る **jisho o miru** (_to see a dictionary_)

_____

2. クレジットカードで払う **kurejittokādo de harau** (_to pay by a credit card_)

_____

3. ちょっと聞く **chotto kiku** (_to ask about something_)

_____

4. ちょっとお願いする **chotto onegai suru** (_to request something_)

_____

5. ちょっと食べてみる **chotto tabete miru** (_to try eating a little bit_)

_____

Translate the following sentences into Japanese.

1. *You can use my car.*

_____

2. *You are not allowed to smoke here.*

_____

3. *You cannot speak here.*

_____

4. *You may go home early.*

_____

5. *You must not use a dictionary.*

_____

The constructions . . . てもいい **te mo ii** and . . . てはいけない **te wa ikenai** can be used not only with verbs but also with a copular verb and adjectives to express minimum conditions, qualifications, or requirements. For example:

部屋は狭くてもいいです。
Heya wa semakute mo ii desu.
The room is okay to be small. / A small room is acceptable.

暗くてはいけません。
Kurakute wa ikemasen.
It's not okay if it is dark. / A dark (room) is not acceptable.

ジーパンでもいいですよ。
Jīpan de mo ii desu yo.
Jeans are fine.

ジーパンではいけません。
Jīpan de wa ikemasen.
Jeans are not acceptable.

Suppose that you must find an apartment. Answer the following questions in Japanese.

1. 狭くてもいいですか。**Semakute mo ii desu ka.** (*Is a small (room) allowed?*)

_____

2. うるさくてもいいですか。**Urusakute mo ii desu ka.** (*Is it okay to be noisy?*)

_____

3. 古くてもいいですか。**Furukute mo ii desu ka.** (*Is an old one allowed?*)

_____

4. 家賃がちょっと高くてもいいですか。**Yachin ga chotto takakute mo ii desu ka.** (*Is it okay if the rent is a bit expensive?*)

_____

5. 交通が不便でもいいですか。**Kōtsū ga fuben de mo ii desu ka.** (*Is it okay if the transportation methods are inconvenient?*)

_____

Obligation and discretion

Obligation is expressed by combining a negative conditional phrase in the form . . . なくては **nakute wa** (*if you do not . . .*) and a disagreement phrase like いけません **ikemasen** (*it is bad*). For example, 帰らなくてはいけません **kaeranakute wa ikemasen** literally means *if I do not go home, it is bad*, which actually means *I must go home*.

You can express discretion by combining a negative conditional phrase like . . . なくても **nakute mo** (*even if you do not . . .*) and an agreement phrase like いいです **ii desu** (*it is fine*). For example, 帰らなくてもいいです **kaeranakute mo ii desu** literally means *even if I do not go home, it is fine*, which actually means *I do not have to go home*. For example:

> あしたまでに家賃を払わなくてはいけません。
> **Ashita made ni yachin o harawanakute wa ikemasen.**
> *I have to pay the rent by tomorrow.*

> あしたは仕事に行かなくてもいいです。
> **Ashita wa shigoto ni ikanakute mo ii desu.**
> *I don't have to go to work tomorrow.*

EXERCISE
13·17

In Japanese, ask whether you have to do each of the following.

1. 送料を払う **sōryō o harau** (*to pay the delivery fee*)

_____

2. 数学のクラスを取る **sūgaku no kurasu o toru** (*to take a math course*)

_____

3. 漢字を覚える **kanji o oboeru** (*to memorize kanji*)

_____

4. 電話をする **denwa o suru** (*to make a phone call*)

_____

Translate the following sentences into Japanese.

1. *You don't have to pay the delivery fee.*

   _____

2. *You don't have to go to Osaka.*

   _____

3. *You need to go to Kyōto.*

   _____

4. *You have to read kanji.*

   _____

5. *You have to be able to read kanji.*

   _____

You can use these obligation and discretion constructions with adjectives and nouns also. For example:

> 安くなくてもいいですよ。
> **Yasukunakute mo ii desu yo.**
> *It's fine not to be cheap.*

> 安くなくてはいけません。
> **Yasukunakute wa ikemasen.**
> *It has to be cheap.*

> ダイヤじゃなくてもいいです。
> **Daiya ja nakute mo ii desu.**
> *It's okay not to be diamond. (Any gemstone is fine.)*

> ダイヤじゃなくてはいけません。
> **Daiya ja nakute wa ikemasen.**
> *It has to be diamond. (No other gemstone is acceptable.)*

EXERCISE
13·19

Suppose that you must find a job. Answer the following questions in Japanese.

1. 給料が安くてもいいですか。

   Kyūryō ga yasukute mo ii desu ka.

   Is it okay if the salary is low?

   _____

2. 難しい仕事でもいいですか。

Muzukashii shigoto de mo ii desu ka.

Is it okay if the job is difficult?

---

3. 小さい会社でもいいですか。

Chīsai kaisha de mo ii desu ka.

Is it okay if the company is small?

---

4. 夜勤でもいいですか。

Yakin de mo ii desu ka. (夜勤 **yakin**: *night shift*)

Is it okay if you have to do night shift?

---

5. 交通が不便でもいいですか。

Kōtsū ga fuben de mo ii desu ka.

Is it okay if the commute is inconvenient?

Occasionally, . . . なければ **nakereba** is used instead of . . . なくては **nakute wa**. For example, 帰らなければいけません **kaeranakereba ikemasen** and 帰らなくてはいけません **kaeranakute wa ikemasen** are more or less synonymous, both meaning *(I) have to go home*. In addition, いけません **ikemasen** can be replaced with なりません **narimasen** in this construction. They are almost synonymous, but なりません **narimasen** gives the impression that the obligatory situation is somewhat inevitable and has arisen naturally. For example:

> 私は大阪に行かなければなりません。
> **Watashi wa Ōsaka ni ikanakereba narimasen.**
> *I have to go to Osaka.*

Passives and causatives

·14·

A particular situation can be stated in different ways, depending on the speaker's perspective. This chapter shows how to create passive sentences and causative sentences that allow you to express facts from different perspectives.

Passive verbs

To form a passive sentence, you need to create a passive verb. You can convert a Japanese verb into a passive verb by dropping the final **ru** or **u** in the dictionary form and adding **rareru** or **areru**. To conjugate a verb, look at the following table and follow the pattern of the verb with the same ending and in the same category:

	Ending	Dictionary Form	Passive Form
Ru verbs	-eる -eru	かえる kaeru (*change*)	かえられる kaerareru
	-iる -iru	きる kiru (*wear*)	きられる kirareru
U verbs	-す -su	はなす hanasu (*speak*)	はなされる hanasareru
	-く -ku	かく kaku (*write*)	かかれる kakareru
	-ぐ -gu	およぐ oyogu (*swim*)	およがれる oyogareru
	-む -mu	よむ yomu (*read*)	よまれる yomareru
	-ぬ -nu	しぬ shinu (*die*)	しなれる shinareru
	-ぶ -bu	とぶ tobu (*jump*)	とばれる tobareru
	-う -(w)u	かう kau (*buy*)	かわれる kawareru
	-る -ru	きる kiru (*cut*)	きられる kirareru
	-つ -tsu	まつ matsu (*wait*)	またれる matareru
Irregular verbs		くる kuru (*come*)	こられる korareru
		する suru (*do*)	される sareru

Convert each of the following verbs into its passive form, as shown in the example.

EXAMPLE   食べる **taberu** (*eat*)   →   食べられる **taberareru**

1. 盗む **nusumu** (*steal*)   →   _____

2. たたく **tataku** (*hit*)   →   _____

3. こわす **kowasu** (*break*)   →   _____

4. 運ぶ **hakobu** (*carry*)   →   _____

5. 使う **tsukau** (*use*)   →   _____

6. 取る **toru** (*take*)   →   _____

7. 誘う **sasou** (*invite*)   →   _____

8. しかる **shikaru** (*scold*)   →   _____

9. ほめる **homeru** (*praise*, **ru** verb)   →   _____

10. する **suru** (*do*)   →   _____

The passive verbs are **ru** verbs, and you can conjugate them accordingly, as in 食べられる **taberare-ru**, 食べられない **taberare-nai**, 食べられます **taberare-masu**, and so on.

Passive verbs are used in two different constructions: direct passive and indirect passive.

Direct passive

Just like English passive sentences, direct passive sentences in Japanese bring the speaker's attention to the direct object of the verb by making it a subject noun. In this case, the performer of the action is marked by the particle に **ni**, the receiver of the action (direct object) is marked by the subject particle が **ga**, and the verb is in the passive form. See the contrast between the active sentence and the passive sentence below:

> メアリーさんがマイクさんの手紙を読みました。
> **Mearī-san ga Maiku-san no tegami o yomimashita.**
> *Mary read Mike's letter.* (active)

> マイクさんの手紙がメアリーさんに読まれました。
> **Maiku-san no tegami ga Mearī-san ni yomaremashita.**
> *Mike's letter was read by Mary.* (direct passive)

Convert the following active sentences into direct passive sentences in Japanese.

1. 弟が私のカメラをこわしました。

   Otōto ga watashi no kamera o kowashimashita.

   My little brother broke my camera.

2. 父が弟をしかりました。

Chichi ga otōto o shikarimashita.

My father scolded my little brother.

_____

3. 猫が魚を取りました。

Neko ga sakana o torimashita.

A cat took the fish.

_____

4. アメリカ人が日本語を話しています。

Amerika-jin ga Nihon-go o hanashite imasu.

Americans are speaking Japanese.

_____

Indirect passive

Indirect passive sentences do not have English equivalents. Unlike direct passive sentences, indirect passive sentences do not shift the speaker's attention to the direct object of the verb. Therefore, the direct object of the verb, if any, does not undergo any changes. Furthermore, the verb can be an intransitive verb such as *to cry* or *to die*. Instead, indirect passive sentences bring the speaker's attention to the person who was indirectly but negatively affected by what happened. In indirect passive sentences, the action performer is marked by the particle に **ni**; the person who was annoyed, inconvenienced, disturbed, troubled, or saddened is treated as the subject, marked by が **ga**, which is often covered by the topic particle は **wa**; and the verb must be in the passive form. For example, compare the two sentences below:

> メアリーさんがマイクさんの手紙を読みました。
> **Mearī-san ga Maiku-san no tegami o yomimashita.**
> *Mary read Mike's letter.* (active)

> マイクさんはメアリーさんに手紙を読まれました。
> **Maiku-san wa Mearī-san ni tegami o yomaremashita.**
> *Mike was unhappy because Mary read his letter.* (indirect passive)

EXERCISE
14·3

Translate the following sentences into English.

1. 兄は昨日雨にふられました。

Ani wa kinō ame ni furaremashita.

_____

2. 私は弟に先に卒業されました。

Watashi wa otōto ni sakini sotsugyō saremashita.

_____

3. 真さんは彼女に泣かれました。

Makoto-san wa kanojo ni nakaremashita.

_____

4. またマイクさんにうちに来られました。

Mata Maiku-san ni uchi ni koraremashita.

_____

5. 猫に魚を取られました。

Neko ni sakana o toraremashita.

_____

6. 試験の時、先生に横に立たれました。

Shiken no toki, sensei ni yoko ni tataremashita.

_____

EXERCISE 14·4

Convert the following sentences into indirect passive in Japanese.

1. 5年前に子供が死にました。

Go-nen mae ni kodomo ga shinimashita.

My child died five years ago.

_____

2. 子供が家出をしました。

Kodomo ga iede o shimashita.

My child ran away from home.

_____

3. 隣の席の男の人がタバコを吸いました。

Tonari no seki no otoko no hito ga tabako o suimashita.

A man in the next seat smoked.

_____

4. 犬が逃げました。

   Inu ga nigemashita.

   My dog ran away.

   _____

5. 私が100点を取ったと言ったら、みんながびっくりしました。

   Watashi ga hyaku-ten o totta to ittara, minna ga bikkuri shimashita.

   When I said I got a 100, everyone was surprised.

   _____

Causative verbs

To form a causative sentence, you need to create a causative verb. You can convert a Japanese verb into a causative verb by dropping the final **ru** or **u** in the dictionary form and adding **saseru** or **aseru**. To conjugate a verb, look at the following table and follow the pattern of the verb with the same ending and in the same category:

	Ending	Dictionary Form	Causative Form
Ru verbs	-eる -eru	かえる **kaeru** (*change*)	かえさせる **kaesaseru**
	-iる -iru	きる **kiru** (*wear*)	きさせる **kisaseru**
U verbs	-す -su	はなす **hanasu** (*speak*)	はなさせる **hanasaseru**
	-く -ku	かく **kaku** (*write*)	かかせる **kakaseru**
	-ぐ -gu	およぐ **oyogu** (*swim*)	およがせる **oyogaseru**
	-む -mu	よむ **yomu** (*read*)	よませる **yomaseru**
	-ぬ -nu	しぬ **shinu** (*die*)	しなせる **shinaseru**
	-ぶ -bu	とぶ **tobu** (*jump*)	とばせる **tobaseru**
	-う -(w)u	かう **kau** (*buy*)	かわせる **kawaseru**
	-る -ru	きる **kiru** (*cut*)	きらせる **kiraseru**
	-つ -tsu	まつ **matsu** (*wait*)	またせる **mataseru**
Irregular verbs		くる **kuru** (*come*)	こさせる **kosaseru**
		する **suru** (*do*)	させる **saseru**

EXERCISE
14·5

Convert each of the following verbs into its causative form, as shown in the example.

EXAMPLE   食べる **taberu** (*eat*)   →   食べさせる **tabesaseru**

1. 書く **kaku** (*write*)   →   _____

2. 読む **yomu** (*read*)   →   _____

3. 運ぶ **hakobu** (*carry*)   → _____

4. 洗う **arau** (*wash*)   → _____

5. 取る **toru** (*take*)   → _____

6. 着る **kiru** (*wear*, **ru** verb)   → _____

7. 切る **kiru** (*cut*, **u** verb)   → _____

8. する **suru** (*do*)   → _____

9. 来る **kuru** (*come*)   → _____

The resulting causative verbs are **ru** verbs, and you can conjugate them accordingly, as in 食べさせる **tabesase-ru**, 食べさせない **tabesase-nai**, 食べさせます **tabesase-masu**, and so on.

Make-causative and *let*-causative

Causative verbs can be either *make*-causative, meaning *to make someone do something* or *let*-causative, meaning *to let someone do something*. Which they mean depends on whether you think the action performer is willing to perform the action or not. For example, in the two sentences below, the first one is understood as *make*-causative and the second one as *let*-causative because washing dishes is usually considered to be work, while reading a comic book is usually considered to be entertainment:

> 母が妹に皿を洗わせました。
> **Haha ga imōto ni sara o arawasemashita.**
> *My mother made my younger sister wash dishes.*

> 母が妹にマンガを読ませました。
> **Haha ga imōto ni manga o yomasemashita.**
> *My mother let my little sister read a comic book.*

As you can see in these sentences, the person who enforces or allows the action appears as the subject noun in a causative sentence. The person who actually performs the action is marked by the particle に **ni** if the verb is transitive but by を **o** if the verb is intransitive. See the contrast between the two sentences below:

> 母が妹に皿を洗わせました。
> **Haha ga imōto ni sara o arawasemashita.**
> *My mother made my younger sister wash dishes.*

> 母は妹を走らせました。
> **Haha wa imōto o hashirasemashita.**
> *My mother made my sister run.*

EXERCISE

14·6

Translate the following sentences into English.

1. 昨日、兄が弟を泣かせました。

   Kinō, ani ga otōto o nakasemashita.

   _____

2. 母を休ませました。

   Haha o yasumasemashita.

   _____

3. 弟は野菜が嫌いですが、母は弟に毎日野菜を食べさせます。

   Otōto wa yasai ga kirai desu ga, haha wa otōto ni mainichi yasai o tabesasemasu.

   _____

4. 弟はチョコレートが大好きです。母は少しなら弟にチョコレートを食べさせます。

   **Otōto wa chokorēto ga daisuki desu. Haha wa sukoshi nara otōto ni chokorēto o
   tabesasemasu.**

   _____

EXERCISE

14·7

Change the following sentences to indicate, in Japanese, that you caused the actions.

1. 妹が部屋を掃除しました。

   Imōto ga heya o sōji shimashita.

   My little sister cleaned her room.

   _____

2. 弟が鞄を持ちました。

   Otōto ga kaban o mochimashita.

   My little brother held my bag.

   _____

3. 子供が薬を飲みました。

   Kodomo ga kusuri o nomimahsita.

   My child took medicine.

   _____

4. 犬が歩きました。

Inu ga arukimashita.

My dog walked.

_____

5. 学生が漢字を練習しました。

Gakusei ga kanji o renshū shimashita.

My student practiced kanji.

_____

Causative with auxiliary verbs of giving and receiving

Let-causative sentences are usually accompanied by auxiliary verbs such as あげる **ageru**, くれる **kureru**, and もらう **morau**, which implicitly show who was benefited by whose kindness. For example:

> 母は私に料理をさせてくれました。でも、てんぷらは作らせてくれませんでした。
> **Haha wa watashi ni ryōri o sasete kuremashita. Demo, tenpura wa tsukurasete kuremasendeshita.**
> *My mother let me cook. However, she did not let me make tempura.*

> 子供に専攻を決めさせてあげます。
> **Kodomo ni senkō o kimesasete agemasu.**
> *I'll let my child decide his major.*

> 父の車は使わせてもらえませんでした。でも、兄の車を使わせてもらいました。
> **Chichi no kuruma wa tsukawasete moraemasendeshita. Demo, ani no kuruma o tsukawasete moraimashita.**
> *I was not allowed to use my father's car. However, I was allowed to use my big brother's car.*

You can use *let*-causative sentences with honorific verbs of giving and receiving to very politely seek permission to do something. All of the following sentences mean *Am I allowed to go home a little bit early today?* For example:

> 今日はちょっと早く帰らせてくださいませんか。
> **Kyō wa chotto hayaku kaerasete kudasai masen ka.**

> 今日はちょっと早く帰らせていただきたいんですが。
> **Kyō wa chotto hayaku kaerasete itadakitai ndesu ga.**

> 今日はちょっと早く帰らせていただけますか。
> **Kyō wa chotto hayaku kaerasete itadakemasu ka.**

Use くれます *kuremasu* to share three things that your parents kindly allowed you to do when you were younger.

1. _____

2. _____

3. _____

Use くれませんでした *kuremasendeshita* to share three things that your parents did not allow you to do when you were younger.

1. _____

2. _____

3. _____

Suppose you want to very politely ask permission to do the following actions. State what you would say, using くださいませんか *kudasai masen ka*.

1. この部屋を使う **kono heya o tsukau** (*to use this room*)

   _____

2. ちょっと休む **chotto yasumu** (*to take a short rest*)

   _____

3. 理由を聞く **riyū o kiku** (*to hear the reason*)

   _____

Causative passive

Make-causative sentences are often converted to passive to indicate *to be made to do something*. Such situations commonly occur when one is being taught, trained, or employed, and they also occur due to obligations that result from many kinds of human relationships. This construction often implicitly shows the discontent of the person who is forced to do something. Compare the following causative sentence and causative-passive sentence:

先生が学生に漢字を練習させました。
Sensei ga gakusei ni kanji o renshū-sasemashita.
The teacher made his students practice kanji. (causative)

学生が先生に漢字を練習させられました。
Gakusei ga sensei ni kanji o renshū-saseraremashita.
The students were made to practice kanji by their teacher. (causative passive)

As you can see, in a causative-passive sentence, the one who was made to do something appears as the subject, the person who enforced the action is marked by the particle に **ni**, and the verb carries both the causative suffix and the passive suffix. You can create a causative-passive verb by inserting **rare** in the causative verb, right before **ru**, as in 食べさせられる **tabe-sase-rare-ru** (*to be made to eat*). However, in case of **u** verbs other than those that end in す **su**, the latter part of the causative suffix せ **se** and the initial part of the passive suffix ら **ra** very commonly merge to become one syllable, さ **sa**. That is, せられる **serareru** is shortened to される **sareru**. To conjugate a verb, look at the following table and follow the pattern of the verb with the same ending and in the same category:

	Ending	Dictionary Form	Causative-Passive Form
Ru verbs	-eる -eru	かえる**kaeru** (*change*)	かえさせられる **kaesaserareru**
	-iる -iru	きる**kiru** (*wear*)	きさせられる **kisaserareru**
U verbs	-す -su	はなす **hanasu** (*speak*)	はなさせられる **hanasaserareru**
	-く -ku	かく **kaku** (*write*)	かかせられる **kakaserareru** かかされる **kakasareru**
	-ぐ -gu	およぐ **oyogu** (*swim*)	およがせられる **oyogaserareru** およがされる **oyogasareru**
	-む -mu	よむ **yomu** (*read*)	よませられる **yomaserareru** よまされる **yomasareru**
	-ぬ -nu	しぬ **shinu** (*die*)	しなせられる **shinaserareru** しなされる **shinasareru**
	-ぶ -bu	とぶ **tobu** (*jump*)	とばせられる **tobaserareru** とばされる **tobasareru**
	-う -(w)u	かう **kau** (*buy*)	かわせられる **kawaserareru** かわされる **kawasareru**
	-る -ru	きる **kiru** (*cut*)	きらせられる **kiraserareru** きらされる **kirasareru**
	-つ -tsu	まつ **matsu** (*wait*)	またせられる **mataserareru** またされる **matasareru**
Irregular verbs		くる **kuru** (*come*)	こさせられる **kosaserareru**
		する **suru** (*do*)	させられる **saserareru**

EXERCISE
14·11

Convert the following verbs into their causative-passive forms. If a contracted form is possible, indicate it also.

EXAMPLE   食べる **taberu** (*eat*)   →   食べさせられる **tabesaserareru**

1. 磨く **migaku** (*polish*)   →   _____

2. 歌う **utau** (*sing*)   →   _____

3. 運ぶ **hakobu** (*carry*)   →   _____

4. 習う **narau** (*learn*)   →   _____

5. 待つ **matsu** (*wait*)   →   _____

6. する **suru** (*do*)   →   _____

7. 来る **kuru** (*come*)   →   _____

EXERCISE
14·12

Translate the following sentences into English.

1. 僕は母に荷物を持たせられました。

   Boku wa haha ni nimotsu o motaseraremashita.

   _____

2. 私は父に書道を習わせられました。

   Watashi wa chichi ni shodō o narawaseraremashita.

   _____

3. カラオケで歌を歌わされました。

   Karaoke de uta o utawasaremashita.

   _____

4. 病院で3時間待たせられました。

   Byōin de san-jikan mataseraremashita.

   _____

5. 高いプレゼントを買わせられました。

   Takai purezento o kawaseraremashita.

   _____

EXERCISE
14·13

In Japanese, indicate that you are made to do each of the following.

1. 犬の世話をする **inu no sewa o suru** (*to take care of a dog*)

   _____

2. 塾に行く **juku ni iku** (*to go to a cram school*)

   _____

3. 文句を聞く **monku o kiku** (*to listen to the complaints*)

   _____

4. 仕事を辞める **shigoto o yameru** (*to quit a job*)

   _____

5. 罰金を払う **bakkin o harau** (*to pay fines*)

   _____

6. 靴を磨く **kutsu o migaku** (*to polish shoes*)

   _____

EXERCISE

14·14

Complete each sentence with the appropriate particle. For a greater challenge, cover the English translations as you work on this exercise.

1. マンガ _____ 読みました。

   Manga _____ yomimashita.

   I read a comic book.

2. アメリカではマンガ _____ 読まれています。

   Amerika de wa manga _____ yomarete imasu.

   Comic books are being read in the United States.

3. 私は手紙 _____ 兄 _____ 読まれました。とても嫌でした。

   Watashi wa tegami _____ ani _____ yomaremashita. Totemo iya deshita.

   My letter was read by my brother. I was very annoyed by it.

4. 先生は日本語の本を学生 _____ 読ませました。

   Sensei wa Nihon-go no hon o gakusei _____ yomasemashita.

   The teacher made her students read a Japanese book.

5. 私は先生 _____ 中国語の本を読ませられました。

   Watashi wa sensei _____ Chūgoku-go no hon o yomaseraremashita.

   I was made to read a Chinese book by my teacher.

6. 先生は私 _____ 先生の本 _____ 読ませてくださいました。

   Sensei wa watashi _____ sensei no hon _____ yomasete kudasaimashita.

   My teacher kindly allowed me to read her book.

Honorifics

·15·

Japanese has a rich and complex honorific system that is very sensitive to the distinction between one's in-group and out-group. A person's family members definitely belong to his in-group. Close friends and even those who work or study in the same institution may also belong to his in-group, depending on the context. Everyone else belongs to his out-group. The Japanese honorific system employs a variety of words, prefixes, suffixes, and sentence endings that can apply to verbs, nouns, adjectives, and sentence constructions and fall under five categories:

- **Respectful language:** respectfully describes the referent's or addressee's actions, states, belongings, and so on. For example, いらっしゃる **irassharu** (*to go*).
- **Humble language:** humbly describes the speaker's or speaker's in-group member's actions, belongings, and so on, which are directed to the referent or addressee. For example, 伺う **ukagau** (*to go*).
- **Courteous language:** courteously describes the speaker's or others' actions, belongings, and so on. For example, 参る **mairu** (*to go*).
- **Polite language:** makes utterances polite with grammatical items such as です **desu** (*to be*) and ます **masu** (polite suffix).
- **Word beautification:** graciously refers to things and concepts. For example, お野菜 **o-yasai** (*vegetables*).

Special honorific verbs

The honorific system applies most extensively to verbs. There are some grammatical constructions and suffixes that apply to verbs, but there are also specific honorific vocabulary words. The following are very commonly used special honorific words:

Plain/Neutral Verb	Respectful Verb	Humble/Courteous Verb
いる **iru** (*exist*)	いらっしゃる **irassharu**[1]	おる **oru** (courteous)
行く **iku** (*go*)	いらっしゃる **irassharu**[1]	参る **mairu**[2] (courteous) 伺う **ukagau**[2] (humble)
来る **kuru** (*come*)	いらっしゃる **irassharu**[1]	参る **mairu** (courteous)
する **suru** (*do*)	なさる **nasaru**[1]	致す **itasu** (courteous)
食べる **taberu** (*eat*) 飲む **nomu** (*drink*)	召し上がる **meshiagaru**	頂く **itadaku** (humble)

continued

Plain/Neutral Verb	Respectful Verb	Humble/Courteous Verb
見る miru (*look*)	ご覧になる go-ran ni naru	拝見する haiken suru[3] (*humble*)
言う iu (*say*)	おっしゃる ossharu[1]	申し上げる mōshiageru (*humble*) 申す mōsu (*courteous*)
知る shiru (*know*)	ご存知だ gozonji da	存じ上げる zonjiageru (*humble*) 存じる zonjiru (*courteous*)
あげる ageru (*give*) やる yaru (*give*)	not applicable	差し上げる sashiageru (*humble*)
くれる kureru (*give*)	下さる kudasaru[1]	not applicable
尋ねる tazuneru (*ask*)	not applicable	伺う ukagau (*humble*)
ある aru (*exist, have*)	not applicable	ごさる gozaru[1] (*humble/courteous*)
…だ da (copula)	…でいらっしゃる de irassharu[1]	…でござる de gozaru[1] (*humble/courteous*)

[1] These verbs are **u** verbs, but り **ri** that appears right before the polite suffix (ます **masu**, ません **masen**, etc.) changes to い **i**, as in いらっしゃいます **irasshaimasu**, なさいます **nasaimasu**, おっしゃいます **osshaimasu**, and 下さいます **kudasaimasu**. In addition, the plain command form of なさる **nasaru** is なさい **nasai**.
[2] If the speaker is going to the place of the addressee, use 伺う **ukagau** rather than 参る **mairu**.
[3] Use 拝見する **haiken suru** only if the item to be seen belongs to the addressee.

The following are examples of the use of honorific verbs:

田中さんはいらっしゃいますか。
Tanaka-san wa irasshaimasu ka.
Is Mr. Tanaka there?

では、明日伺います。
De wa, asu ukagaimasu.
Then I will come to visit you tomorrow.

今から叔父の所に参ります。
Ima kara oji no tokoro ni mairimasu.
I'm now going to go to my uncle's house.

EXERCISE
15·1

In Japanese, change the following sentences to make them sound more polite by using special respectful verbs.

1. 食べませんか。

Tabemasen ka.

Wouldn't you like to eat?

2. 先生は今日は来ません。

   Sensei wa kyō wa kimasen.

   The professor will not come (here) today.

   _____

3. 社長さんはいますか。

   Shachō-san wa imasu ka.

   Is the president here?

   _____

4. 見てください。

   Mite kudasai.

   Please take a look at it.

   _____

...られる (r)areru (respectful form of verbs)

You can convert a verb from the dictionary form into its respectful form by dropping the final **ru** or **u** and adding **rareru** or **areru**. This is the same form as the passive form discussed in Chapter 14. To conjugate a verb, look at the following table and follow the pattern of the verb with the same ending and in the same category:

	Ending	Dictionary Form	Respectful Form
Ru verbs	-える -eru	かえる **kaeru** (*change*)	かえられる **kaerareru**
	-いる -iru	きる **kiru** (*wear*)	きられる **kirareru**
U verbs	-す -su	はなす **hanasu** (*speak*)	はなされる **hanasareru**
	-く -ku	かく **kaku** (*write*)	かかれる **kakareru**
	-ぐ -gu	およぐ **oyogu** (*swim*)	およがれる **oyogareru**
	-む -mu	よむ **yomu** (*read*)	よまれる **yomareru**
	-ぬ -nu	しぬ **shinu** (*die*)	しなれる **shinareru**
	-ぶ -bu	とぶ **tobu** (*jump*)	とばれる **tobareru**
	-う -(w)u	かう **kau** (*buy*)	かわれる **kawareru**
	-る -ru	きる **kiru** (*cut*)	きられる **kirareru**
	-つ -tsu	まつ **matsu** (*wait*)	またれる **matareru**
Irregular verbs		くる **kuru** (*come*)	こられる **korareru**
		する **suru** (*do*)	される **sareru**

For example:

> この本は先生が書かれたのですか。
> **Kono hon wa sensei ga kakareta no desu ka.**
> *Did you write this book, Professor?*

Note that the respectful form of いる **iru** (*to be*) is おられる **orareru**, which is replaced by いらっしゃる **irassharu** depending on the context.

EXERCISE

15·2

In Japanese, change the following sentences to make them sound more polite by using the respectful forms discussed earlier.

1. メアリーさんと話しましたか。

   Mearī-san to hanashimashita ka.

   Did you talk with Mary?

   _____

2. ゴルフはしますか。

   Gorufu wa shimasu ka.

   Do you play golf?

   _____

3. 今日の新聞を読みましたか。

   Kyō no shinbun o yomimashita ka.

   Did you read today's newspaper?

   _____

お + stem + になる o . . . ni naru (respectful)

To respectfully express the referent's or the addressee's action, you can use a verb with the prefix お **o** and になる **ni naru**. For example:

> この本は先生がお書きになったのですか。
> **Kono hon wa sensei ga o-kaki ni natta no desu ka.**
> *Did you write this book, Professor?*

Using お...になる **o...ni naru**, *rephrase the following sentences in Japanese to make them more polite.*

1. ゆっくり休みましたか。

   Yukkuri yasumimashita ka.

   Did you rest (well, taking enough time)?

   _____

2. 山田さんと会いましたか。

   Yamada-san to aimashita ka.

   Did you meet with Ms. Yamada?

   _____

3. もう決めましたか。

   Mō kimemashita ka.

   Have you already decided?

   _____

4. 社長はもう帰りました。

   Shachō wa mō kaerimashita.

   The president has already returned home.

   _____

Some verbs that are Sino-Japanese words (words of Chinese origin) can be used in this construction, but ご **go** must be used instead of お **o**. For example:

> 社長が今ご到着になりました。
> **Shachō ga ima go-tōchaku ni narimashita.**
> *The president (of the company) has just arrived.*

お + stem + する o...suru (humble)

To express your or your in-group member's action in a humble manner, use a verb in the stem form, preceded by お **o** and followed by the verb する **suru**. The verb する **suru** can be replaced by いたす **itasu**. Do not use this construction if your action does not affect the other person at all. For example, 私はお帰(りい)たします **Watashi wa o-kaeri (ita)shimasu** (*I will return home*) is not appropriate. Use this construction when your action somehow affect the other person. For example:

> 電話をお借り(いた)します。
> **Denwa o o-kari (ita)shimasu.**
> *I'd like to use your telephone.*

> 兄がお荷物をお預かり(いた)します。
> **Ani ga o-nimotsu o o-azukari (ita)shimasu.**
> *My older brother will keep your luggage.*

*Using お…いたす **o…itasu**, rephrase the following sentences in Japanese to make them sound humble.*

1. 私が調べます。

   Watashi ga shirabemasu.

   I will investigate it.

   _____

2. 私が運びました。

   Watashi ga hakobimashita.

   I carried them.

   _____

3. 私が作りましょう。

   Watashi ga tsukurimashō.

   I will make it.

   _____

4. 私が集めましょうか。

   Watashi ga atsumemashō ka.

   Shall I collect them?

   _____

Some verbs that are Sino-Japanese words can be used in this construction, but ご **go** must be used instead of お **o**. For example:

ご協力いたしますよ。
Go-kyōryoku itashimasu yo.
I'll cooperate with you.

In each of the following, choose the correct answer from the options in parentheses.

1. 私がお運び（になります, いたします）。

   Watashi ga o-hakobi (ni narimasu, itashimasu).

   I will carry (them).

2. 先生がお書き（になりました, いたしました）。

   Sensei ga o-kaki (ni narimashita, itashimashita).

   The professor wrote it.

3. 母がお送り（になりました，いたしました）。

Haha ga o-okuri (ni narimashita, itashimashita).

My mother sent it (to him/you).

4. 妹が（召し上がりました，頂きました）。

Imōto ga (meshiagarimashita, itadakimashita).

My younger sister ate (it).

5. 私が（いらっしゃいます，伺います）。

Watashi ga (irasshaimasu, ukagaimasu).

I will come (to your place).

Asking for permission very politely

The *let*-causative discussed in Chapter 14 is often used to very politely seek permission to do something. For example, instead of saying うちに帰ってもいいですか **Uchi ni kaette mo ii desu ka**, you can say any of the following:

うちに帰らせてください。
Uchi ni kaerasete kudasai.
Please let me go home.

うちに帰らせていただけませんか。
Uchi ni kaerasete itadakemasen ka.
Could I go home? (Literally: *Could I receive your letting me go home?*)

うちに帰らせていただきたいんですが。
Uchi ni kaerasete itadaki-tai n desu ga.
I'd like to go home. (Literally: *I want to receive your letting me go home, but . . .*)

EXERCISE
15·6

Make the following questions polite by using a causative verb and いただけませんか *itadakemasen ka so you can politely ask for permission in Japanese.*

1. 今日は早く帰ってもいいですか。

Kyō wa hayaku kaette mo ii desu ka.

Is it okay to go home early today?

_____

2. この車を使ってもいいですか。

Kono kuruma o tsukatte mo ii desu ka.

Is it okay to use this car?

_____

3. その手紙を読んでもいいですか。

Sono tegami o yonde mo ii desu ka.

Is it okay to read that letter?

4. ここで待ってもいいですか。

Koko de matte mo ii desu ka.

Is it okay to wait here?

Making a request very politely

To very politely request that someone do something, you can add ください **kudasai** after a verb in the stem form preceded by お **o**. So, instead of saying 入ってください **haitte kudasai**, you can say:

お入りください。
O-hairi kudasai.
Please come in.

In addition, you can use a verb in the te form followed by いただけませんか **itadakemasen ka** or いただきたいんですが **itadakitai n desu ga**. For example:

この手紙を英語に翻訳していただけませんか。
Kono tegami o eigo ni hon'yaku shite itadakemasen ka.
Could you please translate this letter into English? (Literally: *Couldn't I receive your translating this letter into English?*)

この手紙を翻訳していただきたいんですが。
Kono tegami o hon'yaku shite itadaki-tai n desu ga.
I'd like you to translate this letter. (Literally: *I want to receive your translating this letter, but . . . .*)

EXERCISE
15·7

Make the following requests politely in Japanese by using いただけませんか *itadakemasen ka.*

1. 推薦状を書いてください。

Suisenjō o kaite kudasai.

Please write a letter of recommendation.

2. 車を貸してください。

Kuruma o kashite kudasai.

Please lend me your car.

3. タバコを吸わないでください。

Tabako o suwanai de kudasai.

Please do not smoke.

_____

4. 考えてみてください。

Kangaete mite kudasai.

Please try thinking (about it).

_____

EXERCISE
15·8

Translate each of the following sentences into English.

1. 今日は早く帰らせていただけないでしょうか。

Kyō wa hayaku kaerasete itadakenai deshō ka.

_____

2. どうぞお座りください。

Dōzo o-suwari kudasai.

_____

3. メールアドレスをお教えくださいませんか。

Mēru adoresu o o-oshie kudasai masen ka.

_____

4. 今日で会社を辞めさせていただきたいんです。

Kyō de kaisha o yamasasete itadaki-tai n desu.

_____

5. 少々お待ちください。

Shōshō o-machi kudasai.

_____

Using お **o** and ご **go** before a noun

You can place the polite prefixes お **o** and ご **go** before a noun to show respect to the person you're talking to or about or to the things that belong to that person. Make sure not to use a polite prefix for yourself or for your in-group members. The basic rule is to use お **o** before a native Japanese word and ご **go** before a Sino-Japanese word, but there are numerous exceptions. The following are some of the frequently used words with お **o** or ご **go**:

- お名前 **o-namae** (*name*)
- ご住所 **go-jūsho** (*address*)
- お電話番号 **o-denwa-bangō** (*telephone number*)
- お勉強 **o-benkyō** (*study*)
- お車 **o-kuruma** (*car*)
- ご結婚 **go-kekkon** (*marriage*)
- お食事 **o-shokuji** (*meal*)
- ご家族 **go-kazoku** (*family*)
- ご注文 **go-chūmon** (*order*)

Some nouns are always preceded by a polite prefix, regardless of who is talking to whom or to whom an item belongs to. For example, the following words almost always appear with a polite prefix:

- お金 **o-kane** (*money*)
- お茶 **o-cha** (*tea*)
- お湯 **o-yu** (*hot water*)
- ご飯 **go-han** (*(cooked) rice*)

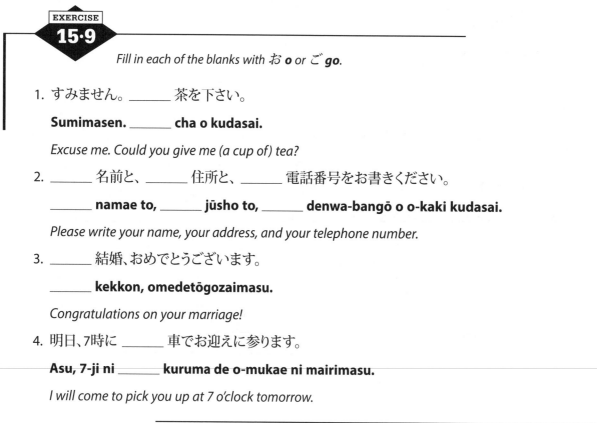

EXERCISE
15·9

Fill in each of the blanks with お **o** *or* ご **go**.

1. すみません。＿＿＿＿ 茶を下さい。

   Sumimasen. ＿＿＿＿ cha o kudasai.

   Excuse me. Could you give me (a cup of) tea?

2. ＿＿＿＿ 名前と、＿＿＿＿ 住所と、＿＿＿＿ 電話番号をお書きください。

   ＿＿＿＿ namae to, ＿＿＿＿ jūsho to, ＿＿＿＿ denwa-bangō o o-kaki kudasai.

   Please write your name, your address, and your telephone number.

3. ＿＿＿＿ 結婚、おめでとうございます。

   ＿＿＿＿ kekkon, omedetōgozaimasu.

   Congratulations on your marriage!

4. 明日、7時に ＿＿＿＿ 車でお迎えに参ります。

   Asu, 7-ji ni ＿＿＿＿ kuruma de o-mukae ni mairimasu.

   I will come to pick you up at 7 o'clock tomorrow.

Family terms

Family terms have different forms, depending on the use. You use plain forms such as 父 **chichi** (*father*) and 母 **haha** (*mother*) to refer to your own family members in front of outsiders. You can use honorific forms such as お父さん **otōsan** (*father*) and お母さん **okāsan** (*mother*) to politely refer to someone else's family members. See the following table for examples:

Meaning	Plain Form	Honorific Form
grandfather	祖父 **sofu**	おじいさん **ojīsan**
grandmother	祖母 **sobo**	おばあさん **obāsan**
uncle	おじ **oji**	おじさん **ojisan**
aunt	おば **oba**	おばさん **obasan**
husband	主人 **shujin**	ご主人 **go-shujin**
wife	家内 **kanai**, 妻 **tsuma**	奥さん **okusan**
child	子供 **kodomo**	お子さん **okosan**
son	息子 **musuko**	息子さん **musukosan**
daughter	娘 **musume**	お嬢さん **ojōsan**
grandchildren	孫 **mago**	お孫さん **omagosan**
parents	両親 **ryōshin**	ご両親 **go-ryōshin**
siblings	兄弟 **kyōdai**	ご兄弟 **go-kyōdai**
relatives	親戚 **shinseki**	ご親戚 **go-shinseki**

Honorific forms for adjectives

You can use the prefixes お **o** and ご **go** with adjectives just as you do with nouns. For example:

最近はお忙しいですか。
Saikin wa o-isogashii desu ka.
Have you been busy lately?

お肌がおきれいですね。
O-hada ga o-kirei desu ne.
You have beautiful skin.

ご立派です。
Go-rippa desu.
You are great.

ピアノがお上手ですね。
Piano ga o-jōzu desu ne.
You are good at (playing) the piano.

Honorific/polite question words

Some question words have polite counterparts. For example, the polite counterparts of だれ **dare** (*who*) and どこ **doko** (*where*) are どなた **donata** and どちら **dochira**, respectively. Similarly, the polite counterpart of どう **dō** (*how*) is いかが **ikaga** (*how*). For example:

あの方はどなたですか。
Ano kata wa donata desu ka.
Who is that person?

どちらへいらっしゃるんですか。
Dochira e irassharu n desu ka.
Where are you going?

ブラウンさんはどちらからですか。
Buraun-san wa dochira kara desu ka.
Where is Mr. Brown from?

ご旅行はいかがでしたか。
Go-ryokō wa ikaga deshita ka.
How was your trip?

コーヒーはいかがですか。
Kōhī wa ikaga desu ka.
How about some coffee?

EXERCISE
15·10

Complete the following sentences using question words in honorific style.

1. _____ で働いていらっしゃるんですか。

   _____ **de hataraite irassharu n desu ka.**

   Where do you work?

2. お仕事は _____ ですか。

   O-shigoto wa _____ **desu ka.**

   How is your job?

3. 担当の方は _____ ですか。

   Tantō no kata wa _____ **desu ka.**

   Who is in charge of this?

Review exercises

1 Introducing Japanese sounds, word order, and writing systems

EXERCISE
16·1

Read the following words written in hiragana aloud. Romanization is provided in the answer key.

1. やま   *mountain*
2. じかん   *time*
3. てんぷら   *tempura*
4. きって   *postage stamps*
5. でんしゃ   *train*

EXERCISE
16·2

Read the following words written in katakana aloud. Romanization is provided in the answer key.

1. アメリカ   *America*
2. イギリス   *England*
3. ブラジル   *Brazil*
4. ボストン   *Boston*
5. ピアノ   *piano*
6. ゲーム   *game*

EXERCISE 16·3

Read the following Japanese words written in kanji aloud. Romanization is provided in the answer key.

1. 私   *I*
2. 人   *person*
3. 日本人   *a Japanese person*
4. 三人   *three people*
5. 高い   *expensive*
6. 学ぶ   *to learn*

EXERCISE 16·4

Reorder the items in each set to form a grammatical sentence.

1. です, 日本人, 私は

   desu, Nihon-jin, watashi wa

   I am Japanese.

   _____

2. じゃありません, 私は, 学生

   ja arimasen, watashi wa, gakusei

   I'm not a student.

   _____

3. 来た, 川口さんが, うちに

   kita, Kawaguchi-san ga, uchi ni

   Mr. Kawaguchi came to my home.

   _____

4. アンさんを, 誘った, ケンさんが

   Ann-san o, sasotta, Ken-san ga

   Ken invited Ann.

   _____

5. 犬が, 食べた, ケーキを

   Inu ga, tabeta, kēki o

   The dog ate the cake.

   _____

2 Nouns

**EXERCISE
16·5**

Choose the appropriate item in parentheses.

1. (この, これ, nothing) はスキャナーです。(スキャナー **sukyanā:** scanner)

   (Kono, Kore, nothing) wa sukyanā desu.

2. (あの, あれ, nothing) 人は先生です。

   (Ano, Are, nothing) hito wa Nihon-jin desu.

3. (その, それ, nothing) は私のペンです。

   (Sono, Sore, nothing) wa watashi no pen desu.

4. 私の犬は(あの, あれ, nothing)です。

   Watashi no inu wa (ano, are, nothing) desu.

5. (あの, あれ, nothing) 山田さんは学生です。

   (Ano, Are, nothing) Yamada-san wa gakusei desu.

**EXERCISE
16·6**

Translate the following sentences into Japanese.

1. This one is my mother's book.

   _____

   _____

2. That one is Ann's mother's book.

   _____

   _____

3. Mr. Tanaka is my father's friend's friend.

   _____

   _____

4. This is a children's book.

   _____

   _____

5. This is a children's book in China.

   _____

   _____

Which noun, appearing after the particle の, can be omitted if contextually understood in each of the following sentences?

1. あれは私の本です。

   Are wa watashi no hon desu.

   That one is my book.

   _____

2. 私の車はそれです。

   Watashi no kuruma wa sore desu.

   My car is that one (near you).

   _____

3. 父の車はあれです。

   Chichi no kuruma wa are desu.

   My father's car is that one.

   _____

4. あれは山田さんの友達のお父さんの車です。

   Are wa Yamada-san no tomodachi no otōsan no kuruma desu.

   That one over there is Ms. Yamada's friend's father's car.

   _____

5. これは日本の会社の建物です。

   Kore wa Nihon no kaisha no tatemono desu.

   This is a building that belongs to a Japanese company.

   _____

3 Numbers

EXERCISE
16·8

Give the pronunciation of each of the following numbers.

1.   6 _____

2.   15 _____

3.   23 _____

4. 3,333 _____

5. 99,999 _____

EXERCISE
16·9

Specify the number of each of the following items, using appropriate class counters such as 匹 **hiki** (the class counter for cats), *as in* 2匹 **ni-hiki**.

1. five dogs _____

2. three students _____

3. two apples _____

4. five books _____

5. three pens _____

EXERCISE
16·10

Give the pronunciation of each of the following time references in Japanese.

1. 5 o'clock _____

2. 2:20 pm _____

3. 8:15 am _____

4. April 1st _____

5. December 20th _____

Give the following amounts and quantities in Japanese.

1. 5 hours _____

2. 4 months _____

3. 100 yen _____

4. 9 pages _____

5. 3 minutes _____

4 Basic verb forms

*Convert the following u-verbs into the **masu** form.*

EXAMPLE 　　生まれる **umareru** (to be born) → 生まれます **umaremasu**

1. 話す **hanasu** (to talk) 　　→ _____

2. 運ぶ **hakobu** (to carry) 　→ _____

3. 買う **kau** (to buy) 　　　　→ _____

4. 取る **toru** (to take) 　　　→ _____

5. 待つ **matsu** (to wait) 　　→ _____

*Convert the following ru-verbs into the **masu** form.*

EXAMPLE 　　貸す **kasu** (to loan) 　→ 　貸します **kashimasu**

1. 食べる **taberu** (to eat) 　　　　→ _____

2. 寝る **neru** (to sleep) 　　　　　→ _____

3. 変える **kaeru** (to change) 　　　→ _____

4. 着る **kiru** (to wear) 　　　　　→ _____

5. 借りる **kariru** (to borrow) 　　→ _____

EXERCISE 16·14

Convert the following verbs, which may be ru-verbs or u-verbs, into the **masu** form.

EXAMPLE 飲む **nomu** (to drink) → 飲みます **nomimasu**

1. 着る **kiru** (to wear, ru-verb) → _____
2. 切る **kiru** (to cut, u-verb) → _____
3. 変える **kaeru** (to change, ru-verb) → _____
4. 帰る **kaeru** (to go home, u-verb) → _____
5. いる **iru** (to need, u-verb) → _____

EXERCISE 16·15

Convert the following verbs into the **nai** form.

EXAMPLE 出る **deru** (to leave somewhere) → 出ない **denai**

1. 書く **kaku** (to write) → _____
2. 読む **yomu** (to read) → _____
3. 会う **au** (to meet) → _____
4. ある **aru** (to exist) → _____
5. いる **iru** (to exist) → _____

EXERCISE 16·16

Convert the following verbs into the **ta** form (the plain past affirmative form).

EXAMPLE 開ける **akeru** (to open) → 開けた **aketa**

1. 飛ぶ **tobu** (to fly) → _____
2. 見る **miru** (to look) → _____
3. 言う **iu** (to say) → _____
4. 来る **kuru** (to come) → _____
5. する **suru** (to do) → _____

Convert each of the following verbs into the potential form.

EXAMPLE　　　食べる **taberu** (to eat)　→　食べられる **taberareru** (to be able to eat)

1. 泳ぐ **oyogu** (to swim)　　→　　_____

2. 寝る **neru** (to sleep)　　→　　_____

3. 起きる **okiru** (to get up)　→　　_____

4. 動く **ugoku** (to move)　　→　　_____

5. 持つ **motsu** (to hold)　　→　　_____

Convert the following phrases into the progressive form.

EXAMPLE　　　歩く **aruku** (to walk)　→ 歩いています **aruite imasu** (I am walking)

1. 泳ぐ **oyogu** (to swim)　　　　　　　　　→　_____

2. 休む **yasumu** (to take a rest)　　　　　　→　_____

3. 走る **hashiru** (to run)　　　　　　　　　→　_____

4. かたづける **katadzukeru** (to put things away)　→　_____

5. 考える **kangaeru** (to think about something)　→　_____

Convert the following Japanese sentences into polite counterparts.

EXAMPLE　　　あれは犬だ。 **Are wa inu da.** (That is a dog.)
　　　　　　　→ あれは犬です。 **Are wa inu desu.**

1. これは私の本じゃない。 **Kore wa watashi no hon ja nai.** (This is not my book.)

→ _____

_____

2. 昨日はコーヒーを飲まなかった。**kinō wa kōhī o nomanakatta.** (I did not drink coffee yesterday.)

→ _____

_____

3. カタカナが書ける。**Katakana ga kakeru.** (I can write katakana.)

→ _____

_____

4. 兄は泳げない。**Ani wa oyogenai.** (My brother cannot swim.)

→ _____

_____

5. スミスさんは空手ができる。**Sumisu-san wa karate ga dekiru.** (Mr. Smith can do karate.)

→ _____

_____

5 Verb types

Choose the appropriate item in parentheses.

1. 昨日、火事が（ありました, いました）。

   Kinō, kaji ga (arimashita, imashita).

   There was a fire yesterday.

2. 明日、数学の試験が（あります, います）。

   Ashita, sūgaku no shiken ga (arimasu, imasu).

   I have a math exam tomorrow.

3. 私は妹が二人（あります, います）。

   Watashi wa imōto ga futari (arimasu, imasu).

   I have two younger sisters.

4. あそこに猫が（あります, います）。

   Asoko ni neko ga (arimasu, imasu).

   There is a cat over there.

5. 富士山を見たことが（あります, います）。

   Fujisan o mita koto ga (arimasu, imasu).

   I have seen Mt. Fuji.

Fill in the blanks with either が **ga** *or* を **o.**

1. 窓 _____ あきました。

   Mado _____ akimashita.

   The window opened.

2. 窓 _____ あけました。

   Mado _____ akemashita.

   (I) opened the window.

3. 富士山 _____ 見えました。

   Fujisan _____ miemashita.

   (I) saw Mt. Fuji.

4. 富士山 _____ 見ました。

   Fujisan _____ mimashita.

   (I) saw Mt. Fuji.

5. かばんにペン _____ 入れました。

   Kaban ni pen _____ iremashita.

   (I) put a pen in (my) bag.

Choose the appropriate item in parentheses.

1. 私は妹に本を (あげました, くれました)。

   Watashi wa imōto ni hon o (agemashita, kuremashita).

2. 田中さんは妹にチョコレートを (あげました, くれました)。

   Tanaka-san wa imōto ni chokorēto o (agemashita, kuremashita).

3. 妹は母から1万円 (くれました, もらいました)。

   Imōto wa haha kara ichi-man-en (kuremashita, moraimashita).

4. 私は先生に本を (もらいました, いただきました)。

   Watashi wa sensei ni hon o (moraimashita, itadakimashita).

5. 山田さんが私に数学を教えて (くれました, もらいました)。

   Yamada-san ga watashi ni sūgaku o oshiete (kuremashita, moraimashita).

6 Auxiliaries that follow verbs in the te form

EXERCISE
16·23

Choose the appropriate item in parentheses.

1. あしたは母の誕生日です。プレゼントを買って（行きました, おきました）。

   Ashita wa haha no tanjōbi desu. Purezento o katte (ikimashita, okimashita).

   Tomorrow is my mother's birthday. I bought a present ...

2. もう９月です。すずしくなって（きました, ありました）。

   Mō ku-gatsu desu. Suzushiku natte (kimashita, arimashita).

   It's already September. It ... cool ...

3. へんですね。窓が開けて（もらいますよ, ありますよ）。

   Hen desu ne. Mado ga akete (moraimasu yo, arimasu yo).

   It's strange. The window is ... open ...

4. 高い時計をなくして（おきました, しまいました）。

   Takai tokei o nakushite (okimashita, shimaimashita).

   I lost an expensive watch ...

5. おいしいですよ。食べて（みて, すぎて）ください。

   Oishii desu yo. Tabete (mite, sugite) kudasai.

   It's delicious, I tell you. Please eat ...

EXERCISE
16·24

Translate the following sentences into Japanese.

1. I want a new car.

   _____

   _____

2. I want to sleep.

   _____

   _____

3. I want to go to Canada.

   _____

   _____

4. I want my little brother to study Japanese.

   _____

   _____

5. I want my little brother to make his room clean.

   _____

   _____

7 Particles

*Complete each of the following sentences with が **ga** or を **o**.*

1. マイクさん _____ 来ました。

   Maiku-san _____ kimashita.

   Mike came.

2. マイクさん _____ 誘いました。

   Maiku san _____ sasoimashita.

   (I) invited Mike.

3. あそこにマイクさん _____ いますよ。

   Asoko ni Maiku-san _____ imasu yo.

   Mike is over there.

4. 車 _____ 買いました。

   Kuruma _____ kaimashita.

   (I) bought a car.

5. 車 _____ ほしいです。

   Kuruma _____ hoshii desu.

   I want a car.

EXERCISE 16·26

Complete each of the following sentences with を **o**, *に* **ni**, *or で* **de**.

1. 車 _____ ボストン _____ 行きました。

   Kuruma _____ Bosuton _____ ikimashita.

   (I) went to Boston by car.

2. 手 _____ すし _____ 食べました。

   Te _____ sushi _____ tabemashita.

   (I) ate sushi by hand.

3. クレジットカード _____ テレビ _____ 買いました。

   Kurejittokādo _____ terebi _____ kaimashita.

   I bought a TV with (my) credit card.

4. テーブルの下 _____ 猫がいます。

   Tēburu no shita _____ neko ga imasu.

   There is a cat under the table.

5. 日本 _____ 日本語 _____ 勉強しました。

   Nihon _____ Nihongo _____ benkyō shimashita.

   I studied Japanese in Japan.

EXERCISE 16·27

Select the appropriate item in the parentheses.

1. 病院 (で, まで) 歩きました。

   Byōin (de, made) arukimashita.

   I walked to the hospital.

2. テレビ (と, や, か) 冷蔵庫を買いました。

   Terebi (to, ya, ka) reizōko o kaimashita.

   I bought a TV, a refrigerator, etc.

3. 日本（から, へ）来ました。

Nihon (kara, e) kimashita.

(I) came from Japan.

4. テニスが好きです。水泳（は, も）好きです。

Tenisu ga suki desu. Suiei (wa, mo) sukidesu.

I like tennis. I also like swimming.

5. あのレストランでアイスランド（の, が）料理を食べました。

Ano resutoran de Aisurando (no, ga) ryōri o tabemashita.

I ate Icelandic cuisine at that restaurant.

EXERCISE
16·28

Complete the Japanese sentences so that they match the meaning of the
English sentences provided.

1. 弟は寝て _____ 。

Otōto wa nete _____ .

My younger brother does nothing but sleep.

2. 自転車しか _____ 。

Jitensha shika _____ .

I only have a bicycle.

3. 姉は高いもの _____ 。

Ane wa takai mono _____ .

My older sister even buys expensive things.

4. 去年、中国に行きました。韓国 _____ 。

Kyonen, Chūgoku ni ikimashita. Kankoku _____ .

(I) went to China last year. (I) also went to South Korea.

5. クッキー _____ 。

Kukkī _____ .

(I) just ate cookies.

8 Adjectives and adverbs

EXERCISE
16·29

Translate the following sentences into Japanese.

1. Ken is a serious student.

   _____

   _____

2. This *kanji* is not very difficult.

   _____

   _____

3. Tanaka-san is kind and smart.

   _____

   _____

4. Please write neatly.

   _____

   _____

5. Please be quiet.

   _____

   _____

EXERCISE
16·30

Ask the following questions in Japanese.

1. Which is easier, Chinese or Korean?

   _____

   _____

2. Which do you like better, watching movies or reading books?

   _____

   _____

3. Out of all the fruit, what do you like the best?

_____

_____

4. Among strawberries, bananas, and peaches, which do you like the best?

_____

_____

5. Who is the tallest: Ann, Mike, or Tom?

_____

_____

9 Sentence types

Complete the following sentences with だれ **dare**, どこ **doko**, 何 **nani**, いつ **itsu**, *or* どう**dō**.

1. 朝御飯は _____ で食べましたか。

   Asa-gohan wa _____ de tabemashita ka.

   Where did (you) eat (your) breakfast?

2. 昨日の晩御飯は _____ を食べましたか。

   Kinō no ban-gohan wa _____ o tabemashita ka.

   What did you eat for supper yesterday?

3. 昨日の試験は _____ でしたか。

   Kinō no shiken wa _____ deshita ka.

   How was yesterday's exam?

4. 試験は _____ ですか。

   Shiken wa _____ desu ka.

   When is (your) exam?

5. その本は _____ からもらいましたか。

   Sono hon wa _____ kara moraimashita ka.

   From whom did you get that book?

Translate the following sentences into Japanese.

1. There was someone in that room.

   _____

   _____

2. Did you go anywhere during summer vacation?

   _____

   _____

3. I did not go anywhere yesterday.

   _____

   _____

4. I did not eat anything yesterday.

   _____

   _____

5. Did you talk with anyone yesterday?

   _____

   _____

Complete the following sentences appropriately.

1. 今日は雨が降る _____ しれません。傘を持って行ってください。

   Kyō wa ame ga furu _____ shiremasen. Kasa o motteitte kudasai.

   It may rain today. Please bring an umbrella with you.

2. 東京で地震があった _____ ですよ。

   Tōkyō de jishin ga atta _____ desu yo.

   They say that there was an earthquake in Tokyo.

3. あのレストランはおいしい _____ 。いっしょに行きましょう。

   Ano resutoran wa oishii _____ . Isshoni ikimashō.

   That restaurant is probably good. Let's go there together.

4. モントリオールの友達のうちに _____ つもりです。いっしょに行きませんか。

   Montoriōru no tomodachi no uchi ni _____ tsumori desu. Isshoni ikimasen ka.

   I plan to go to my friend's house in Montreal. Why don't you come (go) with me?

5. 何かかくしている _____ ですね。見せなさい。

   Nanika kakukshite iru _____ desu ne. Misenasai.

   You appear to be hiding something, don't you? Show (it) to me.

6. ボタンを _____ と説明書に書いてあります。

   Botan o _____ to setsumeisho ni kaite arimasu.

   The instruction manual says to press the button.

10   Complex words and phrases

EXERCISE
16·34

Complete the following sentences with やすい **yasui**, にくい **nikui**, or たい **tai**.

1. カタカナは書き _____ です。

   Katakana wa kaki _____ desu.

   Katakana is easy to write.

2. 田中さんはちょっと話し _____ です。

   Tanaka-san wa chotto hanashi _____ desu.

   Mr. Tanaka is a bit hard to talk to.

3. 祖母に会い _____ です。

   Sobo ni ai _____ desu.

   (I) want to see my grandmother.

4. ロブスターは食べ _____ です。

   Robusutā wa tabe _____ desu.

   Lobsters are difficult to eat.

5. てんぷらが食べ _____ です。

   Tenpura ga tabe _____ desu.

   I want to eat tempura.

Complete the following sentences appropriately.

1. 兄は新しい車を _____。

   Ani wa atarashii kuruma o _____ .

   My big brother wants a new car.

2. 昨日の晩はワインを _____。

   Kinō no ban wa wain o _____ .

   (I) drank too much wine last night.

3. 本を _____。

   Hon o _____ .

   (I) started writing a book.

4. 日本語を勉強 _____。

   Nihongo o benkyō _____ .

   (I) will continue studying Japanese.

5. この本はもう読み _____。

   Kono hon wa mō yomi _____ .

   (I) finished reading this book.

Translate the following sentences into English.

1. 納豆を食べようとしましたが、食べられませんでした。

   Mattō o tabeyō to shimashita ga, taberaremasendeshita.

   _____

2. 来年、結婚しようと思っています。

   Rainen, kekkon shiyō to omotte imasu.

   _____

3. この映画は面白そうですね。

   Kono eiga wa omoshiro sō desu ne.

   _____

4. 父は子供のような人です。

Chichi wa kodomo no yō na hito desu.

_____

5. 田中さんはあまり日本人らしくありません。

Tanaka-san wa amari Nihonjin rashiku arimasen.

_____

**EXERCISE
16·37**

Choose the appropriate item in the parentheses.

1. できるだけ毎日運動するように（なって, して）います。

   Dekirudake mainichi undō suru yō ni (natte, shite) imasu.

   I try my best to do exercise every day as much as possible.

2. 最近日本語が話せるように（なり, し）ました。

   Saikin Nihongo ga hanaseru yō ni (nari, shi) mashita.

   (I) started to be able to speak Japanese lately.

3. ここではタバコがすえない（こと, よう）になりました。

   Koko de wa tabako ga suenai (koto, yō) ni narimashita.

   It has been decided that we cannot smoke here.

4. 漢字を読む（こと, よう）ができますか。

   Kanji o yomu (koto, yō) ga dekimasu ka.

   Can you read kanji?

5. うなぎを食べた（こと, よう）がありますか。

   Unagi o tabeta (koto, yō) ga arimasu ka.

   Have you eaten eel before?

11 Clauses

EXERCISE
16·38

Choose the most appropriate item in parentheses.

1. このフライトが一番（便利だ, 便利）と思います。

   Kono furaito ga ichiban (benri da, benri) to omoimasu.

   (I) think this flight is most convenient.

2. いつできる（か, かどうか）教えてください。

   Itsu dekiru (ka, ka dōka) oshiete kudasai.

   Please let me know when (it) can be completed.

3. 映画を見る（前, 後）にポップコーンを作ります。

   Eiga o miru (mae, ato) ni poppukōn o tsukurimasu.

   Before I watch a movie, I make popcorns.

4. ごはんを（食べる, 食べている）間にテレビは見ません。

   Gohan o (taberu, tabete iru) aida ni terebi wa mimasen.

   (I) don't watch TV while eating.

5. 空港に（着きました, 着いた）ときに電話してください。

   Kūkō ni (tsukimashita, tsuita) toki ni denwa shite kudasai.

   Please call (me) when you arrive at the airport.

6. 音楽を（聞いて, 聞き）ながら車を運転します。

   Ongaku o (kiite, kiki) nagara kuruma o unten shimasu.

   (I) drive while listening to music.

7. 雨が（降っている, 降らない）うちに帰りましょう。

   Ame ga (futte iru, furanai) uchi ni kaerimashō.

   Let's go home before it starts raining.

Complete the following sentences creatively.

1. _____ ので今日は勉強します。

_____**node kyō wa benkyō shimasu.**

2. _____ から今日は勉強します。

_____**kara kyō wa benkyō shimasu.**

3. _____ のに兄はぜんぜん勉強していません。

_____**noni ani wa zenzen benkyō shite imasen.**

4. _____ が今日は勉強しません。

_____**ga kyō wa benkyō shimasen.**

Translate the following Japanese sentences into English.

1. 昨日見た映画はあまり面白くありませんでした。

Kinō mita eiga wa amari omoshiroku arimasendeshita.

_____

2. だれとでも話せるということはいいことですよ。

Dare to demo hanaseru to iu koto wa ii koto desu yo.

_____

3. 筑波というところで研究をしました。

Tsukuba to iu tokoro de kenkyū o shimashita.

_____

4. 近藤恵美子という人を知っていますか。

Kondō Emiko to iu hito o shitte imasu ka.

_____

12 Conjunctions

EXERCISE 16·41

Translate the following sentences into Japanese.

1. I go shopping, cook, and do laundry on weekends.

   _____

   _____

2. I watched TV, did my homework, and slept yesterday.

   _____

   _____

3. I cleaned my room and got tired.

   _____

   _____

4. Ann is pretty and kind.

   _____

   _____

5. I went to work without eating breakfast yesterday.

   _____

   _____

6. I ate rice instead of bread this morning.

   _____

   _____

EXERCISE 16·42

Using each of the following phrases, make a sentence creatively.

1. 頭もいいし **atama mo ii shi**

   _____

2. 掃除もしたし **sōji mo shitashi**

   _____

3. 本を読んだり **hon o yondari**

_____

4. テニスをして **tenisu o shite**

_____

Choose the most appropriate item in parentheses.

1. 今日はテニスをします。それから、買い物に (行きました, 行きます)。

   Kyō wa tenisu o shimasu. Sorekara, kaimono ni (ikimashita, ikimasu).

2. この部屋は明るいです。それに、(きたない, きれい) です。

   Kono heya wa akarui desu. Soreni, (kitanai, kirei) desu.

3. 大学に入りました。そして、言語学(を勉強しました, が好きです)。

   Daigaku ni hairimashita. Soshite, gengogaku (o benkyō shimashita, ga suki desu).

4. この道をまっすぐ行ってください。そうすると、(駅があります, 右に曲がってください)。

   Kono michi o massugu itte kudasai. Sōsuruto, (eki ga arimasu, migi ni magatte kudasai).

5. よく勉強しました。(それで, それから)、いい成績をとりました。

   Yoku benkyō shimashita. (Sorede, sorekara), ii seiseki o torimashita.

6. 兄の車は高いです。(でも, ですから)、よく 壊れます。

   Ani no kuruma wa takai desu. (Demo, Demo), yoku kowaremasu.

7. 英語を話しますか。(それか, それとも) フランス語を話しますか。

   Eigo o hanashimasu ka. (Soreka, Soretomo) Furansugo o hanashimasu ka.

13 Conditionals

Choose the appropriate item in parentheses.

1. このドアは (押したら, 押すなら) 開きます。

   Kono doa wa (oshitara, osunara) akimasu.

2. 中国に（行ったら, 行くなら）ビザをとってください。

Chūgoku ni (ittara, ikunara) biza o totte kudasai. (ビザ **biza**: visa)

3. （安かったら, 安いと）買いませんか。

(Yasukattara, yasui to), kaimasen ka.

4. このドアを（押したら, 押せば）開きました。

Kono doa o (oshitara, oseba) akimashita.

16·45

Translate the following Japanese sentences into English.

1. 早く帰ってもいいですか。

Hayaku kaette mo ii desu ka.

_____

2. クレジットカードを使ってはいけません。

Kurejittokādo o tsukatte wa ikemasen.

_____

3. クレジットカードを使わなくてはいけません。

Kurejittokādo o tsukawanakute wa ikemasen.

_____

4. 宿題はしなくてもいいです。

Shukudai wa shinakute mo ii desu.

_____

5. 高くてもいいです。

Takakute mo ii desu.

_____

EXERCISE

16·46

Complete the following sentences creatively.

1. いい本なら高くても _____ 。

Ii hon nara takakutemo _____.

2. 高いなら便利でも _____ 。

   Takai nara benri demo _____ .

3. いくらがんばっても _____ 。

   Ikura ganbatte mo _____ .

4. 私は何でも _____ 。

   Watashi wa nan demo _____ .

5. 姉は何を食べても _____ 。

   Ane wa nani o tabete mo _____ .

14   Passives and causatives

EXERCISE
16·47

Convert each of the following sentences into direct passive sentences in Japanese.

EXAMPLE   弟が私のカメラを壊しました。

   Otōto ga watashi no kamera o kowashimashita.

   → 私のカメラが弟に壊されました。

   Watashi no kamera ga otōto ni kowasaremashita.

1. 父が兄をほめました。

   Chichi ga ani o homemashita.

   _____

2. 犬が弟を噛みました。

   Inu ga otōto o kamimashita.

   _____

3. 田中さんが伊藤さんを誕生日パーティーに招待しました。

   Tanaka-san ga Itō-san o tanjōbi pātī ni shōtai shimashita.

   _____

EXERCISE
16·48

Convert each of the following sentences into indirect passive sentences in Japanese.

EXAMPLE　　　弟が私のカメラを壊しました。

Otōto ga watashi no kamera o kowashimashita.

→ 弟に私のカメラを壊されました。

Otōto ni watashi no kamera o kowasaremashita.

1. 去年父が死にました。

   Kyonen chichi ga shinimashita.

   _____

2. レストランでとなりの人がタバコをすいました。

   Resutoran de tonari no hito ga tabako o suimashita.

   _____

3. 私が１００点をとったら、みんながびっくりしました。

   Watashi ga 100-ten o tottara, minna ga bikkuri shimashita.

   _____

EXERCISE
16·49

Convert each of the following sentences into causative sentences in Japanese.

EXAMPLE　　　弟が車を洗いました。

Otōto ga kuruma o araimashita.

→ 弟に車を洗わせました。

Otōto ni kuruma o arawasemashita.

1. 妹が料理をしました。

   Imōto ga ryōri o shimashita.

   _____

2. 妹がテレビを見ました。

   Imōto ga terebi o mimashita.

   _____

3. 妹が泣きました。

   Imōto ga nakimashita.

   _____

Translate the following sentences into English.

1. 私は父に習字を習わせられました。

   Watashi wa chichi ni shūji o narawaseraremashita.

   _____

2. 友達に２時間待たせられました。

   Tomodachi ni 2-jikan mataseraremashita.

   _____

3. 母に部屋を掃除させられました。

   Haha ni heya o sōji saseraremashita.

   _____

4. 先生は私に先生の本を読ませてくださいました。

   Sensei wa watashi ni sensei no hon o yomasete kudasaimashita.

   _____

5. 私は先生に漢字を１００回書かせられました。

   Watashi wa sensei ni kanji o 100-kai kakaseraremashita.

   _____

15   Honorifics

Choose the appropriate item from the options in parentheses.

1. 先生は（い, いらっしゃい）ますか。

   Sensei wa (i, irasshai) masu ka.

   Is the teacher here?

2. 社長、（みて, ご覧になって）ください。

   Shachō, (mite, goran ni natte) kudasai.

   President, please take a look.

3. 私がお書き（になり, いたし）ました。

Watashi ga o-kaki (ni nari, itashi) mashita.

I wrote (it).

4. 先生がお書き（になり, いたし）ました。

Sensei ga o-kaki (ni nari, itashi) mashita.

The teacher wrote (it).

5. 今日は早く帰らせて（ください, いただけない）でしょうか。

Kyō wa hayaku kaerasete (kudasai, itadakenai) deshō ka.

Today, would it be alright if I go (home) early?

EXERCISE 16·52

Convert the underlined word to their polite counterparts.

1. <u>どこ</u>へいらっしゃるんですか。

<u>Doko</u> e irassharun desu ka.

Where are you going?

_____

2. ご旅行は<u>どう</u>でしたか。

Go-ryokō wa <u>dō</u> deshita ka.

How was your trip?

_____

3. <u>だれ</u>がいらっしゃったんですか。

<u>Dare</u> ga irasshatta n desu ka.

Who came?

_____

4. ピアノが<u>上手</u>ですね。

Piano ga <u>jōzu</u> desu ne.

You are good at playing the piano.

_____

5. <u>車</u>でお迎えに参ります。

<u>Kuruma</u> de o-mukae ni mairimasu.

I'll come to pick you up by car.

_____

APPENDIX A
Basic verb forms

See the table of basic verb forms on the following page.

Ending of the Dictionary Form		Dictionary Form	Nai Form	Stem Form	Te Form	Potential Form	Command Form	Ba Form	Volitional Form	Causative Form	Passive Form
Ru verb	-eる -eru	かえる kaeru (*change*)	かえない kaenai	かえ kae	かえて kaete	かえられる kaerareru	かえろ kaero	かえれば kaereba	かえよう kaeyō	かえさせる kaesaseru	かえられる kaerareru
	-iる -iru	きる kiru (*wear*)	きない kinai	き ki	きて kite	きられる kirareru	きろ kiro	きれば kireba	きよう kiyō	きさせる kisaseru	きられる kirareru
U verb	-す -su	はなす hanasu (*speak*)	はなさない hanasanai	はなし hanashi	はなして hanashite	はなせる hanaseru	はなせ hanase	はなせば hanaseba	はなそう hanasō	はなさせる hanasaseru	はなされる hanasareru
	-く -ku	かく kaku (*write*)	かかない kakanai	かき kaki	かいて kaite	かける kakeru	かけ kake	かけば kakeba	かこう kakō	かかせる kakaseru	かかれる kakareru
	-ぐ -gu	およぐ oyogu (*swim*)	およがない oyoganai	およぎ oyogi	およいで oyoide	およげる oyogeru	およげ oyoge	およげば oyogeba	およごう oyogō	およがせる oyogaseru	およがれる oyogareru
	-む -mu	よむ yomu (*read*)	よまない yomanai	よみ yomi	よんで yonde	よめる yomeru	よめ yome	よめば yomeba	よもう yomō	よませる yomaseru	よまれる yomareru
	-ぬ -nu	しぬ shinu (*die*)	しなない shinanai	しに shini	しんで shinde	しねる shineru	しね shine	しねば shineba	しのう shinō	しなせる shinaseru	しなれる shinareru
	-ぶ -bu	とぶ tobu (*jump*)	とばない tobanai	とび tobi	とんで tonde	とべる toberu	とべ tobe	とべば tobeba	とぼう tobō	とばせる tobaseru	とばれる tobareru
	-vowel + u -う	かう kau (*buy*)	かわない kawanai	かい kai	かって katte	かえる kaeru	かえ kae	かえば kaeba	かおう kaō	かわせる kawaseru	かわれる kawareru
	-る -ru	きる kiru (*cut*)	きらない kiranai	きり kiri	きって kitte	きれる kireru	きれ kire	きれば kireba	きろう kirō	きらせる kiraseru	きられる kirareru
	-つ -tsu	まつ matsu (*wait*)	またない matanai	まち machi	まって matte	まてる materu	まて mate	まてば mateba	まとう matō	またせる mataseru	またれる matareru
Irregular verb		くる kuru (*come*)	こない konai	き ki	きて kite	こられる korareru	こい koi	くれば kureba	こよう koyō	こさせる kosaseru	こられる korareru
		する suru (*do*)	しない shinai	し shi	して shite	できる dekiru	しろ shiro	すれば sureba	しよう shiyō	させる saseru	される sareru

Slightly irregular u verbs

◆ The **nai form** of ある **aru** (*exist*) is ない **nai**.
◆ The **te form** of 行く **iku** (*go*) is 行って **itte**.
◆ The **masu form** of いらっしゃる **irassharu** (*exist*) and くださる **kudasaru** (*give*) are いらっしゃいます and くださいます... respectively.

Nakatta form
The **nakatta** form can be created by replacing the final ない **nai** in the **nai form** with なかった **nakatta**.

Masu form
The **masu** form can be created by adding ます **masu** at the end of the stem form.

Ta form, tara form, and tari form
The **ta** form can be created by replacing the final **e** in the **te** form with **a**.
The **tara** form and the **tari** form can be created by adding ら **ra** and り **ri** after the **ta** form, respectively.

APPENDIX B

Basic sentence predicate forms

See the table of basic sentence predicate forms on the following page.

			Verb	I Adjective	Na Adjective	Noun + Copula
Plain	Non-past	Affirmative	食べる **taberu** *(eats, will eat)*	高い **takai** *(is expensive)*	高価だ **kōka da** *(is expensive)*	犬だ **inu da** *(is a dog)*
		Negative*	食べない **tabenai** *(doesn't/won't eat)*	高くない **takaku nai** *(isn't expensive)*	高価じゃない **kōka ja nai** *(isn't expensive)*	犬じゃない **inu ja nai** *(isn't a dog)*
	Past	Affirmative	食べた **tabeta** *(ate)*	高かった **takakatta** *(was expensive)*	高価だった **kōka datta** *(was expensive)*	犬だった **inu datta** *(was a dog)*
		Negative*	食べなかった **tabenakatta** *(didn't eat)*	高くなかった **takaku nakatta** *(wasn't expensive)*	高価じゃなかった **kōka ja nakatta** *(wasn't expensive)*	犬じゃなかった **inu ja nakatta** *(wasn't a dog)*
Polite	Non-past	Affirmative	食べます **tabemasu** *(eats, will eat)*	高いです **takai desu** *(is expensive)*	高価です **kōka desu** *(is expensive)*	犬です **inu desu** *(is a dog)*
		Negative*	食べません **tabemasen** or 食べないです **tabenai desu** *(doesn't/won't eat)*	高くありません **takaku arimasen** or 高くないです **takaku nai desu** *(isn't expensive)*	高価じゃありません **kōka ja arimasen** or 高価じゃないです **kōka ja nai desu** *(isn't expensive)*	犬じゃありません **inu ja arimasen** or 犬じゃないです **inu ja nai desu** *(isn't a dog)*
	Past	Affirmative	食べました **tabemashita** *(ate)*	高かったです **takakatta desu** *(was expensive)*	高価でした **kōka deshita** *(was expensive)*	犬でした **inu deshita** *(was a dog)*
		Negative*	食べませんでした **tabemasendeshita** or 食べなかったです **tabenakatta desu** *(didn't eat)*	高くありませんでした **takaku arimasendeshita** or 高くなかったです **takaku nakatta desu** *(wasn't expensive)*	高価じゃありませんでした **kōka ja arimasendeshita** or 高価じゃなかったです **kōka ja nakatta desu** *(wasn't expensive)*	犬じゃありませんでした **inu ja arimasendeshita** or 犬じゃなかったです **inu ja nakatta desu** *(wasn't a dog)*

* じゃ **ja** in the negative forms of **na** adjectives and copula in this table can be では **de wa**.

Japanese–English glossary

A

abunai: *dangerous*
abura: *oil*
agaru (**u** verb): *to rise*
ageru (**ru** verb): *to raise* (上げる, 揚げる),
　to give (あげる)
ago: *chin, jaw*
ahiru: *duck*
ai: *love*
aida: *between*
aimai na: *vague*
aisukurīmu: *ice cream*
Ajia: *Asia*
aka: *red*
akachan: *baby*
akeru (**ru** verb): *to open*
aki: *autumn, fall*
ame: *rain* (雨), *candy* (飴)
Amerika: *America*
Amerika-jin: *American person*
anata: *you*
ane: *older sister* (plain)
ani: *older brother* (plain)
anime: *anime*
anzen na: *safe*
ao: *blue*
apāto: *apartment*
arau (**u** verb): *to wash*
are: *that one* (over there)
Arigatō gozaimasu.: *Thank you!*
aru (slightly irregular **u** verb): *to exist*
aruku (**u** verb): *to walk*
asa: *morning*
asa-gohan: *breakfast*
asai: *shallow*
asatte: *day after tomorrow*
ashi: *foot, leg*
ashita: *tomorrow*
asobu (**u** verb): *to play*
asoko: *over there*
atama: *head*
atarashii: *new*
atatakai: *warm*

atsui: *hot* (weather) (暑い), *hot* (temperature)
　(熱い), *thick* (厚い)
atsumeru (**ru** verb): *to collect*
au (**u** verb): *to meet* (会う), *to encounter*
　(遭う), *to fit* (合う)

B

bā: *bar* (serving drinks)
banana: *banana*
ban-gohan: *dinner*
basu: *bus*
basukettobōru: *basketball*
batā: *butter*
beddo: *bed*
bengoshi: *lawyer*
benkyō-suru (irregular verb): *to study*
benri na: *convenient*
bijutsukan: *art museum*
bīru: *beer*
biza: *visa*
bōeki: *trading*
bōshi: *hat*
bun: *sentence*
bungaku: *literature*
burausu: *blouse*
buta: *pig*
butaniku: *pork*
butsuri: *physics*
byōin: *hospital*
byōki: *illness*

C

chairo: *brown*
chawan: *teacup, rice bowl*
chichi: *father* (plain)
chika: *basement*
chikaku: *near*
chikatetsu: *subway*
chīsai: *small*
chīzu: *cheese*
chizu: *map*
chōshoku: *breakfast*
chotto: *a little bit*

Chūgoku: *China*
chūshajō: *parking lot*
chūshoku: *lunch*

D

daidokoro: *kitchen*
daigaku: *university*
daigakuin: *graduate school*
daijōbu na: *all right*
dainingu: *dining room*
damasu (**u** verb): *to deceive*
dare: *who* (plain)
dareka: *somebody*
deguchi: *exit*
dekiru (**ru** verb): *to be able to do*
demo: *but*
denki: *electricity*
densha: *train*
denwa: *telephone*
denwa-bangō: *telephone number*
depāto: *department store*
dezāto: *dessert, sweets*
dō: *how*
dōbutsu: *animal*
dōbutsuen: *zoo*
dochira: *which one* (of the two)
Doitsu: *Germany*
doko: *where*
dokoka: *somewhere*
Dōmo.: *Thank you!*
donata: *who* (honorific)
dore: *which one* (of the three or more items or in a group of items)
dorobō: *thief*
doru: *dollar*
dōryō: *co-worker*
dōshite: *why*
Doyōbi: *Saturday*

E

e: *picture* (painting or drawing)
eakon: *air conditioning*
ebi: *shrimp*
eiga: *movie*
eigakan: *movie theater*
eigo: *English*
eikyō: *influence*
eki: *station* (for trains and subways)
enpitsu: *pencil*
enpitsu kezuri: *pencil sharpener*
erabu (**u** verb): *to select, to choose*
erebētā: *elevator*

F

fakkusu: *fax*
Firipin: *Philippines*
fōku: *fork*

fude: *brush* (for calligraphy)
fugu: *blowfish*
Fujisan: *Mt. Fuji*
fukai: *deep*
fuku (**u** verb): *to wipe*
fuku: *clothes*
fukuro: *sack* (bag)
-fun: *-minute*
fune: *ship*
Furansu: *France*
furoba: *bathing room*
furui: *old* (for inanimate things)
fūtō: *envelope*
fuyu: *winter*

G

ga: *moth*
gaika: *foreign money*
gaikoku: *foreign country*
gaikoku-jin: *foreigner*
gakkō: *school*
gakusei: *students*
ganko na: *stubborn*
garō: *gallery*
gasorin sutando: *gas station*
geijutsu: *art*
geijutsuka: *artist*
geki: *play*
gekijō: *theater* (for plays and performances)
gengo: *language*
genkan: *entryway*
genki na: *fine* (healthy)
genkin: *cash*
geta: *clogs*
Getsuyōbi: *Monday*
gin: *silver* (metal)
ginkō: *bank*
gitā: *guitar*
go: *five*
go-gatsu: *May*
gogo: *PM, afternoon*
gohan: *rice* (cooked)
gomi: *garbage, trash*
gomibako: *trash can*
gorufu: *golf*
gōtō: *burglar*
gyūniku: *beef*
gyūnyū: *milk*
gozen: *AM*

H

ha: *leaf* (葉), *tooth* (歯)
hachi: *eight* (八), *bee* (蜂)
hachi-gatsu: *August*
hachimitsu: *honey*
hae: *fly* (insect)
haha: *mother* (plain)

hairu (**u** verb): *to enter*
haisha: *dentist*
haitatsu: *delivery*
haiyū: *actor*
hajimeru (**ru** verb): *to begin* (something)
hako: *box*
hakobu (**u** verb): *to carry*
hakubutsukan: *museum*
hamigakiko: *toothpaste*
hana: *flower* (花), *nose* (鼻)
hanabi: *fireworks*
hanashi: *story*
hanasu (**u** verb): *to speak*
hanbun: *half*
harau (**u** verb): *to pay*
hari: *needle*
haru: *spring*
hasami: *scissors*
hashi: *chopsticks* (箸), *bridge* (橋)
hashira: *pillar*
hashiru (**u** verb): *to run*
hata: *flag*
hataraku (**u** verb): *to work*
hatsuon: *pronunciation*
hayai: *early* (早い), *fast* (速い) (adjectives)
hayaku: *early* (早く), *fast* (速く) (adverbs)
hayashi: *woods*
hazukashii: *embarrassing*
hebi: *snake*
heiwa: *peace*
hen na: *weird, strange*
henji: *reply* (response)
heya: *room*
hi: *day* (日), *fire* (火), *sun* (日)
hidari: *left*
hidoi: *terrible*
higashi: *east*
hikari: *light* (illumination)
hikidashi: *drawer*
hikōki: *airplane*
hiku (**u** verb): *to pull*
hikui: *low*
hima: *free time*
himitsu: *secret*
hiroi: *wide, spacious*
hiru-gohan: *lunch*
hisho: *secretary*
hitai: *forehead*
hito: *person*
hitsuji: *sheep*
hitsuyō na: *necessary*
hiza: *knee*
hō: *cheek*
hochikisu: *stapler*
hōgen: *dialect*
hōki: *broom*
hon: *book*

hon'ya: *bookstore*
hon'yaku: *translation*
hon'yakusha: *translator*
honbako: *bookcase*
hondana: *bookshelf*
hone: *bone*
hontō ni: *really* (truly)
hōrensō: *spinach*
hōritsu: *law*
hoshi: *star* (in the sky)
hoshii: *to want* (adjective)
hosoi: *slim*
hoteru: *hotel*
hyaku: *hundred*

I

i: *stomach*
ichi: *one*
ichi-gatsu: *January*
ichigo: *strawberry*
ichiman: *ten thousand*
ie: *house*
Igirisu: *England*
ii: *good*
ijiwaru na: *mean* (unkind)
ika: *squid*
ike: *pond*
iku (slightly irregular **u** verb): *to go*
ikura: *how much* (price); *salmon roe*
ikutsu: *how many*
ima: *now, living room*
imi: *meaning*
imin: *immigrant*
imōto: *younger sister*
inaka: *countryside*
infuruenza: *flu*
inu: *dog*
irassharu (slightly irregular **u** verb): *to exist* (honorific)
iriguchi: *entrance*
iro: *color*
iroiro na: *various*
iru (**ru** verb): *to exist*
iru (**u** verb): *to need*
isha: *physician*
ishi: *stone*
isogashii: *busy*
isogu (**u** verb): *to hurry*
issho ni: *together*
isu: *chair*
itadaku (**u** verb): *to receive* (honorific)
itai: *painful*
itami: *pain*
Itaria: *Italy*
ito: *thread*
itoko: *cousin*
itsu: *when*
itsuka: *someday*

itsumo: *always*
iu (u verb): *to say*

J

jagaimo: *potato*
jaketto: *jacket*
-ji: *. . . o'clock*
jigoku: *hell*
jijitsu: *fact*
-jikan: *hour* (length of time)
jikan: *time*
jiko: *accident*
jīnzu: *jeans*
jishin: *earthquake*
jisho: *dictionary*
jitensha: *bicycle*
jiyū: *liberty*
jōdan: *joke*
joyū: *actress*
jū: *ten*
jū-gatsu: *October*
jūgyōin: *employee*
jūichi-gatsu: *November*
jūni-gatsu: *December*
jūsho: *address*
jūsu: *juice*

K

kaban: *bag*
kabe: *wall*
kabin: *vase*
kaeru (ru verb): *to change*
kaeru (u verb): *to return*
kaeru: *frog*
kagaku: *science* (科学), *chemistry* (化学)
kagami: *mirror*
kagi: *key*
kagu: *furniture*
kai: *shellfish*
kaisha: *company*
kaishain: *company employee*
kaiwa: *conversation*
kaji: *fire* (conflagration)
kakegoto: *gambling*
kaki: *oyster* (牡蠣), *persimmon* (柿)
kakkoii: *cool-looking*
kaku (u verb): *to write* (書く), *to draw* (描く)
kakusu (u verb): *to hide* (something)
kame: *turtle*
kamera: *camera*
kami: *hair* (髪), *paper* (紙), *god* (神)
kaminari: *thunder*
Kanada: *Canada*
kanari: *quite*
kanashii: *sad*
kanban: *sign* (for shops)

kangoshi: *nurse*
kani: *crab*
kanja: *patient* (of a doctor)
kankō: *sightseeing*
Kankoku: *South Korea*
kanojo: *she, girlfriend*
kanpai: *toast* (ceremonial drink)
kantan na: *easy, simple*
kao: *face*
karada: *body* (of a person or an animal)
karai: *hot* (spicy)
kare: *he, boyfriend*
karendā: *calendar*
kariru (ru verb): *to borrow*
karui: *light* (weight)
kasa: *umbrella*
kasu (u verb): *to lend*
kata: *shoulder*
katsu (u verb): *to win*
kau (u verb): *to buy*
kawa: *river* (川), *leather* (革)
kawaii: *cute*
Kayōbi: *Tuesday*
kazan: *volcano*
kaze: *wind* (風), *cold* (virus) (風邪)
keimusho: *jail*
keisatsu: *police*
keisatsukan: *police officer*
keitai (denwa): *cell phone*
keizaigaku: *economics*
kēki: *cake*
ki: *tree*
kibishii: *strict*
kiiro: *yellow*
kiken na: *dangerouns*
kiku (u verb): *to listen*
kinō: *yesterday*
Kinyōbi: *Friday*
kirei na: *beautiful, clean*
kiru (ru verb): *to wear*
kiru (u verb): *to cut*
kisetsu: *season*
kita: *north*
kitanai: *dirty*
kitchin: *kitchen*
kitte: *postage stamp*
kōban: *koban* (police box)
kodomo: *child*
kōen: *park*
kōhī: *coffee*
koi: *carp* (鯉), *love* (恋)
kōjō: *factory*
kōka na: *expensive*
koko: *here*
kōkō: *high school*
kokuseki: *nationality*

kome: *uncooked rice*
komugiko: *flour*
konban: *tonight*
konbini: *convenience store*
kongetsu: *this month*
Konnichiwa.: *Hello!, Good afternoon!*
konshū: *this week*
kore: *this one*
kōri: *ice*
korosu (u verb**):** *to kill*
kōsaten: *intersection*
koshi: *hip*
kōsui: *perfume*
kotae: *answer*
kotoshi: *this year*
kowai: *scary*
kowasu (u verb**):** *to break* (something)
kubi: *neck*
kuchi: *mouth*
kudamono: *fruit*
kudasaru (slightly irregular **u** verb**):** *to give (to me/us)* (honorific)
ku-gatsu: *September*
kūkō: *airport*
kumo: *cloud* (雲)*, spider* (蜘蛛)
kuni: *country*
kurai: *dark*
kurejitto kādo: *credit card*
kureru (ru verb**):** *to give* (to me/us)
kuro: *black*
kuru (irregular verb)**:** *to come*
kuruma: *car*
kusuri: *medicine*
kusuriya: *drugstore*
kutsu: *shoe*
kutsushita: *socks*
kyō: *today*
kyōkai: *church*
kyonen: *last year*
kyōshi: *teacher* (plain)
kyū: *nine*
kyūkyūsha: *ambulance*
kyūryō: *salary*

M

mado: *window*
mae: *front*
magaru (u verb**):** *to (make a) turn*
mago: *grandchildren*
maguro: *tuna*
majime na: *serious*
makura: *pillow*
mame: *beans*
manabu (u verb**):** *to learn*
manga: *cartoon*
massugu: *straight*

mata: *again*
matsu (u verb**):** *to wait*
me: *eye*
megane: *eyeglasses*
mendō na: *troublesome*
meron: *melon*
michi: *street*
midori: *green*
migi: *right*
mikan: *orange* (fruit)
mimi: *ear*
minami: *south*
mise: *store*
mizu: *water*
mizuumi: *lake*
Mokuyōbi: *Thursday*
mono: *thing*
morau (u verb**):** *to receive* (plain)
mori: *forest*
moshi: *if*
moshimoshi: *hello* (telephone answer)
motsu (u verb**):** *to hold* (to have in hand)
mukai gawa: *opposite side*
mune: *chest*
mura: *village*
murasaki: *purple*
mushi: *insect*
musuko: *son*
musume: *daughter*
muzukashii: *difficult*

N

nabe: *pot*
naifu: *knife*
naka: *inside*
namae: *name*
nami: *wave*
namida: *tear*
nana: *seven*
nani: *what*
nanika: *something*
naru (u verb**):** *to become*
nashi: *pear*
natsu: *summer*
naze: *why*
nedan: *price*
nekkuresu: *necklace*
neko: *cat*
nekutai: *tie*
nemui: *sleepy*
neru (ru verb**):** *to sleep*
netsu: *fever*
ni: *two*
Nichiyōbi: *Sunday*
nigai: *bitter*
ni-gatsu: *February*

Nihon: *Japan*
Nihon-go: *Japanese language*
Nihon-jin: *Japanese person*
niku: *meat*
nimotsu: *luggage*
ningyō: *doll*
ninjin: *carrot*
Nippon: *Japan*
nishi: *west*
nodo: *throat*
nomu (**u** verb): *to drink*
noru (**u** verb): *to get on* (transportation)

O

oba: *aunt* (plain)
obasan: *aunt* (polite)
obāsan: *grandmother* (polite)
oboeru (**ru** verb): *to memorize*
o-cha: *(green) tea*
odoru (**u** verb): *to dance*
Ohayō gozaimasu.: *Good morning!* (honorific)
Ohayō.: *Good morning!* (plain)
o-isha-san: *physician* (honorific)
oishii: *delicious*
oji: *uncle* (plain)
ojīsan: *grandfather* (polite)
ojisan: *uncle* (polite)
o-kane: *money*
okāsan: *mother* (polite)
ōkii: *big*
okiru (**ru** verb): *to get up*
oku (**u** verb): *to put*
omiyage: *souvenir*
omoi: *heavy*
omoshiroi: *interesting*
omou (**u** verb): *to think*
onaji: *same*
onaka ga suite iru: *hungry*
onaka: *abdomen*
onēsan: *older sister* (polite)
ongaku: *music*
onīsan: *older brother* (polite)
onna: *female*
onna no hito: *woman*
oriru (**ru** verb): *to get off* (transportation)
osoi: *late, slow*
Ōsutoraria: *Australia*
otoko: *male*
otoko no hito: *man*
otōsan: *father* (polite)
otōto: *younger brother*
ototoi: *day before yesterday*
otto: *husband*
owaru (**u** verb): *to end*
Oyasuminasai.: *Good night!*
oyogu (**u** verb): *to swim*

P

pan: *bread*
pan'ya: *bakery*
pasokon: *computer*
pasupōto: *passport*
pātī: *party* (event)
piano: *piano*
piza: *pizza*
poketto: *pocket*

R

raigetsu: *next month*
rainen: *next year*
raishū: *next week*
rajio: *radio*
rei: *zero*
reizōko: *refrigerator*
rekishi: *history*
remon: *lemon*
renshū: *practice* (exercise)
reshīto: *receipt*
resutoran: *restaurant*
ribingu: *living room*
rimokon: *remote control*
ringo: *apple*
roku: *six*
roku-gatsu: *June*
ryōjikan: *consulate*
ryokō: *trip*
ryōri: *cooking*
ryōshūsho: *receipt*

S

sagasu (**u** verb): *to search*
saifu: *wallet*
sakana: *fish*
sake: *rice wine, salmon*
sakkā: *soccer*
sakka: *writer* (author)
sakura: *cherry* (tree)
samishii: *lonely*
samui: *cold* (weather)
san: *three*
sandaru: *sandal*
san-gatsu: *March*
sangurasu: *sunglasses*
sankaku: *triangle*
sara: *dish* (plate)
sarada: *salad*
saru: *monkey*
sashiageru (**ru** verb): *to give* (honorific)
satō: *sugar*
Sayōnara.: *Goodbye!*
seiseki: *grade* (rating in school)
seito: *pupil*

sekai: *world*
semai: *narrow*
sengetsu: *last month*
sensei: *teacher*
senshū: *last week*
sensō: *war*
sētā: *sweater*
shachō: *company president*
shakaigaku: *social studies*
shakkuri: *hiccup*
shako: *garage*
shashin: *photograph*
shatsu: *shirt*
shi: *four*
shichi: *seven*
shichi-gatsu: *July*
shi-gatsu: *April*
shigoto: *job*
shikaku: *square*
shimauma: *zebra*
shinbun: *newspaper*
shinshitsu: *bedroom*
shinu (**u** verb): *to die*
shio: *salt*
shiriai: *acquaintance*
shiro: *white* (白), *castle* (城)
shita: *under*
shitsumon: *question*
shitte iru: *to know*
shizen: *nature*
shizuka na: *quiet*
shōhizei: *sales tax*
shokubutsu: *plant*
shokugyō: *occupation*
shokuji: *meal*
shomei: *signature*
shōtai: *invitation*
shū: *week*
shukudai: *homework*
shumi: *hobby*
sobo: *grandmother* (plain)
soba: *buckwheat noodle*
sofu: *grandfather* (plain)
soko: *there* (near you)
sore: *that one* (near you)
soto: *outside*
sūgaku: *mathematics*
sugiru (**ru** verb): *to pass by*
suiei: *swimming*
Suiyōbi: *Wednesday*
sukāto: *skirt*
suki na: *to like*
sūpā: *supermarket*
supagettī: *spaghetti*
Supein: *Spain*
suru (irregular verb): *to do*

sūtsu: *suit*
sūtsukēsu: *suitcase*
suwaru (**u** verb): *to sit down*
suzushii: *cool* (weather)

T
tabako: *tobacco*
taberu (**ru** verb): *to eat*
tabi: *journey*
tabun: *probably*
tadashii: *correct*
taishikan: *embassy*
taitei: *usually*
taiyō: *sun*
takai: *expensive*
takushī: *taxi*
tamago: *egg*
tamani: *occasionally*
tanjōbi: *birthday*
tatemono: *building*
te: *hand, arm*
tēburu: *table*
tegami: *letter*
tengoku: *heaven*
tenisu: *tennis*
terebi: *TV*
tochi: *land*
tōi: *far*
tomodachi: *friend*
tonari: *next door*
toriniku: *chicken* (meat)
toru (**u** verb): *to take*
toshi: *year*
totemo: *very*
tsukau (**u** verb): *to use*
tsuku (**u** verb): *to arrive*
tsukue: *desk*
tsukuru (**u** verb): *to make*
tsuma: *wife*
tsume: *nail*
tsumetai: *cold* (temperature other than weather)
tsunami: *tsunami*

U
uchi: *home*
ude: *arm*
ue: *above*
ukeru (**ru** verb): *to receive*
uma: *horse*
umi: *ocean*
unagi: *eel*
undō-suru: *to exercise* (physical)
unten-suru (irregular verb): *to drive*
ureshii: *glad*
uru (**u** verb): *to sell*
urusai: *noisy*

usagi: *rabbit*
ushi: *cow*
ushiro: *behind*
uso: *lie*
uta: *song*
utau (**u** verb): *to sing*
utsukushii: *beautiful*

W

wain: *wine*
wakai: *young*
wakaru (**u** verb): *to understand*
warau (**u** verb): *to laugh*
warui: *bad*
wasureru (**ru** verb): *to forget*
wataru (**u** verb): *to cross over*
watashi: *I*

Y

yakusoku: *promise*
yakyū: *baseball*
yama: *mountain*

yasai: *vegetable*
yasui: *cheap* (inexpensive)
yasumi: *vacation*
yasumu (**u** verb): *to rest*
yōfuku: *clothes* (Western clothes)
yomu (**u** verb): *to read*
yon: *four*
Yōroppa: *Europe*
yoyaku: *reservation* (appointment)
yubi: *finger*
yūbin bangō: *zip code*
yūbinkyoku: *post office*
yuki: *snow*
yume: *dream*
yūmei na: *famous*
yūshoku: *dinner*

Z

zasshi: *magazine*
zenzen: (*not*) *at all*
zero: *zero*
zubon: *pants*

English–Japanese glossary

A
a little bit: **chotto**
abdomen: **onaka**
above: **ue**
accident: **jiko**
acquaintance: **shiriai**
actor: **haiyū**
actress: **joyū**
address: **jūsho**
afternoon: **gogo**
again: **mata**
air conditioning: **eakon**
airplane: **hikōki**
airport: **kūkō**
all right: **daijōbu na**
always: **itsumo**
AM: **gozen**
ambulance: **kyūkyūsha**
America: **Amerika**
American person: **Amerika-jin**
animal: **dōbutsu**
anime: **anime**
answer: **kotae**
apartment: **apāto**
apple: **ringo**
April: **shi-gatsu**
arm: **ude, te**
arrive, to: **tsuku** (**u** verb)
art museum: **bijutsukan**
art: **geijutsu**
artist: **geijutsuka**
Asia: **Ajia**
(not) at all: **zenzen**
August: **hachi-gatsu**
aunt: **oba** (plain)**, obasan** (honorific)
Australia: **Ōsutoraria**
autumn: **aki**

B
baby: **akachan**
bad: **warui**
bag: **kaban**
bakery: **pan'ya**

banana: **banana**
bank: **ginkō**
baseball: **yakyū**
basement: **chika**
basketball: **basukettobōru**
bathing room: **furoba**
be able to do, to: **dekiru** (**ru** verb)
beans: **mame**
beautiful: **kirei na, utsukushii**
become: **naru** (**u** verb)
bed: **beddo**
bedroom: **shinshitsu**
bee: **hachi**
beef: **gyūniku**
beer: **bīru**
begin (something), to: **hajimeru** (**ru** verb)
behind: **ushiro**
between: **aida**
bicycle: **jitensha**
big: **ōkii**
birthday: **tanjōbi**
bitter: **nigai**
black: **kuro**
blouse: **burausu**
blowfish: **fugu**
blue: **ao**
body (of a person or animal): **karada**
bone: **hone**
book: **hon**
bookcase: **honbako**
bookshelf: **hondana**
bookstore: **hon'ya**
borrow, to: **kariru** (**ru** verb)
box: **hako**
boyfriend: **kare**
bread: **pan**
break (something), to: **kowasu** (**u** verb)
breakfast: **asa-gohan, chōshoku**
bridge: **hashi**
broom: **hōki**
brother (older): **ani** (plain)**, onīsan** (honorific)
brother (younger): **otōto**
brown: **chairo**

brush (for calligraphy): **fude**
buckwheat noodle: **soba**
building: **tatemono**
burglar: **gōtō**
bus: **basu**
busy: **isogashii**
but: **demo**
butter: **batā**
buy, to: **kau** (**u** verb)

C

cake: **kēki**
calendar: **karendā**
camera: **kamera**
Canada: **Kanada**
candy: **ame**
car: **kuruma**
carp: **koi**
carrot: **ninjin**
carry, to: **hakobu** (**u** verb)
cartoon: **manga**
cash: **genkin**
castle: **shiro**
cat: **neko**
cell phone: **keitai** (**denwa**)
chair: **isu**
change, to: **kaeru** (**ru** verb)
cheap: **yasui**
cheek: **hō**
cheese: **chīzu**
chemistry: **kagaku**
cherry (tree): **sakura**
chest: **mune**
chicken (meat): **toriniku**
child: **kodomo**
chin: **ago**
China: **Chūgoku**
choose, to: **erabu** (**u** verb)
chopsticks: **hashi**
church: **kyōkai**
clean: **kirei na**
clogs: **geta**
clothes: **fuku, yōfuku**
cloud: **kumo**
coffee: **kōhī**
cold (temperature other than weather): **tsumetai**
cold (virus): **kaze**
cold (weather): **samui**
collect, to: **atsumeru** (**ru** verb)
color: **iro**
come, to: **kuru** (irregular verb)
company: **kaisha**
company employee: **kaishain**
company president: **shachō**
computer: **pasokon**
consulate: **ryōjikan**
convenience store: **konbini**

convenient: **benri na**
conversation: **kaiwa**
cooking: **ryōri**
cool (weather): **suzushii**
cool-looking: **kakkoii**
correct: **tadashii**
country: **kuni**
countryside: **inaka**
cousin: **itoko**
cow: **ushi**
co-worker: **dōryō**
crab: **kani**
credit card: **kurejitto kādo**
cross over, to: **wataru** (**u** verb)
cut, to: **kiru** (**u** verb):
cute: **kawaii**

D

dance, to: **odoru** (**u** verb)
dangerouns: **kiken na**
dark: **kurai**
daughter: **musume**
day after tomorrow: **asatte**
day before yesterday: **ototoi**
day: **hi**
deceive, to: **damasu** (**u** verb)
December: **jūni-gatsu**
deep: **fukai**
delicious: **oishii**
delivery: **haitatsu**
dentist: **haisha**
department store: **depāto**
desk: **tsukue**
dessert (sweets): **dezāto**
dialect: **hōgen**
dictionary: **jisho**
die, to: **shinu** (**u** verb)
difficult: **muzukashii**
dining room: **dainingu**
dinner: **ban-gohan, yūshoku**
dirty: **kitanai**
dish (plate): **sara**
do, to: **suru** (irregular verb)
dog: **inu**
doll: **ningyō**
dollar: **doru**
draw, to: **kaku** (**u** verb)
drawer: **hikidashi**
dress: **wanpīsu**
drink, to: **nomu** (**u** verb)
drive, to: **unten-suru** (irregular verb)
drugstore: **kusuriya**
duck: **ahiru**

E

ear: **mimi**
early: **hayai** (adjective), **hayaku** (adverb)

earthquake: **jishin**
east: **higashi**
easy: **kantan na**
eat, to: **taberu** (**ru** verb)
economics: **keizaigaku**
eel: **unagi**
eight: **hachi**
electricity: **denki**
elevator: **erebētā**
embarrassing: **hazukashii**
embassy: **taishikan**
employee: **jūgyōin**
encounter, to: **au** (**u** verb)
end, to: **owaru** (**u** verb)
England: **Igirisu**
English: **eigo**
enter, to: **hairu** (**u** verb)
entrance: **iriguchi**
entryway: **genkan**
envelope: **fūtō**
Europe: **Yōroppa**
exercise (physical), *to*: **undō-suru**
exist, to: **aru** (slightly irregular **u** verb); **iru** (**ru** verb);
    irassharu (slightly irregular **u** verb)
exit: **deguchi**
expensive: **kōka na, takai**
eye: **me**
eyeglasses: **megane**

F

face: **kao**
fact: **jijitsu**
factory: **kōjō**
fall (autumn): **aki**
famous: **yūmei na**
far: **tōi**
fast: **hayai** (adjective), **hayaku** (adverb)
father: **chichi** (plain), **otōsan** (polite)
fax: **fakkusu**
February: **ni-gatsu**
female: **onna**
fever: **netsu**
fine (healthy): **genki na**
finger: **yubi**
fire (conflagration): **kaji**
fire (flame): **hi**
fireworks: **hanabi**
fish: **sakana**
fit: **au** (**u** verb)
five: **go**
flag: **hata**
flour: **komugiko**
flower: **hana**
flu: **infuruenza**
fly (insect): **hae**
foot: **ashi**
forehead: **hitai**

foreign country: **gaikoku**
foreign money: **gaika**
foreigner: **gaikokujin**
forest: **mori**
forget, to: **wasureru** (**ru** verb)
fork: **fōku**
four: **shi , yon**
France: **Furansu**
free time: **hima**
Friday: **kinyōbi**
friend: **tomodachi**
frog: **kaeru**
front: **mae**
fruit: **kudamono**
furniture: **kagu**

G

gallery: **garō**
gamble: **kakegoto**
garage: **shako**
garbage: **gomi**
gas station: **gasorin sutando**
Germany: **Doitsu**
get off (transportation), *to*: **oriru** (**ru** verb)
get on (transportation), *to*: **noru** (**u** verb)
get up, to: **okiru** (**ru** verb)
girlfriend: **kanojo**
give, to: **ageru** (**ru** verb), **kureru** (**ru** verb),
    sashiageru (**ru** verb), **kudasaru** (slightly irregular
    u verb)
glad: **ureshii**
glasses (eyeglasses): **megane**
go, to: **iku** (slightly irregular **u** verb)
Good afternoon!: **Konnichiwa.**
god: **kami**
golf: **gorufu**
Good morning!: **Ohayō.** (plain), **Ohayō gozaimasu.**
    (honorific)
Good night!: **Oyasuminasai.**
good: **ii** (irregular adjective)
Goodbye!: **Sayōnara.**
grade (rating in school): **seiseki**
graduate school: **daigakuin**
grandchildren: **mago**
grandfather: **ojīsan** (honorific),
    sofu (plain)
grandmother: **obāsan** (honorific),
    sobo (plain)
green: **midori**
guitar: **gitā**

H

hair: **kami**
half: **hanbun**
hand: **te**
hat: **bōshi**
he: **kare**

head: **atama**
heaven: **tengoku**
heavy: **omoi**
hell: **jigoku**
Hello! (telephone greeting): **moshimoshi**
Hello!: **Konnichiwa.**
here: **koko**
hiccup: **shakkuri**
hide (something), *to*: **kakusu** (**u** verb)
high school: **kōkō**
hip: **koshi**
history: **rekishi**
hobby: **shumi**
hold (to have in hand), *to*: **motsu** (**u** verb)
home: **uchi**
homework: **shukudai**
honey: **hachimitsu**
horse: **uma**
hospital: **byōin**
hot (spicy): **karai**
hot (temperature, weather): **atsui**
hotel: **hoteru**
hour: **-ji, -jikan**
house: **ie**
how many: **ikutsu**
how much (price): **ikura**
how: **dō**
hundred: **hyaku**
hungry: **onaka ga suite iru**
hurry, to: **isogu** (**u** verb)
husband: **otto**

I

I: **watashi**
ice: **kōri**
ice cream: **aisukurīmu**
if: **moshi**
illness: **byōki**
immigrant: **imin**
influence: **eikyō**
insect: **mushi**
inside: **naka**
interesting: **omoshiroi**
intersection: **kōsaten**
invitation: **shōtai**
Italy: **Itaria**

J

jacket: **jaketto**
jail: **keimusho**
January: **ichi-gatsu**
Japan: **Nihon, Nippon**
Japanese language: **Nihon-go**
Japanese person: **Nihon-jin**
jaw: **ago**
jeans: **jīnzu**
job: **shigoto**

joke: **jōdan**
journey: **tabi**
juice: **jūsu**
July: **shichi-gatsu**
June: **roku-gatsu**

K

key (to room): **kagi**
kill, to: **korosu** (**u** verb)
kitchen: **daidokoro, kitchin**
knee: **hiza**
knife: **naifu**
know, to: **shitte iru**
koban (police box): **kōban**

L

lake: **mizuumi**
land: **tochi**
language: **gengo**
last month: **sengetsu**
last week: **senshū**
last year: **kyonen**
late: **osoi**
laugh, to: **warau** (**u** verb)
law: **hōritsu**
lawyer: **bengoshi**
leaf: **ha**
learn, to: **manabu** (**u** verb)
leather: **kawa**
left: **hidari**
leg: **ashi**
lemon: **remon**
lend, to: **kasu** (**u** verb)
letter: **tegami**
liberty: **jiyū**
lie: **uso**
light (illumination): **hikari**
light (weight): **karui**
like, to: **suki na**
listen, to: **kiku** (**u** verb)
literature: **bungaku**
living room: **ima, ribingu**
lonely: **samishii**
love: **ai, koi**
low: **hikui**
luggage: **nimotsu**
lunch: **chūshoku, hiru-gohan**

M

magazine: **zasshi**
make, to: **tsukuru** (**u** verb)
male: **otoko**
man: **otoko no hito**
March: **san-gatsu**
mathematics: **sūgaku**
May: **go-gatsu**
meal: **shokuji**

mean (unkind): **ijiwaru na**
meaning: **imi**
meat: **niku**
medicine: **kusuri**
meet: **au** (**u** verb)
melon: **meron**
memorize, to: **oboeru**
    (**ru** verb)
milk: **gyūnyū**
-minute: **-fun**
mirror: **kagami**
Monday: **Getsuyōbi**
money: **o-kane**
monkey: **saru**
morning: **asa**
moth: **ga**
mother: **haha** (plain), **okāsan**
    (honorific)
mountain: **yama**
mouth: **kuchi**
movie theater: **eigakan**
movie: **eiga**
Mt. Fuji: **Fujisan**
museum: **hakubutsukan**
music: **ongaku**

N

nail: **tsume**
name: **namae**
narrow: **semai**
nationality: **kokuseki**
nature: **shizen**
near: **chikaku**
necessary: **hitsuyō na**
neck: **kubi**
need, to: **iru** (**u** verb)
needle: **hari**
new: **atarashii**
newspaper: **shinbun**
next door: **tonari**
next month: **raigetsu**
next week: **raishū**
next year: **rainen**
nine: **kyū**
noisy: **urusai**
north: **kita**
nose: **hana**
November: **jūichi-gatsu**
now: **ima**
nurse: **kangoshi**

O

occasionally: **tamani**
occupation: **shokugyō**
ocean: **umi**
o'clock: **-ji**
October: **jū-gatsu**

old (for inanimate things): **furui**
one: **ichi**
open (something), *to*: **akeru** (**ru** verb)
opposite side: **mukai gawa**
orange (fruit): **mikan**
outside: **soto**
over there: **asoko**
oyster: **kaki**

P

PM: **gogo**
pain: **itami**
painful: **itai**
pants: **zubon**
paper: **kami**
park: **kōen**
parking lot: **chūshajō**
party (event): **pātī**
pass by, to: **sugiru** (**ru** verb)
passport: **pasupōto**
patient (doctor's): **kanja**
pay, to: **harau** (**u** verb)
peace: **heiwa**
pear: **nashi**
pencil: **enpitsu**
pencil sharpener: **enpitsu kezuri**
perfume: **kōsui**
persimmon: **kaki**
person: **hito**
Philippines: **Firipin**
photograph: **shashin**
physician: **isha** (plain), **o-isha-san**
    (honorific)
physics: **butsuri**
piano: **piano**
picture (painting or drawing): **e**
pig: **buta**
pillar: **hashira**
pillow: **makura**
pizza: **piza**
plant: **shokubutsu**
play (drama): **geki**
play, to: **asobu** (**u** verb)
pocket: **poketto**
police: **keisatsu**
police officer: **keisatsukan**
pond: **ike**
pork: **butaniku**
post office: **yūbinkyoku**
pot: **nabe**
potato: **jagaimo**
practice (exercise): **renshū**
price: **nedan**
probably: **tabun**
promise: **yakusoku**
pronunciation: **hatsuon**
pull, to: **hiku** (**u** verb)

pupil: **seito**
purple: **murasaki**
put, to: **oku** (**u** verb)

Q

question: **shitsumon**
quickly: **hayaku**
quiet: **shizuka na**
quite: **kanari**

R

rabbit: **usagi**
radio: **rajio**
rain: **ame**
raise, to: **ageru** (**ru** verb)
read, to: **yomu** (**u** verb)
really (truly): **hontō ni**
receipt: **reshīto**
receive, to: **ukeru** (**ru** verb), **morau** (**u** verb, plain),
   itadaku (**u** verb, honorific)
red: **aka**
refrigerator: **reizōko**
remote control: **rimokon**
reply (response): **henji**
reservation (appointment): **yoyaku**
rest, to: **yasumu** (**u** verb)
restaurant: **resutoran**
return, to: **kaeru** (**u** verb)
rice (cooked): **gohan**
rice (uncooked): **kome**
rice bowl: **chawan**
rice wine: **sake**
right: **migi**
rise, to: **agaru** (**u** verb)
river: **kawa**
room: **heya**
run, to: **hashiru** (**u** verb)

S

sack (bag): **fukuro**
sad: **kanashii**
safe: **anzen na**
salad: **sarada**
salary: **kyūryō**
sales tax: **shōhizei**
salmon: **sake**
salmon roe: **ikura**
salt: **shio**
same: **onaji**
sandal: **sandaru**
Saturday: **Doyōbi**
say, to: **iu** (**u** verb)
scary: **kowai**
school: **gakkō**
science: **kagaku**
scissors: **hasami**
search, to: **sagasu** (**u** verb)

season: **kisetsu**
secret: **himitsu**
secretary: **hisho**
select, to: **erabu** (**u** verb)
sell, to: **uru** (**u** verb)
sentence: **bun**
September: **ku-gatsu**
serious: **majime na**
seven: **nana** or **shichi**
shallow: **asai**
she: **kanojo**
sheep: **hitsuji**
shellfish: **kai**
ship: **fune**
shirt: **shatsu**
shoe: **kutsu**
shoulder: **kata**
shrimp: **ebi**
sightseeing: **kankō**
sign (shop): **kanban**
signature: **shomei**
silver (metal): **gin**
simple: **kantan na**
sing, to: **utau** (**u** verb)
sister (older): **ane** (plain), **onēsan** (honorific)
sister (younger): **imōto**
sit down, to: **suwaru** (**u** verb)
six: **roku**
skirt: **sukāto**
sleep, to: **neru** (**ru** verb)
sleepy: **nemui**
slim: **hosoi**
slow: **osoi**
small: **chīsai**
snake: **hebi**
snow: **yuki**
soccer: **sakkā**
social studies: **shakaigaku**
socks: **kutsushita**
somebody: **dareka**
something: **nanika**
somewhere: **dokoka**
son: **musuko**
song: **uta**
South Korea: **Kankoku**
south: **minami**
souvenir: **omiyage**
spacious: **hiroi**
spaghetti: **supagettī**
Spain: **Supein**
speak, to: **hanasu** (**u** verb)
spider: **kumo**
spinach: **hōrensō**
spring: **haru**
square: **shikaku**
squid: **ika**
stamp (postage stamp): **kitte**

stapler: **hochikisu**

star (in the sky): **hoshi**

station (for trains and subways): **eki**

stomach: **i**

stone: **ishi**

store: **mise**

story: **hanashi**

straight: **massugu**

strange: **hen na**

strawberry: **ichigo**

street: **michi**

strict: **kibishii**

stubborn: **ganko na**

students: **gakusei**

study, to: **benkyō-suru** (irregular verb)

subway: **chikatetsu**

sugar: **satō**

suit: **sūtsu**

suitcase: **sūtsukēsu**

summer: **natsu**

sun: **taiyō, hi**

Sunday: **Nichiyōbi**

sunglasses: **sangurasu**

supermarket: **sūpā**

sweater: **sētā**

swim, to: **oyogu** (**u** verb)

swimming: **suiei**

T

table: **tēburu**

take, to: **toru** (**u** verb)

taxi: **takushī**

tea (green tea): **o-cha**

teacher: **sensei** (honorific), **kyōshi** (plain)

teacup: **chawan**

tear: **namida**

telephone number: **denwa-bangō**

telephone: **denwa**

ten: **jū**

ten thousand: **ichiman**

tennis: **tenisu**

terrible: **hidoi**

Thank you!: **Arigatō gozaimasu., Dōmo.**

that one (near you): **sore**

that one (over there): **are**

theater (for plays and performances): **gekijō**

there (near you): **soko**

thick: **atsui**

thief: **dorobō**

thing: **mono**

think, to: **omou** (**u** verb)

this month: **kongetsu**

this one: **kore**

this week: **konshū**

this year: **kotoshi**

thread: **ito**

three: **san**

throat: **nodo**

thunder: **kaminari**

Thursday: **Mokuyōbi**

tie: **nekutai**

time: **jikan**

toast (ceremonial drink): **kanpai**

tobacco: **tabako**

today: **kyō**

together: **issho ni**

tomorrow: **ashita**

tonight: **konban**

tooth: **ha**

toothpaste: **hamigakiko**

trading: **bōeki**

train: **densha**

translation: **hon'yaku**

translator: **hon'yakusha**

trash: **gomi**

tree: **ki**

triangle: **sankaku**

trip: **ryokō**

troublesome: **mendō na**

tsunami: **tsunami**

Tuesday: **Kayōbi**

tuna: **maguro**

turn, to, or *make a turn, to*: **magaru** (**u** verb)

turtle: **kame**

TV: **terebi**

two: **ni**

U

umbrella: **kasa**

uncle: **oji** (plain), **ojisan** (honorific)

under: **shita**

understand, to: **wakaru** (**u** verb)

university: **daigaku**

use, to: **tsukau** (**u** verb)

usually: **taitei**

V

vacation: **yasumi**

vague: **aimai na**

various: **iroiro na**

vase: **kabin**

vegetable: **yasai**

very: **totemo**

village: **mura**

visa (for traveling): **biza**

volcano: **kazan**

W

wait, to: **matsu** (**u** verb)

walk, to: **aruku** (**u** verb)

wall: **kabe**

wallet: **saifu**

want, to: **hoshii**

war: **sensō**

warm: **atatakai**

wash, to: **arau** (**u** verb)

water: **mizu**

wave: **nami**

wear, to: **kiru** (**ru** verb)

Wednesday: **Suiyōbi**

week: **shū**

weird: **hen na**

west: **nishi**

what: **nani**

when: **itsu**

where: **doko**

which one (of the two): **dochira**

which one (of the three or more items): **dore**

white: **shiro**

who: **dare** (plain), **donata** (honorific)

why: **dōshite, naze**

wide: **hiroi**

wife: **tsuma**

win, to: **katsu** (**u** verb)

wind: **kaze**

window: **mado**

wine: **wain**

winter: **fuyu**

wipe, to: **fuku** (**u** verb)

woman: **onna no hito**

woods: **hayashi**

work, to: **hataraku** (**u** verb)

world: **sekai**

write, to: **kaku** (**u** verb)

writer (author): **sakka**

Y

year: **toshi**

yellow: **kiiro**

yesterday: **kinō**

yogurt: **yōguruto**

you: **anata**

young: **wakai**

Z

zebra: **shimauma**

zero: **zero, rei**

zip code: **yūbin bangō**

zoo: **dōbutsuen**

Answer key

Answers are not given for oral exercises or those that explore personal circumstances.

1 Introducing Japanese sounds, word order, and writing systems

1·10
1. bus
2. necktie
3. TV
4. radio
5. camera
6. iron

1·11
1. person
2. Japanese person
3. to come
4. not to come
5. next year
6. expensive
7. student

1·13
1. が **ga**, を **o**
2. を **o**, が **ga**
3. が **ga**, に **ni**

1·14
1. に **ni**
2. が **ga**
3. に **ni**
4. を **o**

1·15
1. 東京に行った。**Tōkyō ni itta.**
2. すしを食べた。**Sushi o tabeta.**
3. 友達がバナナを食べた。**Tomodachi ga banana o tabeta.**
4. メアリーはボストンに行った。 **Mearī wa Bosuton ni itta.**

1·16
1. a
2. a
3. a or b
4. a or b
5. c
6. c

2 Nouns

2·2
1. b
2. b
3. a
4. a
5. c

2·3
    1. b
    2. c
    3. a
    4. d

2·5
    1. あの **Ano**
    2. あれ **Are**
    3. nothing
    4. それ **Sore**
    5. これ **Kore**

2·6
    1. 田中さんは私の友達です。　**Tanaka-san wa watashi no tomodachi desu.**
    2. これは子供の本です。　**Kore wa kodomo no hon desu.**
    3. あれは山田さんの大学です。　**Are wa Yamada-san no daigaku desu.**
    4. あれは山田さんの友達の車です。**Are wa Yamada-san no tomodachi no kuruma desu.**

2·7
    1. あれは私の本です。　**Are wa watashi no hon desu.** (*That one is my book.*)
        or 私の本はあれです。　**Watashi no hon wa are desu.** (*My book is that one.*)
    2. その車は私のです。　**Sono kuruma wa watashi no desu.** (*That car is mine.*)
    3. 父の車は日本のです。　**Chichi no kuruma wa Nihon no desu.** (*My father's car is Japanese.*)
    4. この鉛筆は田中さんのです。　**Kono enpitsu wa Tanaka-san no desu.** (*This pencil is Mr. Tanaka's.*)

2·8
    1. 母 **haha**
    2. お母さん **okāsan**
    3. お父さん **otōsan**
    4. お兄さん **onīsan**

2·9
    1. は **wa**, の **no**
    2. は **wa**, の **no**, の **no**
    3. の **no**, は **wa**, の **no**
    4. の **no**, の **no**, は **wa**, の **no**

3   Numbers

3·1
    1. はち **hachi**
    2. じゅう に **jū-ni**
    3. に じゅう **ni-jū**
    4. に じゅう に **ni-jū-ni**
    5. なな じゅう きゅう **nana-jū-kyū**

3·2
    1. さんびゃく にじゅう **san-byaku-ni-jū**
    2. ごせん ろっぴゃく きゅうじゅう きゅう **go-sen-rop-pyaku-kyū-jū-kyū**
    3. いちまん にせん **ichi-man ni-sen**
    4. ななまん さんぜん はっぴゃく **nana-man-san-zen-hap-pyaku**
    5. きゅうまん きゅうせんきゅうひゃく きゅうじゅう きゅう **kyū-man kyū-sen kyū-hyaku-kyū-jū kyū**

3·4
    1. 5本 **go-hon**
    2. 3枚 **san-mai**
    3. 2匹 **ni-hiki**
    4. 5人 **go-nin**
    5. 3つ **mit-tsu**
    6. 7冊 **nana-satsu**

3·5
    1. 25ページ **ni-jū-go pēji**
    2. 6階 **rokkai**
    3. 2位 **ni-i**

3·6
    1. さんじ **san-ji**
    2. よじ にじゅうごふん **yo-ji ni-jū-go-fun**
    3. しちじ じゅっぷん **shichi-ji jup-pun**
    4. ごぜん くじ じゅうごふん **gozen ku-ji jū-go-fun**
    5. ごご じゅうにじ じゅうにふん **gogo jū-ni-ji jū-ni-fun**

1. さんがつ **san-gatsu**
2. しがつ **shi-gatsu**
3. ごがつ いつか **go-gatsu itsuka**
4. じゅうがつ とおか **jū-gatsu tōka**
5. くがつ にじゅうよっか **ku-gatsu nijūyokka**

3·9
1. 3時 **san-ji**
2. 3時間 **san-jikan**
3. 100円 **hyaku-en**
4. 8月 **hachi-gatsu**
5. 8ケ月 **hachi-kagetsu**
6. 5メートル **go-mētoru**

3·10
1. 3人目の学生 **san-nin-me no gakusei**
2. 2杯目のコーヒー **ni-hai-me no kōhī**
3. 2つ目の交差点 **futa-tsu-me no kōsaten**
4. 3人目の子供 **san-nin-me no kodomo**

3·11
1. 4 o'clock
2. 4 hours
3. 4th hour
4. April
5. 4th month

4 Basic verb forms

4·1
1. **u** verb
2. ambiguous
3. **u** verb
4. **u** verb
5. ambiguous
6. **u** verb
7. **u** verb

4·2
1. **ru** verb
2. **u** verb
3. **u** verb
4. **ru** verb
5. **u** verb

4·3
1. b
2. c
3. b
4. b

4·4

Masu form	**Nai** form
1. たべます **tabemasu**	たべない **tabenai**
2. ねます **nemasu**	ねない **nenai**
3. みます **mimasu**	みない **minai**
4. あげます **agemasu**	あげない **agenai**
5. かります **karimasu**	かりない **karinai**
6. おしえます **oshiemasu**	おしえない **oshienai**

4·5

Masu form	**Nai** form
1. のみます **nomimasu**	のまない **nomanai**
2. あいます **aimasu**	あわない **awanai**
3. かちます **kachimasu**	かたない **katanai**
4. いきます **ikimasu**	いかない **ikanai**
5. およぎます **oyogimasu**	およがない **oyoganai**
6. うります **urimasu**	うらない **uranai**
7. しにます **shinimasu**	しなない **shinanai**
8. はなします **hanashimasu**	はなさない **hanasanai**
9. あそびます **asobimasu**	あそばない **asobanai**

4·6
1. たべない **tabenai**
2. みない **minai**
3. きらない **kiranai**
4. きます **kimasu**
5. うります **urimasu**, うらない **uranai**
6. とびます **tobimasu**, とばない **tobanai**
7. まちます **machimasu**, またない **matanai**
8. かいます **kaimasu**, かわない **kawanai**
9. します **shimasu**, しない **shinai**
10. きます **kimasu**, こない **konai**

4·7
1. かいて **kaite**
2. いって **itte**
3. かって **katte**
4. かって **katte**
5. とんで **tonde**
6. して **shite**
7. きて **kite**

4·8
1. かいた **kaita**
2. いった **itta**
3. かった **katta**
4. かった **katta**
5. とんだ **tonda**
6. した **shita**
7. きた **kita**

4·9
1. かかなかった **kakanakatta**
2. いかなかった **ikanakatta**
3. かわなかった **kawanakatta**
4. かたなかった **katanakatta**
5. とばなかった **tobanakatta**
6. しなかった **shinakatta**
7. こなかった **konakatta**

4·10
1. 行かない **ikanai**
2. 借りない **karinai**
3. 買う **kau**
4. 書いた **kaita**
5. 読まなかった **yomanakatta**

4·11
1. 行きません **ikimasen**
2. 食べまます **tabemasu**
3. 書きませんでした **kakimasendeshita**
4. 読みました **yomimashita**
5. 休みませんでした **yasumimasendeshita**

4·12
1. *I will drink.* (or *I drink.*)
2. *I drank.*
3. *I am drinking.*
4. *I was drinking.*

4·13
1. かける **kakeru**
2. いえる **ieru**
3. よめる **yomeru**
4. かえる **kaeru**
5. こられる **korareru**
6. たべられる **taberareru**

4·14
1. 昨日は金曜日でした。**Kinō wa Kinyōbi deshita.**
2. あれは猫じゃありません。**Are wa neko ja arimasen.** or あれは猫じゃないです。**Are wa neko ja nai desu.** (じゃ **ja** in these sentences may be では **de wa**.)
3. あの人はスミスさんです。**Ano hito wa Sumisu-san desu.**
4. 昨日の晩ご飯はてんぷらじゃありませんでした。**Kinō no ban-gohan wa tenpura ja arimasendeshita.** or 昨日の晩ご飯はてんぷらじゃなかったです。**Kinō no ban-gohan wa tenpura ja nakatta desu.** (じゃ **ja** in these sentences may be では **de wa**.)

5 Verb types

5·1
1. *to log in*
2. *to send an email*
3. *to start*
4. *to order*
5. *to date*

5·2
1. 私の本はかばんの中にあります。Watashi no hon wa kaban no naka ni arimasu.
2. 私のかばんはいすの後ろにあります。Watashi no kaban wa isu no ushiro ni arimasu.
3. 犬は机の下にいます。Inu wa tsukue no shita ni imasu.
4. 猫は犬の隣にいます。Neko wa inu no tonari ni imasu.

5·3
1. ありました arimashita
2. います imasu
3. あります arimasu
4. ありますか arimasu ka
5. いますか imasu ka

5·4
1. none
2. てんぷら tenpura
3. マイクさん Maiku-san
4. none

5·5
1. が ga
2. を o
3. が ga
4. が ga
5. を o

5·6
1. を o
2. が ga
3. 見られました miraremashita
4. が ga

5·7
1. あげました agemashita
2. くれました kuremashita
3. くれました kuremashita
4. あげました agemashita
5. 下さいました kudasaimashita

5·8
1. もらいました moraimashita
2. 頂きました itadakimashita
3. に ni
4. 兄 ani

5·9
1. 母が隣の方にお菓子を差し上げました。Haha ga tonari no kata ni okashi o sashiagemashita.
2. 私は社長にお酒を差し上げました。Watashi wa shachō ni osake o sashiagemashita.
3. 社長は私にチョコレートを下さいました。Shachō wa watashi ni chokorēto o kudasaimashita. or
   私は社長にチョコレートを頂きました。Watashi wa shachō ni chokorēto o itadakimashita.
4. 母は私にTシャツをくれました。Haha wa watashi ni tīshatsu o kuremashita. or
   私は母にTシャツをもらいました。Watashi wa haha ni tīshatsu o moraimashita.

6 Auxiliaries that follow verbs in the te form

6·1
1. ください kudasai
2. いただき itadaki
3. くれ kure
4. あげ age
5. あげ age or やり yari

6·2
1. habitual
2. resulting
3. progressive
4. habitual
5. resulting

6·4   掃除して sōji shite, 買って katte

6·5   1. 会って atte
2. 使って tsukatte
3. 着て kite
4. 考えて kangaete

6·6   1. 勉強して benkyō shite
2. 忘れて wasurete
3. プレゼントを買って purezento o katte
4. して shite
5. 使って tsukatte

6·7   1. きました kimashita
2. いきます ikimasu
3. いきますよ ikimasu yo
4. きましたね kimashita ne
5. いく iku

6·8   1. 壁にポスターが貼ってあります。　Kabe ni postā ga hatte arimasu.
2. シャツが壁に掛けてあります。　Shatsu ga kabe ni kakete arimasu.
3. 窓が開けてあります。　Mado ga akete arimasu.
4. 電気がつけてあります。　Denki ga tsukete arimasu.
5. 味噌汁が作ってあります。　Miso-shiru ga tsukutte arimasu.

6·9   して shite, 置かないで okanai de, 入れて irete, 洗って aratte, 開けて akete

7   Particles

7·1   1. b
2. d
3. e
4. c
5. a

7·2   1. *I passed the bank.*
2. *I climbed up the mountain.*
3. *I flew through the sky.*
4. *I walked (all over) the park.*
5. *I strolled in Ginza.*

7·3   1. b
2. b
3. b

7·4   1. を o
2. が ga
3. を o
4. が ga
5. が ga

7·5   1. を o
2. を o
3. が ga
4. を o
5. が ga
6. を o
7. が ga

7·6   1. に ni, を o
2. に ni
3. に ni, を o
4. を o, に ni

7·7
1. に **ni**
2. で **de**
3. に **ni**
4. で **de**
5. で **de**, に **ni**

7·8
1. を **o**
2. に **ni**
3. で **de**
4. を **o**
5. に **ni**, で **de**
6. を **o**

7·9
1. に **ni** or へ **e**
2. に **ni**, に **ni**
3. に **ni**, に **ni**
4. に **ni**

7·10
1. へ **e**
2. から **kara**
3. まで **made**
4. に **ni**
5. で **de**

7·11
1. 数学の本と経済学の本を買いました。**Sūgaku no hon to keizaigaku no hon o kaimashita.**
2. 東京や大阪に行きます。**Tōkyō ya Ōsaka ni ikimasu.**
3. 母とてんぷらを作りました。**Haha to tenpura o tsukurimashita.**

7·12
1. にも **ni mo**
2. には **ni wa**
3. も **mo**
4. も **mo**
5. を **o**

7·13
1. 弟は遊んでばかりいます。**Otōto wa asonde bakari imasu.**
2. 妹はマンガばかり読んでいます。**Imōto wa manga bakari yonde imasu.**
3. 姉は買い物ばかりしています。**Ane wa kaimono bakari shite imasu.**

7·14
1. 明子さんはみち子さんとしか話しません。**Akiko-san wa Michiko-san to shika hanashimasen.**
2. チケットが一枚しかありません。**Chiketto ga ichi-mai shika arimasen.**
3. 自転車しかありません。**Jitensha shika arimasen.**
4. ラーメンしか食べませんでした。**Rāmen shika tabemasendeshita.**

7·15
1. だけ **dake**
2. だけ **dake**
3. しか **shika**
4. しか **shika**
5. だけ **dake**

7·16
1. b (*My older sister doesn't eat even delicious things.*)
2. c (*My older brother eats even things that are not delicious.*)
3. d (*My father doesn't buy even cheap things.*)
4. e (*My older brother even buys expensive things.*)
5. a (*My younger brother doesn't read even interesting books.*)

8 Adjectives and adverbs

8·1
1. ジョージさんはまじめです。**Jōji-san wa majime desu.** *George is serious.*
2. 幸子さんの家は大きいです。**Sachiko-san no ie wa ōkii desu.** *Sachiko's house is big.*
3. 私の部屋は広いです。**Watashi no heya wa hiroi desu.** *My room is spacious.*
4. 兄の車は新しいです。**Ani no kuruma wa atarashii desu.** *My older brother's car is new.*
5. これは便利です。**Kore wa benri desu.** *This is convenient.*
6. 恵子さんはきれいです。**Keiko-san wa kirei desu.** *Keiko is pretty.*

8·2
1. 親切じゃありません。or 親切じゃないです。**Shinsetsu ja arimasen.** or **Shinsetsu ja nai desu.** *(He) is not kind.*
2. 優しくありません。or 優しくないです。**Yasashiku arimasen.** or **Yasahiku nai desu.** *(He) is not kind.*
3. 意地悪じゃありません。or 意地悪じゃないです。**Ijiwaru ja arimasen.** or **Ijiwaru ja nai desu.** *(He) is not mean.*
4. こわくありません。or こわくないです。**Kowaku arimasen.** or **Kowaku nai desu.** *(He) is not scary.*
5. かっこよくありません。or かっこよくないです。**Kakkoyoku arimasen.** or **Kakkoyoku nai desu.** *(He) is not good looking.*
6. きれいじゃありません。or きれいじゃないです。**Kirei ja arimasen.** or **Kirei ja nai desu.** *(She) is not pretty.*

8·3
1. 難しかったです。**Muzukashikatta desu.** *(It) was difficult.*
2. 簡単でした。**Kantan deshita.** *(It) was easy.*
3. 面白かったです。**Omoshirokatta desu.** *(It) was interesting.*
4. 大変でした。**Taihen deshita.** *(It) was hard.*
5. つまらなかったです。**Tsumaranakatta desu.** *(It) was boring.*

8·4
1. 私は犬が好きです。**Watashi wa inu ga sukidesu.**
2. 私は猫が好きじゃありません。or 私は猫が好きじゃないです。**Watashi wa neko ga suki ja arimasen.** or **Watashi wa neko ga suki ja nai desu.**
3. 私は虫が嫌いです。**Watashi wa mushi ga kirai desu.**
4. 私は新しいプリンターがほしいです。**Watashi wa atarashii purintā ga hoshii desu.**

8·5 *Sample answers:*
1. やさしくて **yasashikute** *(Mr. Tanaka is a kind and nice person.)*
2. ひどい **hidoi** *(Mr. Kato is a mean and terrible person.)*
3. 痛くて **itakute** *(I had a headache and couldn't go to the class.)*
4. 高くて **Takakute** *(It was expensive, so I couldn't buy it.)*
5. おいしくて **oishikute** *(That restaurant has very delicious (food), and is pretty.)*

8·6
1. 食べませんでした **tabemasendeshita**
2. 歩きます **arukimasu**
3. 飲みません **nomimasen**
4. 泣きます **nakimasu**

8·7
1. はやく **hayaku**
2. 静かに **shizuka ni**
3. まじめに **majime ni**
4. 小さく **chīsaku**

8·8
1. 静かに勉強してください。**Shizuka ni benkyō shite kudasai.**
2. はやく食べてください。**Hayaku tabete kudasai.**
3. 部屋をきれいにしてください。**Heya o kirei ni shite kudasai.**
4. 静かにしてください。**Shizuka ni shite kudasai.**

8·9
1. *lazy*
2. *upset*
3. *smiling*

8·10
1. カナダとアメリカと、どちらの方が大きいですか。**Kanada to Amerika to, dochira no hō ga ōkii desu ka.**
2. 中国語と韓国語と、どちらの方が簡単ですか。**Chūgokugo to Kankokugo to, dochira no hō ga kantan desu ka.**
3. 電車と飛行機と、どちらの方が便利ですか。**Densha to hikōki to, dochira no hō ga benri desu ka.**
4. 日本人と中国人と、どちらの方がよく働きますか。**Nihonjin to Chūgokujin to, dochira no hō ga yoku hatarakimasuka.**
5. ニューヨークとシカゴと、どちらの方が寒いですか。**Nyūyōku to Shikago to, dochira no hō ga samui desu ka.**

8·11 *Sample answers:*
1. クッキーの方が好きです。**Kukkī no hō ga suki desu.**
2. 母の方が厳しいです。**Haha no hō ga kibishii desu.**
3. 猫の方が好きです。**Neko no hō ga suki desu.**

8·12　1. *I'm not as smart as you are.*
　　　2. *The final exam was as difficult as the midterm exam.*
　　　3. *My mother is not as kind as my father.*
　　　4. *This year, it did not snow as much as it did last year.*
　　　5. *Telephones are not as convenient as email.*

8·13　1. *Which do you like better, teaching or learning?*
　　　2. *Teaching is harder than learning.*
　　　3. *Learning is not as hard as teaching.*
　　　4. *I like watching a movie as much as reading a book.*

8·14　1. 私は兄と同じぐらい（よく）食べます。**Watashi wa ani to onaji gurai (yoku) tabemasu.**
　　　2. アメリカは日本より大きいです。**Amerika wa Nihon yori ōkii desu.**
　　　3. 犬は猫より速く走れます。**Inu wa neko yori hayaku hashiremasu.**
　　　4. 漢字を読むのは漢字を書くほど難しくありません。**Kanji o yomu no wa kanji o kaku hodo muzukashiku arimasen.**
　　　5. この本はあの本より高いですか。**Kono hon wa ano hon yori takai desu ka.**

8·15　1. だれ **dare**
　　　2. 何 **nani**
　　　3. どれ **dore**
　　　4. どこ **doko**
　　　5. どれ **dore**

9　Sentence types

9·1　1. どこ **doko**
　　　2. だれ **dare**
　　　3. 何 **nani**
　　　4. どう **dō**
　　　5. いつ **itsu**

9·2　1. *There is someone in that room.*
　　　2. *There is something in this box.*
　　　3. *The criminal is somewhere in this building.*
　　　4. *I will buy a new car someday.*

9·3　1. *I know nothing.* or *I don't know anything.*
　　　2. *I want nothing.* or *I don't want anything.*
　　　3. *I don't want to see anyone.*

9·4　1. どこかに **dokoka ni**, どこにも **doko ni mo**
　　　2. 何か **nanika**, 何も **nani mo**

9·5　1. *In this university, every student lives in a dormitory.*
　　　2. *Every company uses a computer.*
　　　3. *A convenience store can be found in every town.*
　　　4. *I bought every CD of Utada.*

9·6　1. 何でもします。**Nan demo shimasu.**
　　　2. どこにでも行きます。**Doko ni demo ikimasu.**
　　　3. 何でも買います。**Nan demo kaimasu.**

9·7　1. 安い **yasui**
　　　2. 日本人だ **Nihonjin da**
　　　3. ねなかった **nenakatta**
　　　4. よくなかった **yoku nakatta**
　　　5. 見た **mita**
　　　6. 来ない **konai**
　　　7. おもしろかった **omoshirokatta**
　　　8. きれいだった **kirei datta**

9·8　1. 石田さんの奥さんは中国人だそうです。**Ishida-san no oku-san wa Chūgokujin da sō desu.**
　　　2. 日本の牛肉は高いそうです。**Nihon no gyūniku wa takai sō desu.**
　　　3. 高橋さんはイタリア人と結婚したそうです。**Takahashi-san wa Itariajin to kekkon shita sō desu.**
　　　4. 砂糖は健康によくないそうです。**Satō wa kenkō ni yoku nai sō desu.**

9·10
1. あしたは寒いでしょう。**Ashita wa samui deshō.**
2. あさっては寒くないでしょう。**Asatte wa samuku nai deshō.**
3. 今年は雪が降らないでしょう。**Kotoshi wa yuki ga furanai deshō.**
4. あしたのサッカーの試合はないでしょう。**Ashita no sakkā no shiai wa nai deshō.**
5. あの人は韓国人でしょう。**Ano hito wa kankokujin deshō.**

9·11
1. 仕事を変えるかもしれません。**Shigoto o kaeru kamoshiremasen.**
2. あの人は親切じゃないかもしれません。**Ano hito wa shinsetsu ja nai kamoshiremasen.**
3. 大学に行かないかもしれません。**Daigaku ni ikanai kamoshiremasen.**
4. 薬がないかもしれません。**Kusuri ga nai kamoshiremasen.**
5. この車は古いかもしれません。**Kono kuruma wa furui kamoshiremasen.**

9·12
1. 帰りに買い物をするつもりです。**Kaeri ni kaimono o suru tsumori desu.**
2. アトランタの友達のうちに寄るつもりです。**Atoranta no tomodachi no uchi ni yoru tsumori desu.**
3. 新しい車は買わないつもりです。**Atarashii kuruma wa kawanai tsumori desu.**
4. 銀行には就職しないつもりです。**Ginkō ni wa shūshoku shinai tsumori desu.**

9·13
1. 田中さんは昨日ここに来たはずです。**Tanaka-san wa kinō koko ni kita hazu desu.**
2. この本は簡単なはずです。**Kono hon wa kantan na hazu desu.**
3. あしたは山田さんの誕生日のはずです。**Ashita wa Yamada-san no tanjōbi no hazu desu.**
4. 手紙はあした着くはずです。**Tegami wa ashita tsuku hazu desu.**

9·14
1. べき **beki**
2. はず **hazu**
3. はず **hazu**
4. べき **beki**
5. はず **hazu**

9·15
1. 中国では飲料水が足りないらしいです。**Chūgoku de wa inryōsui ga tarinai rashii desu.**
2. 日本の円が安くなったらしいです。**Nihon no en ga yasuku natta rashii desu.**
3. この機械は操作が簡単らしいです。**Kono kikai wa sōsa ga kantan rashii desu.**

9·16
1. よう **yō**
2. らしい **rashii**
3. よう **yō**
4. らしい **rashii**

9·17
1. すう **suu**
2. 買った **katta**
3. ない **nai**
4. な **na**
5. した **shita**

9·18
1. ね **ne**
2. か **ka**
3. よ **yo**

9·19
1. いっしょにレストランに行きませんか。**Issho ni resutoran ni ikimasen ka.**
2. いっしょに宿題をしませんか。**Isshoni shukudai o shimasen ka.**
3. いっしょにコーヒーを飲みませんか。**Isshoni kōhī o nomimasen ka.**
4. いっしょにテニスをしませんか。**Isshoni tenisu o shimasen ka.**

9·20
1. 私が掃除しましょうか。**Watashi ga sōji shimashō ka.**
2. 私が書きましょうか。**Watashi ga kakimashō ka.**
3. 私が運びましょうか。**Watashi ga hakobimashō ka.**
4. 私が運転しましょうか。**Watashi ga unten shimashō ka.**
5. 私が皿を洗いましょうか。**Watashi ga sara o araimashō ka.**

9·21
1. 行こう。**Ikō.**
2. 食べよう。**Tabeyō.**
3. 飲もう。**Nomō.**
4. 帰ろう。**Kaerō.**
5. しよう。**Shiyō.**
6. 見よう。**Miyō.**
7. がんばろう。**Ganbarō.**

9·22 1. ちょっと待ってください。**Chotto matte kudasai.**
2. 入ってください。**Haitte kudasai.**
3. ここに座ってください。**Koko ni suwatte kudasai.**
4. 住所を書いてください。**Jūsho o kaite kudasai.**
5. 静かにしてください。**Shizuka ni shite kudasai.**

9·23 言い **ii**, 洗い **arai**, し **shi**, みがき **migaki**

9·24 1. 書け **kake**
2. 飲め **nome**
3. 頑張れ **ganbare**
4. 立て **tate**
5. 行け **ike**
6. 持て **mote**

9·25 1. 本を貸してくださいませんか。**Hon o kashite kudasai masen ka.**
2. 宿題を出してください。**Shukudai o dashite kudasai.**
3. ここに車をとめないでください。**Koko ni kuruma o tomenai de kudasai.**
4. 歯をみがきなさい。**Ha o migaki nasai.**

10 Complex words and phrases

10·1 1. *I missed watching an interesting movie.*
2. *I might have drunk too much.*
3. *Finish eating quickly.*
4. *Don't forget to take medicine.*

10·2 *Sample answers:*

1. 運転し **unten shi**
2. 持ち **mochi**
3. 使い **tsukai**
4. 書き **kaki**

10·3 1. カナダに行きたいです。**Kanada ni ikitai desu.**
2. 新しい車がほしいです。**Atarashii kuruma ga hoshii desu.**
3. 田中さんに会いたいですか。**Tanaka-san ni ai-tai desu ka.**
4. 日本の映画が見たいです。**Nihon no eiga ga mi-tai desu.** or 日本の映画を見たいです。
Nihon no eiga o mi-tai desu.

10·4 1. 犬を怖がらないでください。**Inu o kowagaranai de kudasai.**
2. 新しいパソコンがほしいです。**Atarashii pasokon ga hoshii desu.**
3. 兄は新しい車をほしがっています。**Ani wa atarashii kuruma o hoshigatte imasu.**
4. 私はピアノがひきたいです。**Watashi wa piano ga hikitai desu.**
5. 父はゴルフをしたがっています。**Chichi wa gorufu o shitagatte imasu.**

10·5 1. *My brother is very manly.*
2. *Ms. Yamaguchi seems to like karaoke.*
3. *Behave as a student.*
4. *My mother was not a typical ideal mother.*
5. *That person is a typical student.* or *That person seems to be a student.*

10·6 1. *My brother is like a superman.*
2. *Mr. Kawaguchi's wife is just like a fashion model.* or *It seems that Mr. Kawaguchi's wife is a fashion model.*
3. *Mr. Tanaka is a person who is like my own father.* or *Mr. Tanaka is like a father to me.*
4. *I want to swim like a dolphin.*

10·7 1. みたい **mitai** or のよう **no yō**
2. らしい **rashii**
3. みたいな **mitai na** or のような **no yō na**
4. みたい **mitai** or のよう **no yō**
5. みたいな **mitai na** or のような **no yō na**

10·8 1. おもしろ **omoshiro**
2. つまらな **tsumarana** or おもしろくなさ **omoshirokunasa**
3. ふり **furi**
4. やさし **yasashi**
5. なき **naki**

10·9   1. 話そうと **hanasō to**
       2. 勉強しようと **benkyō shiyō to**
       3. しようと思っています **shiyō to omotte imasu** (needs to be in the **te iru** form)
       4. できると **dekiru to**
       5. なると思います **naru to omoimasu**

10·10   1. *I tried to tell a lie, but I couldn't.*
       2. *I am thinking of going to Hawaii in summer.*
       3. *When I tried to leave, Mr. Tanaka came in.*
       4. *I almost cried, but I didn't.*

10·11   1. します **shimasu**
       2. なりましたね **narimashita ne**
       3. 読める **yomeru**
       4. して **shite**

10·12   1. *I decided not to take the exam.*
       2. *It has been decided that I won't take the exam.*
       3. *It has been decided that the students can get free admission to this art museum.*
       4. *It has been decided that smoking is not allowed in this building.*

10·13   1. カタカナを読むことができますか。 **Katakana o yomu koto ga dekimasu ka.**
       2. 箸で食べることができますか。 **Hashi de taberu koto ga dekimasu ka.**
       3. 日本語で挨拶をすることができますか。 **Nihongo de aisatsu o suru koto ga dekimasu ka.**
       4. 日本語の新聞を読むことができますか。 **Nihongo no shinbun o yomu koto ga dekimasu ka.**

10·15   1. アイスランドに行ったことがありますか。 **Aisurando ni itta koto ga arimasu ka.**
       2. 納豆を食べたことがありますか。 **Nattō o tabeta koto ga arimasu ka.**
       3. 黒澤の映画を見たことがありますか。 **Kurosawa no eiga o mita koto ga arimasu ka.**
       4. 新幹線に乗ったことがありますか。 **Shinkansen ni notta koto ga arimasu ka.**

11   Clauses

11·1   1. か **ka**
       2. か **ka**, かどうか **ka dō ka**
       3. か **ka**
       4. と **to**
       5. と **to**
       6. だと **da to**
       7. か **ka**

11·2   1. 前 **mae**
       2. 後 **ato**
       3. おきた **Okita**
       4. 行った **itta**

11·3   *Sample answers:*

       1. 夏休みの間にカナダに行こうと思います。 **Natsu-yasumi no aida ni Kanada ni ikō to omoimasu.** (*I'm thinking of going to Canada during the summer vacation.*)
       2. 朝、涼しいうちに仕事をします。 **Asa, suzushii uchi ni shigoto o shimasu.** (*I work while it's cool in the morning.*)
       3. 道が混まないうちに帰りましょう。 **Michi ga komanai uchi ni kaerimashō.** (*Let's go home before the roads get traffic.*)
       4. 忘れないうちに書きます。 **Wasurenai uchi ni kakimasu.** (*I write things down before I forget them.*)
       5. 赤ちゃんが寝ている間に私も寝ます。 **Akachan ga nete iru aida ni watashi mo nemasu.** (*While the baby is sleeping, I also sleep.*)

11·4   1. 暇な **Hima na**
       2. 東京に来る **Tōkyō ni kuru**
       3. 高校生の **Kōkōsei no**
       4. 子供が静かな **Kodomo ga shizuka na**
       5. 運転している **Unten shite iru**

11·6
1. の no
2. な na
3. 食べ tabe
4. 食べている tabete iru
5. 食べている tabete iru

11·7
1. あしたは車があるので心配しないでください。**Ashita wa kuruma ga aru node shinpai shinai de kudasai.**
2. まだ子供なので分からないと思います。**Mada kodomo na node wakaranai to omoimasu.**
3. あしたはテストがないので今日は勉強しません。**Ashita wa tesuto ga nai node kyō wa benkyō shimasen.**
4. 弟はまじめなので宿題は忘れないと思います。**Otōto wa majime na node shukudai wa wasurenai to omoimasu.**

11·8
1. が ga
2. が ga
3. のに noni, が ga
4. のに noni
5. が ga

11·9
1. ので node
2. のに noni
3. から kara
4. ので node

11·10
1. *That person is the person who was walking with Mr. Tanaka yesterday.*
2. *There is a possibility that no one has lived in that building.*
3. *The fact that Takeshi is writing to his father means that he does not have money.*
4. *The restaurant where I ate blowfish for the first time is that one.*
5. *My hobby is to shop on the Internet.*

11·11
1. 宇多田という歌手を知っていますか。**Utada to iu kashu o shitte imasu ka.**
2. 四日市というところに行きました。**Yokkaichi to iu tokoro ni ikimashita.**
3. JLPTという日本語のテストを知っていますか。**JLPT to iu Nihongo no tesuto o shitte imasu ka.**

12 Conjunctions

12·1
1. 私は図書館かうちで勉強します。**Watashi wa toshokan ka uchi de benkyō shimasu.**
2. 私はハンバーガーやホットドッグを食べました。**Watashi wa hanbāgā ya hottodoggu o tabemashita.**
3. 私はイタリアとスペインとフランスに行きました。**Watashi wa Itaria to Supein to Furansu ni ikimashita.**
4. 私は田中さんにも林さんにも会いました。**Watashi wa Tanaka-san ni mo Hayashi-san ni mo aimashita.**

12·2
1. 私は毎日歯をみがいて顔を洗って朝ごはんを食べます。**Watashi wa mainichi ha o migaite kao o aratte asagohan o tabemasu.**
2. 私は漢字を練習してCDを聞いて文法を勉強します。**Watashi wa kanji o renshū shite CD o kiite bunpō o benkyō shimasu.**
3. 母は朝ごはんを作って掃除をしてテレビを見ます。**Haha wa asagohan o tsukutte sōji o shite terebi o mimasu.**
4. 父は昨日5時間運転してとても疲れました。**Chichi wa kinō go-jikan unten shite totemo tsukaremashita.**

12·3
1. 勉強をしないで試験を受けました。**Benkyō o shinai de shiken o ukemashita.**
2. 手を洗わないで食べました。**Te o arawanai de tabemashita.**
3. 靴を履かないで歩きました。**Kutsu o hakanai de arukimashita.**
4. 先月は風邪が治らなくて困りました。**Sengetsu wa kaze ga naoranakute komarimashita.**
5. 本を読まないで映画を見ました。**Hon o yomanai de eiga o mimashita.**

12·4   1. このコースは簡単で宿題が少なくて楽しいです。**Kono kōsu wa kantan de shukudai ga sukunakute tanoshii desu.**

        2. このレストランの食べ物は高くておいしくありません。**Kono resutoran no tabemono wa takakute oishiku arimasen.**

        3. トムさんは頭がよくてかっこよくていい人です。**Tomu-san wa atama ga yokute kakkoyokute ii hito desu.**

12·5   1. 買ったり **kattari**

        2. 食べたり **tabetari**

        3. 飲んだり **nondari**

        4. 寝たり **netari**

        5. したり **shitari**

        6. 作ったり **tsukuttari**

        7. 書いたり **kaitari**

        8. 行ったり **ittari**

12·6   1. 古かったり **furukattari**

        2. 便利だったり **benri dattari**

        3. 楽しかったり **tanoshikattari**

        4. ひどかったり **hidokattari**

        5. 楽だったり **raku dattari**

        6. 優しかったり **yasashikattari**

        7. 厳しかったり **kibishikattari**

        8. よかったり **yokattari**

12·7   1. あしたはメールをチェックしたり映画を見たりしました。**Kinō wa mēru o chekku shitari eiga o mitari shimashita.**

        2. あしたは部屋を掃除したりします。**Ashita wa heya o sōji shitari shimasu.**

        3. 弟は毎日アニメを見たりマンガを読んだりしています。**Otōto wa mainichi anime o mitari manga o yondari shite imasu.**

        4. 私の先生は優しかったり厳しかったりします。**Watashi no sensei wa yasashikattari kibishikattari shimasu.**

        5. メールは便利だったり不便だったりします。**Mēru wa benri dattari fuben dattari shimasu.**

12·8   1. 武さんは意地悪だし、かっこよくないし。**Takeshi-san wa ijiwaru da shi, kakkoyokunai shi.**

        2. 掃除をしたし、買い物もしたし、洗濯もしたし。**Sōji o shita shi, kaimono mo shita shi, sentaku mo shitashi.**

        3. 真さんは勇気があるし、男らしいし、親切だし。**Makoto-san wa yūki ga aru shi, otoko rashii shi, shinsetsu da shi.**

12·10   *Sample answers:*

        1. 掃除をしました **sōji o shimashita** (*Yesterday, I went to shopping in the morning. Then, I cleaned (my rooms).*)

        2. テニスをします **tenisu o shimasu** (*On Sundays, I often go shopping. Then, I play tennis.*)

        3. 宿題が多いです **shukudai ga ōi desu** (*This class is difficult. In addition, there is a lot of homework.*)

        4. 銀行に就職しました **ginkō ni shūshoku shimashita** (*My older brother graduated last year. Then, he was employed by a bank.*)

12·11   1. grammatical

        2. ungrammatical (そうすると **Sōsuruto** should not be used for the speaker's controllable action.)

        3. grammatical

        4. ungrammatical (そうすると **Sōsuruto** should not be used for the speaker's controllable action.)

12·12   それから **Sorekara**, そうすると **Sōsuruto**, それから **Sorekara**, そうすると **Sōsuruto**

12·13   1. grammatical

        2. grammatical

        3. ungrammatical (Rain was not logically expected.)

        4. ungrammatical (Buying a jacket was not done based on logical reasoning.)

12·14 *Sample answers:*

1. 犬は嫌いです **inu wa kirai desu** (*I like cats. However, I hate dogs.*)
2. 毎日アイスクリームを食べています **mainichi aisukurīmu o tabete imasu** (*My younger sister likes ice cream. Therefore, she is eating ice cream every day.*)
3. 食べ物と水を買っておきます **tabemono to mizu o katte okimasu** (*It appears that typhoon is coming tomorrow. Therefore, I will buy food and water in advance.*)
4. 車の事故がありました **kuruma no jiko ga arimashita** (*There was an automobile accident yesterday. However, no one was injured.*)

12·15

1. そうすると **Sōsuruto** (*I opened the door. Then, there was a dog.*)
2. それで **Sorede** or ですから **Desukara** (*I forgot (to bring) my wallet. So, I borrowed money from Mr. Tanaka.*)
3. ですから **Desukara** (*There is a sale at the department store tomorrow. So, why don't we go shopping together?*)

12·16

1. それか **Soreka**
2. それとも **Soretomo**
3. それとも **Soretomo**

13 Conditionals

13·1

1. 読んだら **yondara**
2. 来たら **kitara**
3. 買ったら **kattara**
4. したら **shitara**
5. 書いたら **kaitara**
6. 書かなかったら **kakanakattara**
7. 安かったら **yasukattara**
8. 静かだったら **shizuka dattara**
9. 学生だったら **gakusei dattara**

13·2 *Sample answers:*

1. 春になった **Haru ni natta** (*When spring comes, the snow melts.*)
2. クラスがおわった **Kurasu ga owatta** (*When the class is over, I'll call you.*)
3. 天気がよかった **Tenki ga yokatta** (*If the weather is good, why don't we go to the park?*)
4. いい仕事がもらえた **Ii shigoto ga moraeta** (*If I can get a good job, I'll be very happy.*)

13·3

1. b (*When I opened the window, a bird came in.*)
2. a (*When I tried eating, it was relatively delicious.*)
3. c (*When I listened to music, I started to feel better.*)
4. d (*When I went to the supermarket, I met Mr. Ishida.*)
5. e (*When I drank sake, I started to have a headache.*)

13·4

1. 書けば **kakeba**
2. 飲めば **nomeba**
3. 来れば **kureba**
4. 来なければ **konakereba**
5. あれば **areba**
6. なければ **nakereba**
7. すれば **sureba**
8. いなければ **inakereba**
9. 安ければ **yasukereba**
10. よければ **yokereba**
11. よくなければ **yokunakereba**
12. 静かであれば **shizuka de areba**
13. まじめじゃなければ **majime ja nakereba**
14. 学生じゃなければ **gakusei ja nakereba**

13·5   *Sample answers:*

1. ピアノを習え **piano o narae** (*I should have taken piano lessons when I was young.*)
2. もっと勉強すれ **motto benkyō sure** (*I should have studied more when I was a high school student.*)
3. もっと話せ **motto hanase** (*I should have talked with my mother more when she was alive.*)
4. 富士山をみれ **Fujisan o mire** (*I should have seen Mt. Fuji while I was in Japan.*)
5. 値段をくらべれ **nedan o kurabere** (*I should have compared the price when I was buying a car.*)

13·6
1. b (*If you eat a lot, you'll gain weight.*)
2. h (*If you don't study well, you will not be able to get a 100.*)
3. g (*If you study well, you may be able to get a 100.*)
4. f (*When it is 5 o'clock, it starts to get dark.*)
5. d (*If it is not cheap, it won't sell well.*)

13·7
1. 書かない **kakanai**
2. 飲む **nomu**
3. 足す **tasu**
4. 見る **miru**
5. 安い **yasui**

13·8
1. The main clause expresses suggestion, which is not compatible with a conditional with と **to**.
2. と **to** cannot follow a verb in the past tense.
3. The main clause expresses the speaker's controllable action, which is not compatible with a conditional with と **to**.
4. The action in the conditional clause and the action in the main clause should be switched, because the action in the **to** clause should be followed by the action in the main clause.

13·9
1. 行った **itta**
2. 行く **iku**
3. 暑い **Atsui**
4. 聞きたくない **Kiki-taku nai**
5. 食べない **Tabenai**

13·10   *Sample answers:*

1. 日本に行った **nihon ni itta** (*If you want to study Japanese, you'd better go to Japan.*)
2. パンを買ってきて **pan o katte kite** (*If you are going to the supermarket, please buy some bread (for me).*)
3. 日本語の本が読める **nihongo no hon ga yomeru** (*If you have studied kanji a lot, you should be able to read a Japanese book, right?*)
4. 嫌い **Kirai** (*If you don't like it, you don't need to eat it.*)
5. 高い **Takai** (*If it is expensive, I will not buy it.*)

13·11
1. The **nara** conditional is not sensitive to the order of the events, so it cannot express what consequence holds after a given event.
2. The **nara** conditional is not sensitive to the order of events.
3. The **to** conditional is not compatible with suggestions
4. The **tara** conditional requires the action in the **tara** clause to precede the action in the main clause. A person cannot go to China before getting a visa.
5. The **ba** conditional cannot relate two events that happened in the past.

13·12
1. 押したら **oshitara**, 押すと **osu to**, 押せば **oseba**
2. なったら **nattara**, なると **naru to**, なれば **nareba**
3. なったら **nattara**
4. 開いたら **aitara**, 開くなら **aku nara**
5. 寒かったら **Samukattara**, 寒ければ **Samukereba**, 寒いなら **Samui nara**
6. 安かったら **Yasukattara**, 安いと **Yasui to**, 安ければ **Yasukereba**, 安いなら **Yasui nara**
7. 安かったら **Yasukattara**, 安ければ **Yasukereba**, 安いなら **Yasui nara**
8. 行くなら **iku nara**
9. 開けたら **aketara**, 開けると **akeru to**

13·13
1. *My older brother watches any kind of movies.*
2. *I can sleep anywhere. (Literally: I can sleep well no matter where I sleep.)*
3. *My younger brother does not listen no matter who speaks to him.*
4. *If it is a delicious thing, I'll buy it no matter how expensive it is.*

13·14
1. じしょを見てもいいですか。**Jisho o mite mo ii desu ka.**
2. クレジットカードで払ってもいいですか。**Kurejittokādo de haratte mo ii desu ka.**
3. ちょっと聞いてもいいですか。**Chotto kiite mo ii desu ka.**
4. ちょっとお願いしてもいいですか。**Chotto onegai shite mo ii desu ka.**
5. ちょっと食べてみてもいいですか。**Chotto tabete mite mo ii desu ka.**

13·15
1. 私の車を使ってもいいですよ。**Watashi no kuruma o tsukatte mo ii desu yo.**
2. ここでタバコをすってはいけません。**Koko de tabako o sutte wa ikemasen.**
3. ここでしゃべってはいけません。**Koko de shabette wa ikemasen.**
4. 早く帰ってもいいですよ。**Hayaku kaette mo ii desu yo.**
5. 辞書を使ってはいけません。**Jisho o tsukatte wa ikemasen.**

13·17
1. 送料を払わなくてはいけませんか。**Sōryō o harawanakute wa ikemasen ka.**
2. 数学のクラスを取らなくてはいけませんか。**Sūgaku no kurasu o toranakute wa ikemasen ka.**
3. 漢字を覚えなくてはいけませんか。**Kanji o oboenakute wa ikemasen ka.**
4. 電話をしなくてはいけませんか。**Denwa o shinakute wa ikemasen ka.**

13·18
1. 送料は払わなくてもいいです。**Sōryō wa harawanakute mo ii desu.**
2. 大阪には行かなくてもいいです。**Ōsaka ni wa ikanakute mo ii desu.**
3. 京都に行かなくてはいけません。**Kyōto ni ikanakute wa ikemasen.**
4. 漢字を読まなくてはいけません。**Kanji o yomanakute wa ikemasen.**
5. 漢字が読めなくてはいけません。**Kanji ga yomenakute wa ikemasen.**

14 Passives and causatives

14·1
1. 盗まれる **nusumareru**
2. たたかれる **tatakareru**
3. こわされる **kowasareru**
4. 運ばれる **hakobareru**
5. 使われる **tsukawareru**
6. 取られる **torareru**
7. 誘われる **sasowareru**
8. しかられる **shikarareru**
9. ほめられる **homerareru**
10. される **sareru**

14·2
1. 私のカメラが弟にこわされました。**Watashi no kamera ga otōto ni kowasaremashita.**
2. 弟が父にしかられました。**Otōto ga chichi ni shikararemashita.**
3. 魚が猫に取られました。**Sakana ga neko ni toraremashita.**
4. 日本語がアメリカ人に話されています。**Nihon-go ga Amerika-jin ni hanasarete imasu.**

14·3
1. *My older brother was rained on.*
2. *My younger brother graduated before me (and I was annoyed by it).*
3. *Makoto's girlfriend cried (and he was in trouble).*
4. *Mike came to visit me again (and I was not happy with it).*
5. *The cat took my fish (and I was unhappy).*
6. *During the exam, my teacher stood next to me (and I was disturbed by it).*

14·4
1. 5年前に子供に死なれました。**Go-nen mae ni kodomo ni shinaremashita.**
2. 子供に家出をされました。**Kodomo ni iede o saremashita.**
3. 隣の席の男の人にタバコを吸われました。**Tonari no seki no otoko no hito ni tabako o suwaremashita.**
4. 犬に逃げられました。**Inu ni nigeraremashita.**
5. 私が100点を取ったと言ったら、みんなにびっくりされました。**Watashi ga hyaku-ten o totta to ittara, minna ni bikkuri saremashita.**

14·5
1. 書かせる **kakaseru**
2. 読ませる **yomaseru**
3. 運ばせる **hakobaseru**
4. 洗わせる **arawaseru**
5. 取らせる **toraseru**
6. 着させる **kisaseru**
7. 切らせる **kiraseru**
8. させる **saseru**
9. 来させる **kosaseru**

14·6 1. *My older brother made my younger brother cry yesterday.*
2. *I let my mother rest.*
3. *My younger brother hates vegetables, but my mother makes him eat vegetables every day.*
4. *My younger brother loves chocolate. My mother lets him eat chocolate if it's a little bit.*

14·7 1. 妹に部屋を掃除させました。**Imōto ni heya o sōji sasemashita.**
2. 弟に鞄を持たせました。**Otōto ni kaban o motasemashita.**
3. 子供に薬を飲ませました。**Kodomo ni kusuri o nomasemahsita.**
4. 犬を歩かせました。**Inu o arukasemashita.**
5. 学生に漢字を練習させました。**Gakusei ni kanji o renshū sasemashita.**

14·10 1. この部屋を使わせてくださいませんか。**Kono heya o tsukawasete kudasaimasen ka.** (*Could you please let me use this room?*)
2. ちょっと休ませてくださいませんか。**Chotto yasumasete kudasaimasen ka.** (*Could you please let me take a rest?*)
3. 理由を聞かせてくださいませんか。**Riyū o kikasete kudasaimasen ka.** (*Could you please let me hear the reason (for it)?*)

14·11 1. 磨かせられる **migakaserareru** or 磨かされる **migakasareru**
2. 歌わせられる **utawaserareru** or 歌わされる **utawasareru**
3. 運ばせられる **hakobaserareru** or 運ばされる **hakobasareru**
4. 習わせられる **narawaserareru** or 習わされる **narawasareru**
5. 待たせられる **mataserareru** or 待たされる **matasareru**
6. させられる **saserareru**
7. こさせられる **kosaserareru**

14·12 1. *I was made to carry the luggage by my mother.*
2. *I was made to take calligraphy lessons by my father.*
3. *I was made to sing a song at karaoke.*
4. *I was made to wait for three hours at the hospital.*
5. *I was made to buy an expensive present.*

14·13 1. 犬の世話をさせられました。**Inu no sewa o saseraremashita.**
2. 塾に行かせられました。**Juku ni ikaseraremashita.**
3. 文句を聞かせられました。**Monku o kikaseraremashita.**
4. 仕事を辞めさせられました。**Shigoto o yamesaseraremashita.**
5. 罰金を払わせられました。**Bakkin o harawaseraremashita.**
6. 靴を磨かせられました。**Kutsu o migakaseraremashita.**

14·14 1. を **o**
2. が **ga**
3. を **o**, に **ni**
4. に **ni**
5. に **ni**
6. に **ni**, を **o**

15 Honorifics

15·1 1. 召し上がりませんか。**Meshiagarimasen ka.**
2. 先生は今日はいらっしゃいません。**Sensei wa kyō wa irasshaimasen.**
3. 社長さんはいらっしゃいますか。**Shachō-san wa irasshaimasu ka.**
4. ご覧になってください。**Go-ran ni natte kudasai.**

15·2 1. メアリーさんと話されましたか。**Mearī-san to hanasaremashita ka.**
2. ゴルフはされますか。**Gorufu wa saremasu ka.**
3. 今日の新聞を読まれましたか。**Kyō no shinbun o yomaremashita ka.**

15·3 1. ゆっくりお休みになりましたか。**Yukkuri o-yasumi ni narimashita ka.**
2. 山田さんとお会いになりましたか。**Yamada-san to o-ai ni narimashita ka.**
3. もうお決めになりましたか。**Mō o-kime ni narimashita ka.**
4. 社長はもうお帰りになりました。**Shachō wa mō o-kaeri ni narimashita.**

15·4 1. 私がお調べいたします。**Watashi ga o-shirabe itashimasu.**
2. 私がお運びいたしました。**Watashi ga o-hakobi itashimashita.**
3. 私がお作りいたしましょう。**Watashi ga o-tsukuri itashimashō.**
4. 私がお集めいたしましょうか。**Watashi ga o-atsume itashimashō ka.**

15·5
1. いたします itashimasu
2. になりました ni narimashita
3. いたしました itashimashita
4. 頂きました itadakimashita
5. 伺います ukagaimasu

15·6
1. 今日は早く帰らせていただけませんか。Kyō wa hayaku kaerasete itadakemasen ka.
2. この車を使わせていただけませんか。Kono kuruma o tsukawasete itadakemasen ka.
3. その手紙を読ませていただけませんか。Sono tegami o yomasete itadakemasen ka.
4. ここで待たせていただけませんか。Koko de matasete itadakemasen ka.

15·7
1. 推薦状を書いていただけませんか。Suisenjō o kaite itadakemasen ka.
2. 車を貸していただけませんか。Kuruma o kashite itadakemasen ka.
3. タバコを吸わないでいただけませんか。Tabako o suwanai de itadakemasen ka.
4. 考えてみていただけませんか。Kangaete mite itadakemasen ka.

15·8
1. *May I go home early today?*
2. *Please sit down.*
3. *Could you let me know your email address?*
4. *I would like to quit (working for) this company as of today.*
5. *Please wait a little.*

15·9
1. お o
2. お O, ご go, お o
3. ご Go
4. お o

15·10
1. どちら Dochira
2. いかが ikaga
3. どなた donata

16 Review exercises

16·1
1. やま yama
2. じかん jikan
3. てんぷら tenpura
4. きって kitte
5. でんしゃ densha

16·2
1. アメリカ Amerika
2. イギリス Igirisu
3. ブラジル Burajiru
4. ボストン Bosuton
5. ピアノ piano
6. ゲーム gēmu

16·3
1. 私 watashi
2. 人 hito
3. 日本人 Nihonjin
4. 三人 sannin
5. 高い takai
6. 学ぶ manabu

16·4
1. 私は日本人です。 watashi wa Nihon-jin desu.
2. 私は学生じゃありません。 Watashi wa gakusei ja arimasen.
3. 川口さんがうちに来た。 Kawaguchi-san ga uchi ni kita.
4. ケンさんがアンさんを誘った。 Ken-san ga Ann-san o sasotta.
5. 犬がケーキを食べた。 Inu ga kēki o tabeta.

16·5
1. これ kore
2. あの ano
3. それ sore
4. あれ are
5. nothing

16·6
1. これは母の本です。**Kore wa haha no hon desu.**
2. あれはアンさんのお母さんの本です。**Are wa Ann-san no okāsan no hon desu.**
3. 田中さんは私の父の友達の友達です。**Tanaka-san wa watashi no chichi no tomodachi no tomodachi desu.**
4. これは子供の本です。**Kore wa kodomo no hon desu.**
5. これは中国の子供の本です。**Kore wa Chūgoku no kodomo no hon desu.**

16·7
1. 本 **hon**
2. 車 **kuruma**
3. 車 **kuruma**
4. 車 **kuruma**
5. 建物 **tatemono**

16·8
1. ろく **roku**
2. じゅうご **jūgo**
3. にじゅうさん **nijūsan**
4. さんぜんさんびゃくさんじゅうさん **sanzen sanbyaku sanjūsan**
5. きゅうまんきゅうせんきゅうひゃくきゅうじゅうきゅう **kyūman kyūsen kyūhyaku kyūjūkyū**

16·9
1. 5匹 **go-hiki**
2. 3人 **san-nin**
3. 2つ **futa-tsu**
   or 2個 **ni-ko**
4. 5冊 **go-satsu**
5. 3本 **san-bon**

16·10
1. 5時 **go-ji**
2. 午後2時20分 **gogo ni-ji nijup-pun**
3. 午前8時15分 **gozen hachi-ji jū-go-fun**
4. 4月1日 **shi-gatsu tsuitachi**
5. 12月20日 **jūni-gatsu hatsuka**

16·11
1. 5時間 **go-jikan**
2. 4か月 **yon-kagetsu**
3. 100円 **hyaku-en**
4. 9ページ **kyū-pēji**
5. 3分 **san-pun**

16·12
1. 話します **hanashimasu**
2. 運びます **hakobimasu**
3. 買います **kaimasu**
4. 取ります **torimasu**
5. 待ちます **machimasu**

16·13
1. 食べます **tabemasu**
2. 寝ます **nemasu**
3. 変えます **kaemasu**
4. 着ます **kimasu**
5. 借ります **karimasu**

16·14
1. 着ます **kimasu**
2. 切ります **kirimasu**
3. 変えます **kaemasu**
4. 帰ります **kaerimasu**
5. いります **irimasu**

16·15
1. 書かない **kakanai**
2. 読まない **yomanai**
3. 会わない **awanai**
4. ない **nai**
5. いない **inai**

16·16
1. 飛んだ tonda
2. 見た mita
3. 言った itta
4. 来た kita
5. した shita

16·17
1. 泳げる oyogeru
2. 寝られる nerareru
3. 起きられる okirareru
4. 動ける ugokeru
5. 持てる moteru

16·18
1. 泳いでいます oyoide imasu
2. 休んでいます yasunde imasu
3. 走っています hashitte imasu
4. かたづけています katadzukete imasu
5. 考えています kangate imasu

16·19
1. これは私の本じゃありません。 Kore wa watashi no hon ja arimasen.
or これは私の本じゃないです。 Kore wa watashi no hon ja nai desu.
2. 昨日はコーヒーを飲みませんでした。 Kinō wa kōhī o nomimasendeshita.
3. カタカナが書けます。 Katakana ga kakemasu.
4. 兄は泳げません。 Ani wa oyogemasen.
5. スミスさんは空手ができます。 Sumisu-san wa karate ga dekimasu.

16·20
1. ありました arimashita
2. あります arimasu
3. います imasu
4. います imasu
5. あります arimasu

16·21
1. が ga
2. を o
3. が ga
4. を o
5. を o

16·22
1. あげました agemashita
2. くれました kuremashita
3. もらいました moraimashita
4. いただきました itadakimashita
5. くれました kuremashita

16·23
1. おきました okimashita
2. きました kimashita
3. ありますよ arimasu yo
4. しまいました shimaimashita
5. みて mite

16·24
1. 私は車がほしいです。 Watashi wa kuruma ga hoshii desu.
2. 私はねたいです。 Watashi wa ne-tai desu.
3. 私はカナダに行きたいです。 Watashi wa Kanada ni iki-tai desu.
4. 私は弟に日本語を勉強してほしいです。 Watashi wa otōto ni Nihongo o benkyō shite hoshii desu.
5. 私は弟に部屋をきれいにしてほしいです。 Watashi wa otōto ni heya o kirei ni shite hoshii desu.

16·25
1. が ga
2. を o
3. が ga
4. を o
5. が ga

16·26
1. で, に de, ni
2. で, を de, o
3. で, を de, o
4. に ni
5. で, を de, o

16·27   1. まで made
2. や ya
3. から kara
4. も mo
5. の no

16·28   1. 寝てばかりいます nete bakari imasu
2. ありません arimasen
3. でも買います demo kaimasu
4. にも行きました ni mo ikimashita
5. だけ食べました dake tabemashita

16·29   1. ケンさんは真面目な学生です。Ken-san wa majime na gakusei desu.
2. この漢字はあまり難しくありません。Kono kanji wa amari muzukashiku arimasen.
3. 田中さんはやさしくて、頭がいいです。Tanaka-san wa yasashikute, atama ga ii desu.
4. きれいに書いてください。Kirei ni kaite kudasai.
5. 静かにしてください。Shizuka ni shite kudasai.

16·30   1. 中国語と韓国語と、どちらの方が簡単ですか。 Chūgokugo to Kankokugo to, dochira no hō ga kantan desu ka.
2. 映画を見るのと本を読むのと、どちらの方が好きですか。Eiga o miru no to hon o yomu no to, dochira no hō ga suki desu ka.
3. 果物の中で何が一番好きですか。Kudamono no naka de nani ga ichiban suki desu ka.
4. 苺とバナナと桃の中でどれが一番好きですか。Ichigo to banana to momo no naka de dore ga ichiban suki desu ka.
5. アンさんとマイクさんとトムさんの中でだれが一番背が高いですか。An-san to Maiku-san to Tomu-san no naka de dare ga ichiban se ga takai desu ka.

16·31   1. どこ doko
2. 何 nani
3. どう dō
4. いつ itsu
5. だれ dare

16·32   1. あの部屋にだれかいました。Ano heya ni dareka imashita.
2. 夏休みはどこかに行きましたか。Natsu-yasumi wa dokoka ni ikimashita ka.
3. 昨日はどこにも行きませんでした。Kinō wa doko ni mo ikimasendeshita.
4. 昨日は何も食べませんでした。 Kinō wa nani mo tabemasendeshita.
5. 昨日はだれかと話しましたか。 Kinō wa dareka to hanashimashita ka.

16·33   1. かも kamo
2. そう sō
3. でしょう deshō
4. 行く iku
5. よう yō
6. 押せ ose

16·34   1. やすい yasu
2. にくい nikui
3. たい tai
4. にくい nikui
5. たい tai

16·35   1. ほしがっています hoshigatte imasu
2. 飲みすぎました nomi-sugimashita
3. 書き始めました kaki-hajimemashita
4. しつづけます shi-tsudzukemasu
5. 終わりました owarimashita

16·36   1. I tried to eat nattō (fermented soybeans), but I couldn't.
   2. I'm thinking of getting married next year.
   3. This movie appears interesting.
   4. My father is like a child.
   5. Mr. Tanaka is not like a typical Japanese person.

16·37   1. して **shite**
   2. なり **nari**
   3. こと **koto**
   4. こと **koto**
   5. こと **koto**

16·38   1. 便利だ **benri da**
   2. か **ka**
   3. 前 **mae**
   4. 食べている **tabete iru**
   5. 着いた **tsuita**
   6. 聞き **kiki**
   7. 降らない **furanai**

16·39   *Sample answers.*

   1. あしたは試験がある **Ashita wa shiken ga aru**
   2. あしたは試験があります **Ashita wa shiken ga arimasu**
   3. あしたは試験がある **Ashita wa shiken ga aru**
   4. あしたは試験があります **Ashita wa shiken ga arimasu**

16·40   1. The movie that I watched yesterday was not very interesting.
   2. Being able to talk with anyone is a good thing.
   3. I did research at a place called Tsukuba.
   4. Do you know the person called Emiko Kondō?

16·41   1. 週末は買い物をして料理をして洗濯をします。**Shūmatsu wa kaimono o shite ryōri o shite sentaku o shimasu.**
   2. 昨日はテレビを見て宿題をしてねました。**Kinō wa terebi o mite shukudai o shite nemashita.**
   3. 部屋を掃除して疲れました。 **Heya o sōji shite tsukaremashita.**
   4. アンさんはきれいで優しいです。**An-san wa kireide yasashii desu.**
   5. 昨日は朝ごはんを食べないで仕事に行きました。**Kinō wa asa-gohan o tabenaide shigoto ni ikimashita.**
   6. 今朝はパンを食べないでご飯を食べました。**Kesa wa pan o tabenaide gohan o tabemashita.**

16·42   *Sample answers.*

   1. 田中さんは頭もいいし、やさしいし、かっこいいです。**Tanaka-san wa atama mo ii shi, yasashii shi, kakko ii desu.**
   2. 今日は掃除もしたし、買い物もしたし、洗濯もしました。**Kyō wa sōji mo shitashi, kaimono mo shitashi, sentaku mo shimashita.**
   3. 週末は本を読んだり、映画を見たりします。**Shūmatsu wa hon o yondari, eiga o mitari shimasu.**
   4. テニスをして、シャワーをあびました。 **Tenisu o shite, shawā o abimashita.**

16·43   1. 行きます **ikimasu**
   2. きれい **kirei**
   3. を勉強しました **o benkyō shimashita**
   4. 駅があります **eki ga arimasu**
   5. それで **Sorede**
   6. でも **Demo**
   7. それとも **Soretomo**

16·44   1. 押したら **oshitara**
   2. 行くなら **ikunara**
   3. 安かったら **Yasukattara**
   4. 押したら **oshitara**

16·45   1. Is it okay to go home early?
            2. You are not allowed to use a credit card.
            3. You must use a credit card.
            4. You don't need to do homework.
            5. It is okay to be expensive.

16·46   Sample answers:

            1. 買います **kaimasu**
            2. 買いません **kaimasen**
            3. 100点は取れません **100-ten wa toremasen**
            4. 食べます **tabemasu**
            5. 太りません **futorimasen**

16·47   1. 兄が父にほめられました。**Ani ga chichi ni homeraremashita.**
            2. 弟が犬に噛まれました。**Otōto ga inu ni kamaremashita.**
            3. 伊藤さんが田中さんに誕生日パーティーに招待されました。
              Itō-san ga Tanaka-san ni tanjō pātī ni shōtai saremashita.

16·48   1. 去年父に死なれました。**Kyonen chichi ni shinaremashita.**
            2. レストランでとなりの人にタバコをすわれました。**Resutoran de tonari no hito ni tabako o**
              suwaremashita.
            3. 私が１００点をとったら、みんなにびっくりされました。**Watashi ga 100-ten o tottara, minna ni bikkuri**
              saremashita.

16·49   1. 妹に料理をさせました。**Imōto ni ryōri o sasemashita.**
            2. 妹にテレビを見させました。 **Imōto ni terebi o misasemashita.**
            3. 妹を泣かせました。**Imōto o nakasemashita.**

16·50   1. I was made to take calligraphy lessons by my father.
            2. I was made to wait for two hours by my friend.
            3. I was made to clean rooms by my mother.
            4. The teacher let me read his/her book.
            5. I was made to write a kanji characters 100 times by my teacher.

16·51   1. いらっしゃい **irasshai**
            2. ご覧になって **goran ni natte**
            3. いたし **itashi**
            4. になり **ni nari**
            5. いただけない **itadakenai**

16·52   1. どちら **dochira**
            2. いかが **ikaga**
            3. どなた **donata**
            4. お上手 **o-jōzu**
            5. お車 **o-kuruma**